HOW TO SURVIVE WITHOUT PSYCHOTHERAPY

HOW TO SURVIVE WITHOUT PSYCHOTHERAPY

David Smail

LONDON AND NEW YORK

First published 1996 by Constable and Company Ltd

This edition published in 2015 by
Karnac Books Ltd.

Published 2018 by Routledge
2 Park Square, Milton Park, Abingdon, Oxon OX14 4RN
711 Third Avenue, New York, NY 10017, USA

Routledge is an imprint of the Taylor & Francis Group, an informa business

British Library Cataloguing in Publication Data
A C.I.P. for this book is available from the British Library

ISBN: 9781782202882 (pbk)

For Uta

Contents

Preface

This book is the distillation of over thirty years' experience of talking to people in distress.

At the start of that period I had no reason to suppose that the received wisdom on questions of 'mental illness' would be in any way inadequate to the task of understanding and trying to help those I encountered. My naivety was quickly exposed. Working, as I then was, as an apprentice clinical psychologist in vast Victorian mental hospitals, I soon realised that we were not simply dealing with sick people whose illnesses needed to be diagnosed and cured by appropriate treatments before they were sent on their way.

Yet this was (as it still is) the ruling ideology. We worked in hospitals, with doctors, nurses, medical procedures and a suitably clinical vocabulary with which to describe our activities. The 'patients', though, somehow didn't seem to fit in with the model. Even the most severely disturbed didn't appear ill so much as confused and despairing, beside themselves sometimes with frustration, grief or rage; the less disturbed – the 'personality disorders', 'chronic neurotics' etc. – were at least profoundly unhappy. Though there were many whose case notes might have something like 'childhood uneventful' scribbled in them, there was, if you bothered to talk to them, not one whose life story did not abound with good reasons for their distress. To incarcerate people, drug them, patronise them with facile judgements about their 'adequacy', though one could see well enough how such procedures came about, was just to add insult to injury.

I quickly discovered that I was not the only one to find the orthodox approach to 'mental illness' unconvincing. Medicine wasn't infallible, science was full of uncertainty, the care of the 'mentally ill' was shot through with unexamined social and moral prejudice. And there were alternatives to the orthodoxy.

I changed my place of work to another vast Victorian mental hospital (Claybury Hospital in Essex), but this time one with a difference – a 'therapeutic community'. Here it was recognised that psychological disorder was a matter more of social experience than of illness, and the aim was to rehabilitate people through the experience of living together in a therapeutic environment (the hospital ward) where eccentricity was tolerated and difficulties in relationship reflected upon in daily meetings designed for that purpose.

For a short while the therapeutic-community movement, under the guidance of humane and to an extent charismatic figures like the psychiatrist Denis Martin at Claybury, flourished in the British National Health Service, and I am glad to have had the chance to play my part in it. But this approach, in essence anti-authoritarian in a way which presented an intolerable challenge to a hierarchical NHS bureaucracy as well as to entrenched medical power, was never likely to become the standard form of psychiatric treatment, and it passed its peak in less than a decade. Psychiatry retreated back into its medical/biological stronghold to busy itself with 'severe mental illness', and clinical psychology involved itself in the 'cognitive-behavioural' treatment of anyone whose problems could be seen as the result of their learned experience of life and relationships.

Even though liberated from the distortions and oversimplifications of the 'medical model', I found that there was still not a great deal of satisfaction to be gained from practising within the new orthodoxies of my profession. It was, true enough, a considerable and necessary advance to seek to understand people's distress in the light of their experience of life, but the theoretical background (such as it is) and practical toolkit of 'behavioural' and 'cognitive' approaches in clinical psychology, apart from having a kind of deadening banality about them, *just didn't seem to work*. In fact, *none* of the approaches to 'curing' people's emotional and psychological distress, whether derived from medical psychiatry, clinical psychology or the established approaches of psychoanalysis and psychotherapy, could make out a convincing case for its effectiveness.

Not that working with individuals in distress was itself unrewarding, but I suspect that, certainly in the earlier part of my career, I gained far more from it than they did. There was a huge amount to be learned from the fortitude and resilience with which people struggled with their difficulties, and their gratefulness for the crumb of comfort to be derived from talking to the likes of me about their predicaments was touching and warming. But only at my most self-deceiving could I have claimed that the 'therapy' I was dispensing was making any substantial difference to their lives.

In the early days I assumed that this was because I was simply not doing it as well as I should be. After all, the textbooks and the journal literature were absolutely confident about what could be achieved with the appropriate scientific scrupulousness. However, before long more reassuring and, I think, more likely explanations suggested themselves.

For a start, not *all* the confident pronouncements and scientific demonstrations in the literature could be right, because many of them contradicted each other. There must be another factor at work, and the most likely was professional self-interest. Doctors, behavioural scientists and so on are, sadly perhaps but absolutely inevitably, prey to the same need to justify themselves and earn a living as the rest of society. We told the stories the way we did mainly because that was the way we wanted it to be. That didn't mean that we were liars, charlatans or cheats, merely that we were human beings like everyone else. But it did mean that the very foundations on which our assumptions about mental health were built needed to be re-examined.

Another factor seemed to be that, closeted in our consulting rooms, we were not taking enough account of what went on in the outside world to explain why our patients didn't get better in the way the theory predicted. It wasn't so much what the therapist did to the patient that made him or her better as what *everyone else* did when s/he returned to everyday life.

But it is really Margaret Thatcher I have to thank as much as anybody for opening my eyes fully to what I came to see as the absolutely fundamental and overriding importance of the social environment in the genesis of psychological distress. For it was the utter soulless, callous indifference in the Thatcher years to the welfare and security of ordinary people that finally made it obvious that what mattered to pyschological wellbeing was precisely not interior attributes such as the 'responsibility', 'self-reliance' and 'initiative' beloved of the New Right, but the provision within society of essentially *material* resources. In circumstances where these resources were stripped from whole sections of society and redistributed to another, no clinician with half an eye could fail to see the damage done to those deprived: they came to the consulting room in droves, mostly bemused and blaming themselves for what they saw as their own inadequacies.

Official psychology and psychiatry barely took societal issues into account in their approaches to the understanding and treatment of 'mental illness', and certainly nowhere were they made central to the field of enquiry. We had simply overlooked those factors that give society its dynamic force and most closely affect its members: the distribution, maintenance and embodied effects of *power*. What caused people distress was not so much their own mistakes, inadequacies and illnesses as the powers and influences that bore down upon them from the world beyond their skin.

This discovery was no real surprise. We all know it and enact its consequences in our daily lives: we struggle to wrest our livelihood and the means of our physical and emotional security from the social and material world around us, and the struggle involves almost the whole of our attention. It is only when we become significantly emotionally disturbed, it seems, that we lose sight of what we have taken life to be about and resort to the most abstruse and unlikely theories about what makes us tick.

In the light of this 'revelation', the focus of my clinical work shifted from the patients themselves to the worlds that they inhabited. I found myself spending more and more time trying to persuade people that there was nothing the matter with *them*, but quite a lot the matter with the past and present contexts of their lives.

Although many people find it a considerable relief to discover that they are not 'going out of their minds', not everybody is immediately receptive to this view. Despite its having a good deal to recommend it on the grounds of sheer common sense, the idea that circumstances rather than selves are 'to blame' for emotional distress has a formidable weight of cultural opinion against it, and it takes an unusual independence of spirit to reject institutionalised authority, even in favour of the obvious.

But the more I pursue this line, the more I am persuaded of its fruitfulness. Almost all the mystique falls away from the process of psychotherapy, and patients become equal partners in the conduct of an analysis not of their 'psyches' but of the predicaments that cause them distress. In this there is no need of professional mumbo-jumbo, secrecy or superiority, no necessity to disguise the theory or the therapist's thought processes from supposedly 'manipulative' or 'resistant' clients. And, given a clear enough understanding of the causes of distress – an initial liberating break from the mystifying production of a century of psychology – there is not a great deal of need for psychotherapy itself.

Hence the writing of this book. It attempts to cover the principal themes on which I have found it most useful to concentrate with people struggling to understand the roots of their troubles and to shape strategies for trying to deal with them. These themes – ideas about 'normality', 'responsibility' and 'will power', moral demands, change and, above all, the use and abuse of power – are all closely intertwined, and hence recur throughout the book, but with each being given its principal statement in a chapter of its own.

The book is not intended as a do-it-yourself cure for psychological distress; indeed, its whole point is that such cure is for the most part not within the grasp of the individual sufferer, with or without psychotherapy. If the book can be said to have a 'therapeutic' aim at all, it is to remove from sufferers the burden of responsibility for their pain and to demystify as far as possible some of the ideas and practices that have grown up around psychotherapy during the course of this century.

A note on the use of examples

The use of 'case histories' presents a number of problems. They run the risk of either betraying confidences or straying into fiction, of including too much information or not enough. The more detailed and realistic one tries to make them, the more banal and pallid they seem to sound, or else luridly overdramatised, or (perhaps most often) subtly sentimentalised in a way that distorts reality. I know of no successful attempt to encapsulate people's lives in brief, 'clinical' snapshots of this kind (full-length biographies are problematic enough!). However, the provision of examples in some form is necessary to give shape and organisation to what would otherwise be an uncomfortably abstract discussion, and in what follows I have opted for a schematic oversimplification of types of distress and predicament which are so common as to identify no single individual, but may help to relate different strands of the argument to each other and to link themes that will recur in later chapters. Inevitably, earlier examples anticipate subsequent discussion to some extent.

To make it easier to refer back to them, I have given the examples names in alphabetical order.

Acknowledgements

Acknowledgements are tricky things, mainly because, first, it is so hard to be sure of where the influences upon one have arisen, and, second, because one is almost bound to forget to mention someone of central importance. However, more than churlish, it would be almost dishonest not to give due credit to those who have had, whether or not they intended to, a significant impact on the direction I feel my work has taken.

During the early days at Claybury Hospital, Tom Caine, my first and only real mentor, set me on a course combining respect for evidence with political awareness from which I have not since deviated. Like so many who knew him, I received a great deal of encouragement from the late Don Bannister, and it was his active support that helped to launch my writing career. Jocelyn Burton, through her scrupulous and sensitive editorship of my earlier books, helped enormously in giving my writing what accessibility it has to nonprofessional readers while insisting that I should not sacrifice detail and meaning in pursuit of easy reading. My friend Roger Poole, through countless informal Monday-evening seminars, has contributed hugely to my education beyond the narrow confines of 'psychology'. Too numerous to mention them all, and too invidious to single any of them out, my colleagues in the Nottingham Clinical Psychology Service have over years of conversation, collaboration and friendship contributed incalculably to the ideas to be found in these pages, for which they have my thanks and my affection.

CHAPTER ONE

The Treatment of Distress: Current Approaches

Only the luckiest person gets through life without at some point suffering emotional distress to a degree which could be called 'clinical'. I'm not even sure that anybody is that lucky; if so, I haven't come across them myself. For the majority of us, the periods of our lives when we feel acutely emotionally distressed are usually fairly brief, or the distress itself not so intense that we think immediately of seeking professional help. But even so, there will probably be times in most people's lives when they feel at their wits' end and don't know which way to turn.

When a person does know which way to turn, it will probably be to someone in the family, a spouse or partner, a friend or perhaps a religious community. But sometimes – quite often, in fact – either there is no one immediately available, or those who are, are themselves involved in the problem in a way that makes it impossible for them to stand back and offer the kind of impartial concern necessary for effective support. At these times, the question of professional help may well occur to the person as something to consider.

Whether or not someone in distress consults a doctor (the GP usually being the first recourse), psychotherapist or counsellor, may well depend on a feeling that taking such a step would involve a tacit admission of 'abnormality', of having departed in a radical way from life's usual course. For many people consulting a professional constitutes in this way an expression of desperation.

On the one hand, it seems, there are unhappiness, upset, conflict, confusion, depression and distress (which we expect ourselves to deal with out of our own resources, so to speak), on the other 'breakdown', 'mental illness', 'neurosis', 'psychosis', 'clinical depression' etc., which would mark us out as having departed normal company and in need of people in white coats.

Certainly, the people in white coats do little to disabuse us of the notion that there is a dichotomy between normal and abnormal, 'common unhappiness' and 'hysterical misery',[1] ordinary and 'clinical' types of distress. This is the received opinion, and one that gets endlessly circulated and recirculated via the media, eventually becoming 'common knowledge'. I do not think, however, that there is a great deal of convincing evidence to support it. In the end, what makes the difference between distress that the individual feels somehow able to cope with and distress apparently needing professional help is more a matter of quantity than kind: rather than splitting into a dichotomy, they lie on a continuum.

Usually, of course, it is events that upset us. However unbearable it may feel when it first overcomes us, the often very great pain events may cause us in the course of our lives is quite likely to fade with the passage of time, unless of course the events have effects that persist unchanged (as might be the case, for example, with having been made unemployed). No life could conceivably escape the occurrence of painful events, and, no matter how much we may hope to avoid them, most of us will not be so surprised at being overtaken by them that we feel outside the bounds of normal human experience. But even though painful events are common, most often relatively transitory, and only to be expected, how well we cope with them may depend on what we take to be the norm.

Interestingly, people rarely take their own experience as an indication of what is, so to speak, naturally human, but immediately look round at others to see how they handle similar eventualities.

Rather than reflecting, when something painful happens to them: 'So *this* is how it feels when *x* happens', they tend to wonder: 'Am I reacting as people *normally* do?' Since, for a variety of reasons, it is often very difficult to establish what people normally feel in any given situation, it may often seem that what we are experiencing is significantly *unlike* what is 'normal', and when this happens we are likely to be overtaken by anxiety or shame, or both. This is a theme I shall be returning to in a later chapter. The point I want to make for the moment is that even quite common events that are likely to cause us distress in the course of a life – disappointments, betrayals, losses – may be frightening and isolating to the point where we may start to consider ourselves (and possibly even be considered by others) 'cases'.

It is not just our reaction to disturbing events that may cause us to worry about our normality. Even more problematic is the nature of our private experience. How do you know that the contents of your head from minute to minute, the ceaseless flow of thoughts and feelings which accompany your every waking (not to mention sleeping) moment, are acceptably similar to what's going on inside your fellow creatures? What is it permissible and what not permissible to think and feel? Since people almost never reveal exactly what they're thinking and feeling at any given moment, it is very hard to know whether our own flights of imagination might not be more than slightly crazy. In part, of course, it is precisely this worry that prevents us from revealing the private world of our imagination to others, and in situations where a person loses confidence in the soundness of his or her mental contents, something that is usually just kept to the self may become a source of great anxiety and distress.

In fact, we depend on a *culture* to establish the bounds of normality, within which we are able to feel at ease with our mind, and in this respect the culture may be more or less benign. The closing years of the twentieth century seem to be one of those times when it is less benign.

Cultures that become deformed by ideology tend to generate a kind of policing of thought which attempts to regulate mental life. In some cases, for example under totalitarian political regimes or fundamentalist religions, this process may be quite overt, with secret police and vast bureaucracies for punitive control; in others it may be implicit and informal. Our own culture, driven principally by an ideology determined by commercial interests, offers us a view of mental life which is both impoverished and distorted. On the one hand we are invited to identify with the idealised picture of the happily adjusted consumer, socially perfectly balanced and of impeccable judgement in choosing the options life offers; on the other we are entertained by images of immense violence and sexual prurience, presented to us as features of a kind of alien fantasy world where savagery and madness reign. No wonder we become nervous about our own private experience, for nowhere outside ourselves can we find an indication of how ordinary, real people do actually feel (this, again, is a question I shall be returning to later in this book).

All of us, anyway, live a secret life of doubt and pain which we are quite likely to think is specifically ours. If people become sufficiently troubled by their experience to seek help from a doctor or other professional, they may well do so in fear and trembling that their difference from others will at last come to light and that they will be diagnosed as abnormal.

Some people will be aware that there are brands of psychotherapy designed less to provide solace for troubled minds than to offer the individual some kind of spiritual enrichment or 'personal growth' in the shape of deepened self-understanding and an enhanced ability to live life to the full. For such people, consulting a therapist may constitute more a privilege – even a kind of status symbol – than a badge of shame. It is not for those people that this book is written. Self-exploration, certainly, is a perfectly legitimate activity and may well prove rewarding to those who have the resources to pursue it, but my concern here is with people whose need to understand themselves and their predicament arises out of pain rather than curiosity. My focus is the phenomena of emotional distress and the validity or otherwise of practices that claim to be therapeutic in relation to them.

Principal sources of help

For the person in distress looking for professional help, the prospect is, to put it mildly, confusing and the likely outcome a lottery. If it seems simple and straightforward, either the person is very lucky or very unaware of the sea of complexity surrounding him or her.

There is, to be sure, a more or less standard procedure for seeking help with emotional or psychological problems, and this might lead the innocent to believe that the help they get reflects state-of-the-art treatment, but anyone with experience of the mental-health industry will know how varied practices are and how little control people have over what happens to them.

Most often, people experience their distress as a form of illness (panicky anxiety, for instance, is often experienced initially as imminent physical collapse or even death), but even where they are aware that the core of their troubles is psychological rather than physical, the usual course is to approach the GP. Most GPs will treat the symptoms of distress by offering advice and prescribing the usual tranquillisers and antidepressants, but the pressures of their own job leave them very little time to listen to their patients, and they tend to vary quite markedly both in the way they are likely to view psychological problems and in their awareness of the specialist facilities that exist for treating them.

There are still many GPs of the 'pull yourself together' school and many whose only way of dealing with the mental is to translate it into the physical. These are not the best people to encounter if your distress is anything but temporary or superficial (if it is, on the other hand, these might be the best people to encounter!). Other GPs, an ever dwindling minority, may, in the best traditions of family medicine, use their knowledge of you and call on the wisdom born of years of observation and reflection to offer you sympathetic counselling and sound advice. Most likely, however, the GP will refer you to an expert whom s/he judges the most appropriate person to deal with the kind of problem you are presenting. GPs should have a good knowledge of the treatment facilities available locally (which may vary greatly from place to place), but this will by no means always be the case; there is, therefore, quite an element of luck about whom you may see next.

The options open to the GP for specialist referral are likely to be chosen from psychiatry, clinical psychology or 'counselling' in one or other of its forms. In some case, of course, s/he may wish to involve the social services or other specialist agencies, but probably only if there are obviously prominent factors of material or social deprivation or other practical difficulties involved.

The choice between psychiatry, clinical psychology or counselling is, however, not as straightforward as it may sound, largely because these are not unified disciplines offering standard approaches to treatment which have been tried and tested over time, but broad groupings of professionals who, while for the most part sharing a common and distinctive training, differ widely among themselves both personally (and in this field personality cannot be safely disregarded) and in what they believe about theory and practice. Which group the GP considers appropriate in any particular case is likely to depend on the view s/he takes of your difficulties.

If, for example, the GP considers that you are suffering from a form of 'mental illness', a degree of distress that can in some sense be considered 'clinical', the most likely referral will be to a psychiatrist, i.e. a medical practitioner who has specialised and obtained postgraduate qualifications in psychiatric medicine.

If, on the other hand, the GP considers your problem to be 'behavioural', i.e. arising from situational difficulties or the result of processes of learning that have in some sense been 'maladaptive', you are most likely to be referred to a clinical psychologist, who will have a degree in academic psychology and a subsequent postgraduate qualification, most probably these days as a (non-medical) 'doctor of clinical psychology'. The latter equips him or her to view your problems as having arisen from your experience of life and to treat them from, most likely, a 'cognitive-behavioural' standpoint which attempts to modify your attitude towards your difficulties as well as how you actually deal with them.

In those (frequent) cases where the person's distress seems to arise directly from his or her relations with others, possibly at work but more likely domestically, and where there is otherwise no hint of 'mental illness' or more deep-seated disturbance, there is an increasing likelihood that s/he will be referred to a counsellor. Counsellors may be attached to the GP's practice or may be located elsewhere in their own premises. Counsellors come from a variety of backgrounds. Some, like those who qualified originally as community psychiatric nurses, have professional roots in the mental-health service and considerable experience of people in emotional difficulties. Others have no such experience, but may have received their training on one of the myriad counselling courses that have sprung into existence in recent years. Counsellors may be paid or voluntary and may subscribe to any of a range of theoretical approaches (the most likely being that of the psychologist Carl Rogers). Many counsellors will be without formal qualifications in one of the mental-health 'core professions' such as psychology, medicine, nursing or social work, and though they may well have to conform to the standards of accreditation of the British Association of Counselling, this is not so in every case.

If this is already beginning to sound a little bewildering, it is, I'm afraid, even more complicated than I have so far made it appear. This is partly because, though most GPs are likely to refer roughly in accordance with the way I've indicated, there is in fact a wide overlap between the professions involved, and a lot may depend on who knows whom rather than upon any more reliable guidelines. There is also, as I have already suggested, a wide variation between practitioners within each of these fields, so that one cannot guarantee a standard product, so to speak. If, furthermore, one takes into account the provision of psychological help that exists in the private sector, the complications are greatly compounded and there is virtually no disinterested guidance for the individual to turn to. The major schools of psychoanalysis and analytical psychology (the respective creations of Sigmund Freud and C. G. Jung), for example, exist largely (though not entirely) outside the structure of public health services, as does a vast range of lesser-known approaches to psychotherapy and counselling which the individual may stumble across at some time more or less by chance.

Added to all this is the fact that the lay person has no way of judging the validity of the claims made by the various practitioners for the efficacy of their methods. For obvious reasons, people who depend for their livelihood on their ability to attract patients or clients tend not only to proclaim their wares with confidence, but also to believe their own rhetoric. And yet they cannot all be right. The variations in approach both between and within the broadly 'mental health' professions are not mere matters of emphasis, but are frequently mutually contradictory. This is not the place either to pronounce judgement or to try to reconcile these differences,[2] but it may be instructive to give an indication of some of the difficulties confronting the major approaches.

Psychiatry

Psychiatry is an interesting case in point. Despite having come under increasing, and in my view justified, attack in recent years as promulgating an inappropriate medical model of mental illness, psychiatry still wields considerable influence in the public provision of mental-health services. The clinical head of 'community mental-health teams' will usually be a psychiatrist, and though the teams themselves may involve a range of different professions – nursing, social work, clinical psychology etc. – the structure and content of their operations will be heavily flavoured by psychiatric ideology.

Psychiatry does of course have its uses. A society has to have some way of containing and, where possible, helping people who become so confused, disturbed, excited or frightened that they threaten the safety of themselves or others. Even if mental illness is a myth, as the American psychiatrist Thomas Szasz suggested over twenty years ago, there would have to exist a profession for dealing as humanely as possible with the extremes of human distress. There is, however, a difference between containing distress and curing it, and it is in the latter respect that psychiatry may be said to be found wanting.

Few psychiatrists would agree that mental illness is a myth. Psychiatry has become increasingly biological in its approach in recent times, and huge amounts of effort are put into classifying and diagnosing supposedly clinical conditions ('psychoses', 'neuroses', 'character disorders' etc.) which are taken to have their origin in various forms of genetic and/or biochemical disorder. Psychiatrists are trained according to the established procedures of medicine and their specialism is structured exactly like that of other hospital doctors. They compete for status and reputation with their colleagues in physical medicine, and their credibility would be destroyed if they drifted too far from their medical roots.

The standard psychiatric procedures of treatment and training mean that anyone who becomes a patient is likely to come under the care of a consultant psychiatrist who will be responsible for overseeing his or her 'case'. The doctor doing the actual treatment (most likely the administration of psychoactive drugs of one kind or another) will, however, probably be a more junior psychiatrist whose need to climb the promotional ladder, and so frequently change jobs, means that contact with the patient is unlikely to provide any continuity of care. Indeed, as in other branches of medicine, there is in any case no guarantee that patients will see the same doctor at each outpatient visit. In these circumstances, the patient will probably be treated as someone with an illness, and, though the time spent talking to the psychiatrist may be somewhat longer than that which the GP can afford to give, it is unlikely that a great deal of attention will be given to the *social* significance of his or her 'symptoms', i.e. the underlying traumas and difficulties in background and current circumstances which give rise to distress in the first place.

Of course, not all psychiatrists fit this picture, and there are those whose experience and compassion make them valuable partners in the exploration of patients' emotional pain. There are also psychiatrists who specialise in psychotherapeutic approaches (most usually derived from one or another variation of Freudian psychoanalysis), but they are relatively thin on the ground in Britain and there is no guarantee that the average patient will get the chance of a consultation with one.

Psychiatry has over the last three or four decades had to learn to share the field of 'mental illness' with a number of other professional disciplines and to modify the nature of its once monopolistic claims. It has also had to bend to political changes in the way psychological disorder and its treatment are viewed and funded (the closure of the old mental hospitals and the reliance instead on so-called 'care in the community' have made big differences to psychiatric practice). Always strongly prone to fashions in treatment (one thinks of the crazes not all that long ago for leucotomy and insulin-coma therapy, now mercifully extinct), psychiatry is nothing if not pragmatic, and it is now happy enough to redefine some conditions it might once, for example, have called 'neurotic' as concerns of the 'worried well' and to leave their treatment to various nonmedical professions and voluntary groups of counsellors. These changes have not, however, resulted in psychiatry itself becoming any more liberal.

Increasingly, psychiatrists are having to develop and intensify their role as custodians of those who fall victim to the more extreme forms of distress our society gives rise to, often in very difficult circumstances dictated more by political constraints than by therapeutic concerns, and this, as noted, seems to result in a fortification of the biological approach. To read psychiatric textbooks, or indeed simply to attend to the received opinion reflected in the media, we could be forgiven for thinking that there is no doubt that serious mental illnesses like 'schizophrenia' and 'clinical depression' exist as entities established by medical science. It would seem that the future lies in the further identification of the genetic and biochemical processes underlying disturbed conduct and thinking, and the refinement of the chemical means of modifying them.

Knowledge, as the French philosopher Michel Foucault suggested so persuasively, is inseparable from power,[3] and it certainly seems to be the case that powerful interests within both psychiatry and the wider society have combined since the 1970s to paper over the cracks that critiques by people like Thomas Szasz and R. D. Laing had caused to appear in the notion of mental illness. An explosion of research in the sixties and early seventies which suggested that there could be important psychological causes for so-called psychotic thinking and behaviour has now been largely forgotten or summarily (and quite unjustifiably) discredited. Right-wing political regimes whose economic policies led directly or indirectly to profound psychological distress in whole swathes of the population, the enormously powerful drug companies supplying the vastly lucrative means of 'treatment', and, of course, the profession of psychiatry itself, all had a stake in presenting the concept of 'severe mental illness' as indisputably biological. Even the families of, for example, 'schizophrenic' patients, stung by what they experienced as the blame for their relatives' condition, formed associations to reinforce the indisputability of the illness model.

But disputed it has always been. There is a long tradition within psychiatry and psychology that has sought to establish that underlying even the more puzzling and apparently alien forms of psychological disturbance there are to be found social factors which have little to do with biological ones, except in so far as all thoughts, feelings and actions are mediated through and inseparable from our bodies. In my view, much of this work is far more intellectually convincing and empirically sound than the rough pragmatism of contemporary biological psychiatry, and yet its proponents are often barely heard of by present-day practitioners.[4] I can only account for this with the help of something like Foucault's notion of a 'discourse of power': only certain kinds of 'knowledge' are thinkable and sayable under a given power regime.

Modern psychiatry too has its critics,[5] but, again, their voices tend to be marginal and barely heard behind the chorus of orthodoxy. The view, for instance, that 'schizophrenia' can be called into question as a viable concept is now virtually irreceivable, despite its being one of the most muddled and empirically difficult to establish of all psychiatric diagnoses.[6]

What this means is that the sufferer falling into psychiatric hands cannot automatically expect to receive sympathetic, informed and intelligent help in understanding and alleviating his or her distress from the viewpoint of what it indicates about the nature of his or her world and what s/he can do about it. People in severe difficulties may of course be calmed down by appropriate medication, in some cases be given necessary if not always congenial asylum, and their families may receive much-needed respite. Psychiatry is far more about social control than it is about getting to the roots of psychological illness.

Clinical psychology

By contrast, clinical psychology is very much about understanding people's difficulties as the consequence of their experience of life (what's happening to them in the present as well as their 'learning history') and trying to devise ways of modifying their 'behaviour', as well as their attitudes and 'cognitions', so that the impact of these past and present events is lessened.

Clinical psychologists have nothing like the formal power of psychiatrists – they cannot interfere with or restrain their patients' *bodies* in any significant way – and so their influence over patients is reduced to the power of persuasion. Partly because of this lack of formal power, the kind of patronage or arrogance so frequently experienced with medical doctors is far less likely to be evident among clinical psychologists. They also spend much more time with patients than doctors do – consultations are likely to last for forty-five minutes to an hour at a time – and people are likely to be seen by the same person over the whole period of their treatment. A course of treatment may vary greatly in length, from just one or two consultations to over a hundred, but most will probably be between five and ten.

Although clinical psychology borrows liberally from related disciplines, in particular the various school of psychotherapy (and practitioners may vary widely in their theoretical allegiances), it has its roots in academic psychology, where there is a strong emphasis on experiment and evidence. This has the advantage that there is always an element of pressure on clinical psychologists to justify their procedures according to whether or not they can be shown to be effective, and hence, at least indirectly, to respect the views of their patients in this regard. The disadvantage is that academic psychology itself is a curious patchwork of competing notions (often grandiosely called 'theories'), the superficiality and implausibility of many of which are pretty evident to all except those trying industriously to establish the evidence in their favour.

This means that the ruling dogmas of clinical psychology, usually referred to loosely as 'cognitive behaviourism', embody an, in my view, extraordinarily simplistic collection of ideas about how people come to be the way they are and what they can be expected to be able to do about it. For example, how people learn things, how they form and change 'attitudes', whether and how they can control their 'thoughts', are often dealt with in psychology according to models that have been constructed from a combination of everyday, common-sense (and occasionally contradictory) assumptions and simplified laboratory experiments which scarcely do justice to the complexity of human experience. Such ideas, acceptable enough perhaps to undergraduate students learning the experimental ropes, ring particularly hollow when they come to be applied in the clinical setting, where people's difficulties are often complicated and intractable. Since these issues form the main preoccupations of later chapters, I will not discuss them further here, except to note that, however simplistic, the typical notions of cognitive behaviourism do at least have the merit of treating people as if they exist as social beings in a world that affects them and on which they may, through their own conduct ('behaviour'), have a reciprocal effect.

It is important also to note at this stage that what a practitioner *thinks* about what s/he is doing (and this applies, of course, to all practitioners, not just clinical psychologists), what his or her theories about it are, need not necessarily be all that important to the patient. What matters from the patient's point of view is whether what the practitioner does is helpful. In fact, many studies have shown that, at least for the 'talking therapies', to which, of course, clinical psychology contributes, what counts most towards patients' recovery is precisely not the theoretical inclinations of the practitioners, but their personality, i.e. how far patients feel able to talk to them and to trust them – how likeable they find them.

This is not a particularly convenient finding for those bent on demonstrating that their particular therapy – or even therapy in general – is a *technically* valid form of 'treatment', and any demonstrable advantage for procedures over personalities, however slight, is quickly seized upon. But, time and again, it is so-called nonspecific factors such as those mentioned that research throws up as principally important. This may mean that *only* personalities are important, but it may also mean that so far the active ingredients of successful therapy remain to be discovered. Given the simple-mindedness of many of the ideas about what is technically important in treatment, this latter possibility should not be discounted.

These speculations aside, we may conclude perhaps that what

makes an encounter with clinical psychology more comfortable for many patients than one with psychiatry is as much as anything the time they will be given and the common sense and ordinary humanity with which they will be treated. Since counselling and psychotherapy share with clinical psychology a general lack of formal power (particularly in the case of nonmedical practitioners), the same may be said, to a large extent, for them.

Psychotherapy and counselling

Although clinical psychology is a well-established mental-health profession, there are still only a few thousand clinical psychologists practising in Britain, most of them in the National Health Service. There are undoubtedly many more counsellors and psychotherapists countrywide, though most of them practise outside the NHS. Like every other, the 'market' in psychotherapy and counselling has been largely deregulated over the past decade or so, and there has been a huge increase in the range of therapies available. Even staid institutions of the official health services may now be found offering alternative approaches such as aroma therapy or reflexology as part of their 'package of care', and the criterion of acceptability of therapeutic approaches in general has become one more of saleability than of demonstrable efficacy. It has also become extremely difficult to generalise about counselling and psychotherapy, and a virtual impossibility for the average 'consumer' to be able to make sensible judgements about what may suit him or her.

It would certainly not be possible in the space of a few paragraphs to give anything like a complete and balanced account of all the varieties of psychotherapy and counselling available, and in any case, as already remarked, the 'official' version of their procedures often differs quite radically from what therapists actually do. Anyone wanting to investigate how the various schools of therapy and counselling set about their business is probably best advised to start out with one of the available texts that attempt a general overview.[7] I would, however, like to highlight one or two issues that seem to me particularly important.

The most obvious person to hold responsible for the origination of psychotherapeutic approaches is Sigmund Freud. In the public mind, certainly, Freud's creation, 'psychoanalysis', has achieved a higher profile than any other approach, and many of the basic ideas of psychoanalysis have become part of our everyday thought and language. Freudian psychoanalysis, moreover, having spent, in Britain at least, some of the middle decades of this century on the verge of, if not disrepute, then certainly neglect, has enjoyed a remarkable revival over the last twenty years. But it is important to realise that psychoanalysis is now only one of a vast range of 'talking' approaches to psychological distress, many of which have very little truck with psychoanalytic concepts.

All these approaches tend to differentiate themselves as clearly demarcated 'schools' with restricted entry, established procedures for training, and more or less strict criteria for accreditation. Psychoanalysis was no doubt very influential in setting this trend.

Freud, feeling himself and his colleagues a beleaguered band of scientific pioneers in a hostile and uncomprehending world of Philistines, was almost persecuted by the need to keep the strain of his ideas pure, and the structural development of psychoanalysis resembled more that of a fanatical religious group or a secret society than of a branch of knowledge. Similarly, those renegades who in the early days of psychoanalysis broke away from Freud to form their own systems, also took pains to differentiate themselves from others and to, so to speak, patent their ideas and give their approach a distinctive name. Alfred Adler, for example, developed his 'individual psychology', and C. G. Jung, rather more presumptuously perhaps, called his system 'analytical psychology'.

Throughout this century, ambitious and charismatic characters unable to toe the line of the therapeutic discipline in which they were schooled have continued the tendency to develop a new and distinctive brand, so that now there are literally hundreds of them.

They compete in a flourishing marketplace where there is no shortage of potential consumers, whose only problem is to decide which brand is for them.

There is absolutely no hard and fast evidence that any one approach to counselling or therapy is more effective than any other. This fact is hard to square with the often ferocious lengths a given school will go to to protect its boundaries and preserve the theoretical and practical distinctiveness of its approach. For, if there's nothing much to choose between them, why should they bother? The answer to this question must, I think, lie in the aura of authority which such tight regulation tends to impart. Careful vetting of candidates for training, scrupulous attention to teaching methods and requirements for clinical experience etc., and rigorous accreditation procedures, all of which tend to characterise the more established schools, give an impression to potential consumers that here indeed is a body of knowledge and a set of professional practices demanding veneration and justifying expense.

Psychoanalysis, largely through institutional practices of just the kind outlined above, has probably succeeded more than any other approach in developing a mantle of respectability and authority – with a strong dash of awe-inspiring mystique. The fact that many of its practitioners are medical doctors no doubt also contributes to its competitive edge in this respect. And yet it was precisely the shortcomings of psychoanalytic therapeutic technique – when it was without question the 'market leader' in psychological treatment – that led to the development of alternative approaches.

The psychoanalytic view is, essentially, that at the core of the patient's 'neurotic' difficulties lie the unconscious, wishful impulses of an illicit sexuality and aggression which have, through a process of 'interpretation' by the analyst, to be brought into consciousness and thereby under the disciplined control of the self.[8] The means whereby this was to be achieved, in orthodox analysis, involved an uncomfortably impersonal and distant relationship between patient and analyst, with the latter preserving a kind of neutral anonymity so that patients could 'project' onto him or her (as part of the 'transference relationship') the infantile desires and expectations which supposedly powered the unconscious mind. Quite apart from the fact that this procedure, when put to the test, didn't seem to work,[9] the coldly mechanistic nature of the therapeutic relationship did not endear itself to patients on the whole.[10]

It was probably the work of the psychologist Carl Rogers that did most to challenge the theoretical supremacy of psychoanalysis. Rogers, founder of the school whose 'brand name' is 'client-centred' (or sometimes 'nondirective') therapy, inspired a great deal of research around the mid-twentieth century which demonstrated that the relationship between 'clients' (as Rogerians prefer to call them) and therapists is crucial to the outcome of treatment. Far from preserving a 'neutral screen' for the 'projection' of fantasies by, as in psychoanalysis, sitting out of sight behind a patient stretched out on a couch, Rogerian therapists enter into a more recognisably human exchange with their clients.

In fact, the human characteristics of therapists – their 'warmth', 'empathy' and 'genuineness' – was shown by Rogerian research to be central to the effectiveness of therapy itself. Although, as with all psychological research in this area, these findings have not entirely stood the test of time, they do combine with others to emphasise the 'nonspecificity' of the more potent ingredients of therapy. As far as psychotherapy (including psychoanalysis) and counselling do have a beneficial effect, it is probably as much as anything the way the patient or client perceives the therapist *as a person* that makes the difference. To put it another way, it is solidarity with the therapist that lends heart to patients as they struggle with their difficulties.

Solidarity seems a rather mundane explanation of therapeutic efficacy to arrive at after so much effort and enthusiasm. If this is the conclusion to which experience, as well as the research literature, point us, it is a modest one, and one not easily accepted by either therapists and counsellors or their clients. Perhaps this is why so much energy continues to be invested by the ever-expanding schools of therapy and counselling in the development of distinctive and patentable *techniques* aimed at transforming the individual's distress into, if not happiness, then at least adjustment. And yet, though people's eagerness to believe in the magical promise of change implicit in so much of the therapy industry remains unabated, the evidence that such techniques can be found still stubbornly resists discovery.

The appeal of magic is extremely difficult to resist, and the idea that some kind of transformation takes place in the patient as the direct result of his or her interaction with the therapist is one that neither patients nor therapists find it at all easy to shake off. No less than with the 'mental illness' model of psychiatry, most forms of psychotherapy nurse a conception of the patient as someone *to* whom something is *done* through the technical procedures of the therapy: somehow or other, the *person* is changed, if only through having been moved to 'take responsibility' for his or her life.

This idea of the patient being inspired or transformed through association with an expert in possession of esoteric technical skills has a long history, and even in relatively recent times it is fascinating to see how the form as well as the content of the therapeutic consultation can be traced back to the practices of seventeenth-century magicians and astrologers.[11] So entrenched is this kind of notion in our culture that we can scarcely be blamed for continuing to insist on its validity, and it can probably be seen most clearly at present in the ubiquitous confidence placed in counselling as the antidote to life's commoner cruelties. It is as if anything that disturbs the smooth plastic surface of a 'normal' life, from problems in personal relationships to unexpected human-made or natural disasters, can be eased away with the unction of counselling.[12] It seems that we view psychological pain and emotional trauma as in themselves not only abnormal but unnatural, as something we have a right to have removed through the intervention of professional experts who can rearrange our feelings so that we are left unscarred by events. 'Post-traumatic stress' has thus become a 'disorder' rather than something we might reasonably expect as an entirely natural outcome.

Magic certainly lurks at the centre of a good deal of our thinking about counselling techniques. For example, the notion of 'positive thinking', in one or other of its guises, clearly maintains a widespread appeal. The injunctions of 'rational emotive therapy'[13] to see, and abandon, the folly of our 'irrational' assumptions about ourselves, or the emphasis in 'cognitive therapies' on changing the 'attitudes' that cast a gloom over our world – or even the popular inclination when times are bad to 'look on the bright side' – seem, perhaps, almost a matter of common sense. And yet they embody the profoundly magical idea that merely thinking about the world can change its nature. Noticing that the way we view the world can affect our experience of it misleads us into assuming that we can view it *how we like*: a psychological observation becomes a belief in magic.

The scope of psychotherapy

Limitations of therapy

The idea that individuals are, at least potentially, in charge of their own fate lies at the very heart of therapeutic philosophy. Although this may seem at first sight a healthily optimistic, even necessary view, without which we would wallow in our misery as helpless victims, it is, I believe, an essentially destructive one. The way I have stated it – that people may be in charge of their fate – already, perhaps, begins to show up its inadequacy, but this is basically what ideas about 'changing attitudes', 'assuming responsibility', acting on 'insights' gained, 'cognitive restructuring' and so on, all boil down to. By working on the *self*, people can change their experience of the *world*, and the effects of ravages they have suffered in the *past* can be repaired by them (with, of course, the help of their therapist) in the *present*. This is, certainly, an optimistic view, and it is not one that holds water. Not only does it make very little logical sense, but there is also no convincing empirical evidence that it works in practice.

There are no magical solutions to the damage life inflicts upon us, and to place the burden of change on individuals, to be achieved through some kind of therapeutically mediated internal psychological process, is only in the long run to add to their troubles. For at the end of it all the world is still there, still doing its damage, and all people are likely to feel as the results of their therapists' ministrations is responsibility for their own misery.

What has misled us, I believe, is as much as anything else the environment in which psychotherapy takes place and in which psychotherapeutic theories have therefore been conceived. This is the environment of the consulting room. There are only two animate figures in this space: therapist and patient. In consequence, everything that happens in it comes to be causally attributed to one or the other of them.[14] Even the patient's past is made manifest in the consulting room in the present, so that description of events becomes, almost inevitably, confused with the events themselves. The consulting room becomes, almost by default, a kind of alchemical crucible in which the protagonists can transmute the inert properties of the 'beyond' (whether in space or time) through the passionate force of their intentions and their living interaction. The only thing that seems to matter is what passes between patient and therapist. If the patient improves, for example, it seems self-evident that this must be because of the healing intervention of the therapist – what else could it be, when there is no one else there?

And yet, however much it may be valued – or overvalued – by both patients and therapists, the environment of the consulting room is not the environment in which they live out their lives, and for patients in particular (except those clients of psychoanalysis who spend five hours a week, year in and year out, in the company of an analyst) the influence of therapy is of minute significance in contrast with that of all the other people and things in their lives. Any adequate account of psychological distress, what causes it and what might alleviate it, must surely include the totality of our lives, and as part of that process take due note of the powerful, often inexorable, forces that shape us in the world beyond the consulting room.

Psychological distress, I am suggesting, is not a problem *of* the person or *of* the 'self', but is a problem presented *for* the person by the world.

Even the currently popular notion of 'stress', which would on the face of it seem to suggest a force bearing down on the individual from outside, ends up being represented by most therapeutic approaches as something *inside* people which they have to learn to deal with or 'manage'. Programmes of 'stress management' are in this way directed at manipulating the internal processes through which people are supposedly able to handle stress, rather than at diminishing the stressors in the outside world which have come to make a misery of the lives of so many of us. Once again, it seems to me, this is little more than a disguised form of magic – the belief that we can alter the world by altering the way we imagine it.

It cannot be emphasised too strongly, however, that to suggest that therapeutic magic doesn't cure the ills of the world is *not* to sink into pessimistic resignation. To say that things cannot be changed in the way that most therapeutic approaches imply is not to say that they cannot be changed, nor is it to say that the therapeutic process achieves nothing at all.

The problem with most approaches to psychotherapy and counselling, in my view, is that the theoretical account they give of what they are doing bears very little relation to what actually goes on in therapy, and that, though therapists often *do* do things that are helpful to clients, they have failed to see what these are and to describe them accurately. This is because they have been so anxious to provide the kind of technical analysis of their procedures that would justify their professional stance. There are, of course, exceptions to this rule, and there have been several practitioners of psychotherapy who have had the courage and perspicacity both to take account of the essentially nontechnical, personal nature of much of what they do and to write about the implications of this with power and clarity.[15]

What these writers achieve is to put psychotherapy and counselling in perspective (the perspective of the *relation* between patient and therapist), and in doing so – though this may not always be their main intention – they greatly reduce the grandiosity of its claims. Psychotherapy does not magic away the pains inflicted by the world, but, to some extent and in some cases, provides the patient with a way of understanding his or her predicament, and offers the solidarity of the 'therapeutic relationship' in trying to do something about it.

It is, I think, important to distinguish between three main components of psychotherapy: comfort, clarification and encouragement. These are present in different proportions in different approaches, and the effect of one easily becomes confused with the effect of another – a therapist may assume, for example, that a patient's improvement is due to the power of the 'insights' that have been derived from the explanatory model used in therapy, when it is simply the result of the comfort (solidarity) gained from the mere presence of the therapist.

Comfort

I suspect that it is principally the phenomenon of comfort that maintains the credibility of psychotherapy in the face of all the evidence that its efficacy is in fact only modest. The comfort to be derived from sharing your deepest fears and most shameful secrets with a 'valued other' who does not immediately heap blame or scorn upon you, but who instead listens patiently and sympathetically to what you have to say, is one of the most potently therapeutic experiences to be had. It is this experience that convinces patients and therapists of all persuasions of the validity of their enterprise. Indeed, some writers on psychotherapy, notably Ian Suttie[16] and Paul Halmos[17], have drawn attention to the absolute centrality of love itself to the therapeutic process, suggesting that the therapist's disinterested, loving concern for and acceptance of the patient is the curative factor in therapy.

But there are a number of important limitations to the provision of comfort[18] which must be noted. They are important not because they indicate that therapeutic comfort is somehow bogus, but because they do not square with the 'official' accounts which most therapists offer for the effectiveness of their procedures.

Comfort does not cure anything. Halving a trouble by sharing it does not somehow expunge it from the face of the earth, and when solidarity with the sharer finishes at the termination of therapy, the trouble becomes whole once again. In this way, it is the process of therapy itself that is experienced as therapeutic, and not anything the therapy brings about as a technical achievement.

Sometimes patients recognise the inadequacy of this state of affairs for themselves, especially with those varieties of counselling which consist almost solely of 'empathetic' listening ('it was all very well, but all she did was nod sympathetically'). Perhaps more often, however, they may become dependent on a relationship which, perversely from their point of view, is not intended to be available to them indefinitely: they will be expected to become 'better' at some point. It may well be the case, for example, that some people are sufficiently sustained by their relationship with their therapist to cope with life satisfactorily enough between visits, but it is the boost they get from the visits, rather than anything they have learned from the therapeutic process, that keeps them going. Once the visits have to stop (maybe because of the therapist's worries about 'dependency'), it is quite likely to emerge that nothing has really changed for the patient. The provision of therapeutic comfort of this kind is not unlike the administration of short-acting tranquillisers – it works, it is in a sense addictive, but it will have sooner or later to be withdrawn (with painful consequences).

This is not to say that therapeutic comfort is a bad thing, but it is to suggest that, if it is not to run the risk of becoming a bad thing, it has either to be available unlimitedly, or there have to be other components to the process which enable patients to benefit from it without becoming addicted. As long as comfort is not intended as an end in itself (which might be perfectly acceptable if there were enough comforters to go around), there should be other clear ends to which it may contribute as a means.[19]

Clarification

The component of what I call clarification is seen as essential by most therapeutic approaches. That is to say, it is usually considered necessary to furnish patients with an explanation of their distress – its history and antecedents. Certainly, when they first seek help, people often have no idea why they should be feeling so ill and distressed, and they may themselves attach considerable importance to being told by an expert 'what it is' that is troubling them.

Depending on the theoretical predilections of the therapist, accounts people get of the background to their problems may differ widely, as may the manner in which the information necessary for the construction of an account is extracted from them. It might, for example, take many hours of listening patiently to the sporadic free associations of a 'resistant' patient before a psychoanalyst felt able to lay bare the unconscious sexual wishes and fantasies thought to be at the root of the patient's present difficulties. An expert in 'behaviour modification', on the other hand, might, through a direct and matter-of-fact procedure of question and answer, arrive at a formulation of the client's 'learning history' in half an hour.

The most likely course, perhaps, would be for therapist and patient to collaborate in negotiating a view of the latter's difficulties that accords with the experience of both, so that the therapist will feel happy that the picture emerging of the patient's background and current circumstances is one that makes sense in terms of the kinds of events and relationships likely to give rise to distress, and the patient will feel that the explanations offered by the therapist do not jar too violently with what seems plausible from his or her own perspective. The therapist, in other words, checks the hypotheses that come to mind against the patient's experience.

It is, on the whole, probably not difficult for therapists who are reasonably intelligent, experienced and undogmatic to arrive at quite an accurate picture of what has been and is contributing to a patient's present distress. It may often be the case also that this picture is one which, though the patient eventually accepts it readily enough, came at first as a considerable surprise to him or her. It may be this element of unexpectedness that contributes to the mystique of therapeutic clarification – patients may be startled at what seems to them the almost magical perspicacity of the therapist in unearthing events and feelings in the past of which till then they had little inkling. Therapists are able to do this not because they have uncanny powers of insight (even if some would like to think so), but because they have seen many times before what the patient takes to be his or her utterly idiosyncratic experience. The answer to the question 'How could my therapist possibly have guessed that?' is that the same circumstance has been observed by the therapist in many previous cases.

There is, then, in principle at least, not a great deal of difficulty in arriving at an acceptable account of how people come to be as they are and what are the origins of their distress. Where difficulties do arise is in knowing what is to be done with this information. The idea that 'insight' leads automatically to cure, while figuring largely in many patients' expectations, has long been recognised to be problematic by therapists, even though in their hearts they find it very hard to abandon. Another temptation, touched on earlier, is to try magically to replace the account arrived at with one that offers a rosier prognosis. If we accept, as some 'cognitive' approaches do, that there is no reality beyond our interpretation of it (the way things are is the way we see them), then the possibility of altering history retrospectively becomes quite plausible. Cognitive therapists are fond of pointing out, for example, that a glass may be seen as half empty or half full, with the implication that a gloomy view of the past breeds a pessimism about the future and may be replaced by a more upbeat interpretation of our history.

It seems virtually impossible for almost any therapeutic approach to conceptualise the influence of the patient's past as anything other than something s/he must somehow *alter*, either by interpreting it as not so bad after all, or, having gained 'insight' into it, by deciding (presumably through an act of will) to be a different kind of person in the future; patients are required, that is, somehow to disregard or negate the effects of earlier experience.

Much of this book will be concerned with the impossibility of therapeutic ideas such as these, and with the intellectual and moral confusion which underlies them and which they generate in others. But this is not to say that the investigation of people's background and history is a waste of time. The point of establishing how you got to be the way you are is to disabuse yourself of *mistaken* explanations, not the least of which is that you are somehow responsible for it.

People are often mystified about the causes of their suffering, and an important aspect of their coming to understand what they can and cannot do about their predicament is to be *demystified*. Almost by its very nature (the expectation of magical transformation inherent in the therapeutic situation), psychotherapy is prone to mystify its clients further. For psychotherapy, along with all those approaches that see people's problems as *inside* them (as illnesses, 'character disorders', unconscious complexes, 'maladaptive' learning etc.), obscures the fact that there exists a world *outside* them in which the reasons for their distress are located. Psychotherapy, moreover, very often ends up by insisting, or at least implying, that the way out of their difficulties is up to them, and thereby makes matters worse by adding a moral burden to their troubles.

In this way, it seems to me, psychotherapy can easily become, and indeed frequently does become, a kind of disguised moral campaign which places colossal, and entirely unreasonable, demands on the individual. In suggesting, as many approaches to therapy and counselling do, that people ultimately accept 'responsibility' for themselves, not only do they betray a barely half-baked intellectual grasp of what could possibly be meant by 'responsibility', but they implicitly renounce any claim they could validly make to be offering a professional service.[20]

Encouragement

The third component of psychotherapy to be distinguished is encouragement. By this I mean any kind of influence brought to bear by the therapist on the patient to try actively to make a difference to the factors that are causing him or her distress. Therapies vary quite widely in the extent to which encouraging people to do things is seen as a legitimate role for the therapist. Some psychoanalytically inclined practitioners, as well as many counsellors, would not see it as any part of their business to give people advice or to intervene at all in the way they conduct their daily lives, though in fact there are probably few who can resist doing it at least in subtle ways. Others, like behaviour therapists, would see the prescription of action as an absolutely central plank of their practice.

For nonbehavioural therapists and counsellors (principally those who belong to the 'psychodynamic' tradition of psychoanalysis and its derivatives), the giving of advice to patients is seen as creating dependency and undermining the kind of moral autonomy so important to 'taking responsibility'. Many no doubt slip from this somewhat severe impartiality into encouraging and supporting their clients as the latter, following up on insights gained through therapy, struggle to make new adjustments to their world. But therapists of this persuasion have no developed ideas about what people should do or how they should do it: the theory offers no suggestions in this respect, and the practice, such as it is, is therefore likely to be haphazard, as much a factor of the therapist's personal experience – even whim – as anything else.

Behaviourists, as noted, are different, as are some of the more pragmatic 'cognitive' and 'positive thinking', rationalistic approaches. Courses of action may in these cases be prescribed with great confidence, perhaps even without its being felt necessary to give clients any explanation of why their behaviour is to be shaped in this or that direction. People, it is claimed, become different by acting differently, not by having insights or deciding to become responsible.

In some ways the behavioural view has a good deal to be said for it, and approaches of this kind, largely through the professional development of clinical psychology, have contributed a useful common-sense element to the practice of therapy and counselling. The realisation that insight gets nowhere without action is a necessary step forward. There are, however, difficulties with this kind of approach also.

These stem mainly from the extremely simplistic nature of many of the ideas about learning and change which underlie the cognitive-behavioural approach. These are frequently based on rather crude laboratory experiments in which captive groups of students or hospital patients are subjected to fairly obvious procedures of training or other behavioural manipulation, and the results generalised with little plausibility to the population at large. The intellectual sophistication of ideas about, for example, what constitutes 'learning' or the nature of 'attitudes' may not be great. Much of the earlier behavioural work was based on Pavlovian conditioning, giving rise to oversimplified ideas about positive and negative 'reinforcement' (reward and punishment) as the basis for human learning, and completely overlooking the importance of *meaning* to human beings. While a good deal of the more recent work on cognitive processes makes good this latter defect, it betrays, even so, a surprisingly unsophisticated view of 'cognitions' as things inside people which cause them to behave this way or that, and which can be worked on directly to change the way they behave. The logical mistake is made that, because reality is filtered through our minds, we can alter reality by changing our minds.

What this tends to mean for the patients of cognitive-behavioural therapists is that, though they will certainly be encouraged to tackle difficulties in their lives which the process of clarification has identified, this may often have an unsatisfyingly superficial – and ultimately ineffective – aspect to it.

I have no doubt that it is possible for a person experiencing even severe psychological distress to be helped profoundly and permanently by someone else, whether or not that someone else is a professional helper. However, I do not think that there is so far any convincing indication that any of the orthodox approaches to professional help have a coherent explanation of what makes a relationship 'therapeutic', and in so far as people may at times be therapeutic, it is most often for reasons they do not themselves fully understand.

Frequently, as I have suggested, it is the solidarity with the helper that is found helpful, but this is likely to be a relatively transient phenomenon. There is no evidence that the kind of technical reasons therapists give for the effectiveness, such as it is, of their therapy hold water. Conversely, there is no reason why therapists should be able to say what makes their work effective – the fact that we are unable to give an account of something does not mean that we are unable to *do* it.

Therapists have, I believe, been hampered when trying to account for what they do by the blinkers which the enclosed world of the consulting room has placed on their vision. They have assumed that both the reasons for their clients' distress and the means of alleviating it are to be found within those walls, and they are wrong on both counts. Nevertheless, the experience that comes of trying to help people in emotional difficulties and the immense proliferation of conflicting ideas about therapy which this century has generated make it extremely unlikely that absolutely all therapeutic efforts are going to be in vain and that every theoretical position is vacuous.

There are indeed important lessons to be learned from the practice of psychotherapy, the clues to which are to be found in its three principal components. But, in contemplating the possible benefits of comfort, clarification and encouragement, we need a much more careful and precise analysis of what is really involved in these processes, and whether they could be achieved in other – perhaps more effective – ways than through psychotherapy and counselling. For a further, more negative, but no less important, lesson to be learned from psychotherapy may be that it is possible to survive without it.

To appreciate this we need to see that much of what makes therapeutic intervention seem attractive to people in distress is precisely those elements of its mystique that cannot be fulfilled. Therapists are not the possessors of esoteric knowledge through which people may be transformed – on the whole, as I have suggested, they don't know what they're doing. Furthermore, the very process (the claustrophobic atmosphere of the consulting room) and some of the almost axiomatic beliefs of psychotherapy (e.g. about 'responsibility') militate against an adequate understanding of people's predicaments.

What I shall attempt to do in the remainder of this book is take what I believe can be learned from the practice of psychotherapy both to clarify some of the more common dilemmas people find themselves in and to point to ways of dealing with them which, I hope, may be found encouraging. In suggesting that psychological and emotional distress have their origin in the world rather than in the person, I hope also that there may be some comfort to be derived from these pages.

What I cannot engineer, of course, is a personal relationship with a psychotherapist. Although it is true that this is probably the most immediately potent element in all therapeutic approaches, I am not, for reasons I have already given, convinced that it is the most important one. Nothing will ever change the need for human solidarity, whatever form it comes in, and psychotherapy is only one of many. But the sheer confusion and mystification which still surround our basic notions of mental illness and emotional distress may perhaps best be attacked without the help of a therapy industry which, for the most part, does all too much to maintain them.

CHAPTER TWO

The Experience of Distress

It is not always easy for people in emotional turmoil to shift their attention from *self* to *world*, and yet, if they are to gain an understanding of the origins of their difficulties, that is the most important thing for them to do. We have learned, when in physical pain, to look for the cause inside our bodies, and perhaps that is why we tend to think that the roots of 'psychological' pain are to be found inside our minds. However, when it comes to understanding so-called clinical distress, the causes of our pain are likely to be found in the world beyond our skin.

Psychiatry's obsession with cataloguing the phenomena of distress into diagnostic syndromes of illness is rendered ultimately futile precisely because the supposed victims of such illness are not carriers of clear-cut cultures of disease, but in essence ordinary human beings struggling to cope with a disordered world. The continued efforts of psychiatry to define ever more tightly and exclusively the varieties of illness it thinks are to be discerned in emotional suffering borders, at the end of the twentieth century, on farce. Psychiatrists seem to hope that if, like Victorian gentleman scholars sorting butterflies, they refine their descriptions carefully enough, they will identify species of disease which can be treated medically in the same way that, for instance, tuberculosis can. Widespread criticism of this approach,[1] not to mention its evident fruitlessness, has done nothing over the past hundred years to diminish the enthusiasm of those who engage in it, nor indeed to cast doubt on its viability in the public mind. There are all sorts of reasons for this, but the point I want to emphasise here is that we should not allow the apparent authoritativeness of the medical model to distract us from the search for a more satisfactory alternative.

It is of course possible to arrive at broad descriptions of the kinds of distress that human beings are prone to. As embodied creatures, we have only a limited number of ways to react to the blows life inflicts upon us: the way we express our thoughts and feelings will depend on the physical structure of our bodies. For example, I weep with sadness because that is how human beings are constructed to express the feeling we call sadness, but the physical process of weeping is not the cause of my sadness. On the whole we have no difficulty with the idea that, to understand the meaning of sadness, we need to look to the outside world to see what is making us sad. 'Meaning' points us outside ourselves. Similarly, we can talk about 'anxiety' and 'depression' reasonably comprehensibly because pretty well everybody knows how it feels to be anxious or depressed, and we understand, too, that people are anxious or depressed *about* something. When it comes to 'clinical' distress, however, we suddenly, and quite erroneously, abandon the quest for meaning and divert our gaze instead to the purely physical forms in which distress is given expression and the supposed interior 'pathogenic' process which, we assume, gives rise to them.

Psychiatry, of course, derives its plausibility from precisely those states where people feel anxious or depressed in the apparent absence of there being anything to be anxious or depressed about. It is in these circumstances, for example, that 'depression' may be characterised as 'clinical depression'. But the fact that you can't immediately tell why you're depressed doesn't mean that you have nothing to be depressed about, and that the depression is therefore simply a physical reaction which has got out of hand. It is, I believe, far more sensible and accurate to suggest that it is possible *not to know* why you are depressed than it is to maintain that you are suffering from a 'depressive illness'.[2]

The situation may seem more problematic in the case of the diagnostic labels psychiatrists have concocted to describe complex syndromes of feeling-states and behaviour, for example, 'schizophrenia'. The existence of a 'mental illness' corresponding to this label is nowhere near as well established as the orthodoxy would suggest, but, no doubt, its imposingly medical title deters the ordinary person from questioning it too profoundly. We may feel that our personal familiarity with depression and anxiety authorises us to talk knowledgeably about them, but how many of us would claim to feel schizophrenic from time to time?[3] In fact, there may well be ways for us to begin to understand the experience of 'schizophrenia': try, for example, to imagine feeling unbearably confused, excited and suspicious all at once and you should get quite a good idea.[4] There are times in most people's lives when they become so disturbed and distraught that a ten-minute talk with a psychiatrist could quite easily get them diagnosed as 'psychotic'.

The huge effort put by psychiatry into refining a set of diagnostic labels for the ways in which people exhibit 'signs and symptoms' of distress has become self-perpetuating: if you enforce a standard descriptive vocabulary and insist on similar methods of observation, you can indeed demonstrate a degree of consistency between observers. But the fact that people can agree reliably on a description of how someone is behaving does not say anything about the significance of that description. The fact that someone is showing signs of what psychiatrists have agreed among themselves to call 'paranoid schizophrenia' carries absolutely no implication that there is such a thing as 'paranoid schizophrenia'. This is the problem with psychiatry: there *are* no illnesses corresponding to the labels it has succeeded in agreeing upon.

However watertight and exhaustive a list of descriptions of distress can be made, it is bound not to throw any light on how those states arise, simply because it has nothing to say about the world in which they occur. The way we feel depends on a combination of our past experience and what happens to us in the present, both in the setting of our cultural expectations. We are in a continuous process of interchange with our social and cultural environment, so that the way we experience and express emotional distress depends on a whole range of factors outside ourselves and will also change significantly with the times.[5]

In fact, as I tried to show in *The Origins of Unhappiness*, it makes in many ways much more sense to diagnose the ways in which the *environment* can be damaging than it does the *people* who are damaged by it. I have no doubt, for example, that the radical shift to a 'business culture' which took place in Britain and elsewhere over the decade of the eighties rendered whole sections of the population vulnerable to forms of distress that had touched them only minimally before, as well as creating forms of 'pathology', especially in the young, which are only now becoming evident. (I shall return to this later.)

What is important, then, is not to categorise individuals according to a descriptive typology of emotional distress, but to seek to understand how their distress, whatever form it takes, arises out of their interaction with the world and to identify the kinds of situation in the social environment that can be particularly damaging.

In the rest of this chapter, I shall try to relate some of the commoner ways in which distress is experienced to the kinds of predicaments typically giving rise to them. In order to simplify the discussion, I shall divide the latter into background and current predicaments. Both have their own distinct importance, and it is not really possible to say that one is more significant than the other in accounting for the distress a given individual experiences. Vulnerabilities people have acquired in the past may be brought to the fore by pressing difficulties in the present,[6] and when trying to understand the reasons for anyone's psychological pain it is probably wise to neglect neither the past nor the present.

I want to emphasise as strongly as possible that I am not trying in what follows to compete with psychiatry by setting out an alternative typology of 'mental disorder'. By seeking a structure in which to convey varieties of distress and the kinds of predicaments that may be underlying them, I want only to offer a framework in which they can be discussed without too greatly distorting reality. This is not, in other words, intended as any kind of definitive scientific analysis of the phenomena of emotional distress.

Nor is it intended to be exhaustive. In selecting the material for discussion and the particular examples which I hope may illuminate it, I have in mind a readership not unlike those I encounter in my role as clinical psychologist – people, that is, who have been unable to escape, or hide from themselves, the effect of some of the unkinder lessons of life, and who may perhaps have found the orthodox approaches to their difficulties not particularly helpful. I shall have less to say about the kinds of distress likely to be experienced by people whose fundamental predicaments have been so disabling that they are likely to need, at least occasionally, some form of institutional help. This is not because I regard the nature of such difficulties as qualitatively different from those I shall be considering, but rather because I can speak with confidence only from my own practical experience, which has, for the past twenty-five years, been outside the context of inpatient treatment facilities such as mental hospitals.

One further caveat: when looking, in this chapter, at 'background' and 'current' factors in a given type of predicament, I shall for the most part be doing so from the perspective of the individual occupying that predicament. I shall not, that is to say, be trying at this stage to give an objective account of how distress arises, but one that attempts to adopt the viewpoint of the person suffering it. It is of the utmost importance to distinguish between the way someone *experiences* their problems and what the *causes* of those problems are.

The importance of this distinction applies most strongly in considering the influence of factors in the person's past, in particular the influence of the family. From the personal perspective, injuries suffered at the hands of family members, particularly parents, may very understandably – and in a sense even rightly – be seen as the responsibility of those family members. From an objective perspective, on the other hand, the individual's past was the family's present, and its members no doubt had at the time good reasons for conducting themselves as they did: reasons which they may, indeed, have been unable to resist. These are issues to which we shall return in later chapters, where I hope any apparent paradox will be resolved, but the point of distinguishing here between a subjective and an objective view of cause is to avoid as far as possible the apportionment of blame.

In my view, blame has no legitimate part to play in the objective, psychological understanding of people's conduct, but this is not to say that it is wrong for a person to feel aggrieved at the way, for instance, s/he was treated as a child. For the individual sufferer, that is to say, blame has a legitimacy that it does not have for the psychologist, and it is confusion over this issue that has led so often in the past to misunderstanding, offence and rancour at the suggestion that the nature of early family relations can contribute to later distress.[7] Let it be understood, therefore, that the adoption of the perspective of the sufferer in what follows does not imply an objective attribution of blame to those at whose hands s/he suffered. We all of us try our best, even though much of the time we don't succeed.

Forms of distress – the way it feels

The commonest reaction to adverse events and experiences is unhappiness or, if the events or experiences are severe or prolonged enough, despair. On the whole, people know why they are unhappy or despairing, and, though they may go to the doctor for pills to help them sleep or perhaps for practical advice, they tend not to consult professionals over feelings whose causes are clear to them. It is more when unhappiness takes forms that we cannot immediately understand, or has effects we seem unable to control, that we tend to turn to the experts for help. This is no doubt very largely because of a cultural expectation that suffering of unknown origin is likely to be the result of 'illness'. Freud's distinction between 'hysterical misery' and 'common unhappiness' would tend to bear this out.

In my view this is, however, neither the most productive nor the most accurate way of looking at things. It is not obvious why we should always be able to identify the causes of our feelings, and there is no good reason to conclude that our being unable to do so indicates some kind of 'neurotic' problem. Our disturbed feelings do not necessarily tell us *what* is wrong, but they do all tell us that *something* is wrong. In those cases where we cannot immediately see what is wrong, our potential for understanding may well have been diverted more by the misconceptions of our culture than by some kind of perverse impulse to hide the truth from ourselves. In my experience, people engage in the search for the causes of their unhappiness, when encouraged to do so, with seriousness and determination, and if they appear to be 'resisting' the enlightenment offered them by the so-called experts, that is for the most part out of an entirely healthy suspicion of the unhelpful mystifications they are being fed.[8]

There is, then, no difference in kind between distress caused by circumstances that are immediately identifiable to us and distress whose origins are obscure. The causes of distress may be out of our sight, situated in parts of the environment to which we simply do not have access, or perhaps out of the reach of our memory, having occurred at a time in the past we can no longer recover in words. However, human beings are not content simply to do without explanations, and if a person cannot see the reason why s/he is feeling unhappy or distressed, s/he is likely to invent one. The absence of a reason will be replaced by the most plausible reason that can be invoked. It is this phenomenon that is traded on by the professionals, who are only too ready to jump in with plausible explanations to account for their clients' distress – and plausibility here may be established more by the authority with which the professionals are ready to back their explanations than by any relation they bear to reality.

Establishing the truth of the matter – what the problem 'really is' – is by no means a cut-and-dried procedure, either in principle or in practice, but it does lie in examining precisely the relation between speculation and reality. Any hypothetical explanation for a given individual's distress needs to be validated against his or her experience of the world. In many ways, this is exactly what is meant by 'being scientific', but without any of the mystifying dogmatism and intellectual arrogance that have come to be attached to that expression. We need to be convinced of the truth of an explanation not because we have been impressed or bullied by the status or prestige of an authority, but because it makes sense to us in the context of our knowledge and experience of the world.

The mystique of authority derives at least in part from the notion that establishing the truth of the matter is not something people can do for themselves. It may certainly help to have a guide from time to time, but this does not mean that there is an esoteric access to 'truth' available only to a professional caste of experts. There is, of course, a constant struggle within society for certain professional groups to mystify and monopolise 'truth', but it is still perfectly possible to clarify the reasons for our unhappiness without recourse to a professional psychotherapist. In many respects, it may even be easier.

In those cases where the reasons for unhappiness are not transparent, the experience of distress itself is likely to include a feeling of loss of control – 'not knowing' *puts* one out of control. For the sake of discussion, I shall identify three kinds of loss of control: of feelings, thoughts and actions. This threefold distinction is to an extent artificial, and certainly not mutually exclusive – feelings, thoughts and actions are frequently bundled up inseparably together, and do not occur in neat sequences (one of the grosser errors of cognitive psychology is to assume that they do). I should stress that a feeling of loss of control is just that – a feeling – and does not imply that normally one *is* in control of what one feels, thinks and does. (The issue of control is one to which we shall return in Chapter Six.) Let me also emphasise again that what follows should not be taken as an attempt at a scientific categorisation of types of 'disorder'.

Loss of control of feelings

Being suddenly assailed by feelings of acute fear or panic out of all proportion to the situation in which they occur is probably the commonest form of distress prompting people to seek professional help. So inexplicable do these feelings seem at the time that they are not always immediately recognised as constituting fear, but may be thought by the sufferer to indicate some serious physical problem such as a heart attack. Certainly, the physical concomitants of 'anxiety states' can be extremely unpleasant and frightening in themselves: breathlessness, pounding heart, chest pains, sweating and trembling, faintness and dizziness, inability to swallow and sensations of choking can overtake the individual so rapidly and unexpectedly that the very possibility of a recurrence can itself become a constant fearful preoccupation.

Some people very quickly realise that the sensations they are experiencing do in fact constitute fear, even though it may not be at all clear what they are afraid of. Others may take some time to make the connection, perhaps arriving at this conclusion only after thorough medical examination has failed to reveal any serious physical pathology. Others again may never accept that their feelings have anything to do with fear and anxiety, and may devote years of their lives to the quest for what they are convinced is the physical cause of their troubles.

Our culture certainly doesn't make it easy for us to grasp the relation between what we see as a mental experience, like fear, on the one hand, and physical sensations, like breathlessness and

ANN

Form of distress	Current predicament	Background predicament
Feelings of panic (dizziness, choking, inability to breathe, etc.) in public places like shops, restaurants, buses and trains. Only after a while does Ann begin to experience these 'symptoms' as fear, and a profound loss of confidence in the presence of other people.	After a messy divorce, Ann has married again, this time to a much kinder and more considerate man. However, the children of both their former marriages do not get on well together, and Ann and her new husband are experiencing friction about how to deal with the situation.	Ann's parents split up when she was fourteen, and she, as the eldest of three daughters, had to assume a good deal of responsibility for her sisters. Neither of her parents had taken much interest in her, being preoccupied with their own difficulties, and she had a very poor relationship with her stepfather. She married her first husband at the age of eighteen, thereby getting away from the family home as soon as she could.

dizziness, on the other. We tend to compartmentalise ourselves into 'minds' and 'bodies', and we often take quite a bit of convincing that the two are not separate at all, but expressions of the same thing. We cannot, of course, feel anything without our bodies being involved in producing the feeling, but we still find it hard to shake off the idea that things are either physical events in the material world or are 'all in the mind', perhaps as products of our imagination. In this way, it becomes difficult for people to believe that the absolutely undeniable physicality of their feelings could be put down to anything as insubstantial and 'mental' as fear or anxiety, and they assume, not always wrongly, that an admission that what they feel is fear would be taken by others as evidence that they were 'imagining things'.

There is certainly nothing imaginary about the experience of acute pain and anxiety, though it is also true that it is not nearly as visible to others as the sufferer often fears. The discomfort and misery of such experiences are frequently compounded by the embarrassment the person feels at what s/he assumes is the obviousness of his or her condition to others. This can become a vicious circle, so that, for example, the feelings of shame attached to 'making an exhibition of oneself' – blushing perhaps – can in themselves become the object of phobic dread. The experience of anxiety consists of sensations that have enormous internal saliency but low external visibility: feelings which can be so overwhelming as to make the sufferer afraid s/he is about to faint or may even be dying are likely to go entirely unnoticed by casual passers-by. This is not to say that such feelings are not physical, but that they are mediated by bodily processes on the inside rather than the outside. What feels like a cataclysmic physical event may be externally observable, if at all, as no more than a barely perceptible tremor.

The fear experienced in 'anxiety states' may or may not become attached to specific objects, situations or events. Most commonly, fear of becoming socially conspicuous is what lies behind panic attacks, and the person comes to dread social occasions such as going out shopping or having to use public transport. Sometimes the fear becomes focused on particular situations, again usually in public space – for example, eating in restaurants (and making a spectacle of oneself through choking). Situations where one becomes for an instant the focus of another's attention (filling in forms, signing cheques or papers) can lead to sudden and terrifying panic.

The list of situations (open spaces, enclosed spaces, heights, thunderstorms, wind, snow, meetings, parties, flying, driving) and objects and animals (dogs, cats, spiders, bees and wasps, moths, types of food) to which fear and anxiety can become attached is virtually infinite. People may also fear loss of physical or mental control (often in the absence of any evidence that they have ever done so, or are particularly likely to do so). Dread of loss of bowel or bladder control, for example, may make people's lives a misery as every journey they take becomes a nightmare of planning and every unexpected invitation to go somewhere unfamiliar a cause for panic. Fear of going mad, 'going completely over the top', can often accompany and compound fears and phobias that are already disabling enough.

Most of us are afraid of *something* and could quickly be rendered to jelly by a confrontation with a tarantula, the edge of a steep cliff or an invitation to address a roomful of strangers. As long as such situations as these do not become anything more than rare events in our lives, we are likely not to be particularly troubled by them, and indeed if someone wished to get rid of, say, a fear of spiders, it is not particularly difficult to do so.[9] Sometimes, however, what look like relatively specific objects of fear constitute the visible part of broader or deeper anxieties which are not removed simply by tackling what they seem superficially to be about.

What unites practically all varieties of anxiety, phobia and panic that are not relatively superficial or trivial is a loss of confidence in oneself and one's ability to deal with and earn the attention and respect of others. Often this is a quite conscious part of people's distress, but sometimes, usually because of the kind of social role that is expected of them, it may be quite difficult and painful for them to acknowledge.

To sally out and deal with people in the world, to have 'presence', to appear to others in the way they appear to oneself, i.e. as of consequence, takes a degree of nerve and self-confidence which, when we have it, it is easy to take for granted. This, it seems, is how we are naturally, and to depart from that state is to have 'something wrong' with ourselves. And yet there is probably nothing natural about it. Indeed, I suspect that our culture greatly overvalues the kind of brash independence so many decently sensitive and shy people long to develop.

Be that as it may, there are times in most people's lives when their confidence is eroded to a point where they feel so socially incapable, or so conspicuously incompetent in the eyes of others, that they feel themselves wilting and shrivelling under their scrutiny. In many ways, this *is* the experience of anxiety, and this is what makes it so terrifying: we feel ourselves becoming nothing. We become, it seems, detached from the (social) world in which we are 'normally' rooted, our environment becomes uncannily distant and unreal and we are consumed by panic at the unfamiliarity, isolation and threat that are involved in the experience.

There can be few people who are not familiar with the state of depression. As with anxiety, it is probably when we can't see the reasons for it that it turns from a painful and unpleasant experience into a malign and threatening form of misery.

Being depressed about an event in the world (a loss or disappointment, perhaps) which can be clearly identified by the sufferer as well as those close to him or her is likely to be accepted by all concerned as a temporary phenomenon, and one that may even earn him or her a degree of comforting solidarity with others, which is itself healing. When, however, a black and deadening cloud of despair descends on the individual for no apparent reason, and stays there, perhaps, for weeks at a time, only to disappear as mysteriously as it came, not only does s/he come almost superstitiously to dread its return, but people around him or her are likely to get impatient with what they see as capriciousness. If people don't have a reason to be depressed, so the thinking goes, then they must be 'doing it themselves', so that persisting in being depressed must reflect some kind of wilful refusal to 'snap out of it'.

This virtually inevitable response from the family and friends of 'depressives' serves to compound a condition in which guilt and self-loathing already play only too prominent a part. Depressed people know perfectly well that their state adversely affects those around them, but they are utterly incapable of cheering up to order, and the unhappiness they cause others simply becomes one more reason for self-reproach.

BRENDA

Form of distress	Current predicament	Background predicament
Periods of black depression when she cannot speak without weeping and spends most or all of the day in bed. Unable to go to work and overwhelmed by numbing misery. Only the presence of her small daughter prevents her, she feels, from killing herself.	Brenda seems to have almost no time for herself and no pleasure in life. Her work as a teacher is exhausting and demanding, and her husband sounds like a conceited bully (though she does not herself describe him as such) who constantly undermines her and lives his life entirely to suit himself.	Brenda's mother is a perfectionistic paragon who dominated the family as Brenda and her younger brother were growing up. Brenda felt she could never match her mother's virtue and capability, and it seems she was never able as a child to say how she felt or voice any criticism of anyone in the family. Her father was a weak, rather depressed man who drank a lot and died just before Brenda got married. Both parents, having always wanted a boy, clearly preferred her brother.

Depression, at its worst, is a hopeless, dulled despair from which all vitality has been drained, with a timelessness which abolishes, so it seems, all possibility of future redemption, all ties of love severed in a state of blank, black isolation. What is often striking about it is the degree to which it cannot be put into words: at its centre there seems to be, literally, something indescribable, a black hole impacted with meaning for which no language can be found. It is about something that cannot be said. Nor can it be touched by words of comfort: it is inexorable, and cannot be reasoned away.

There are, to be sure, usually some things sufferers *can* say, for instance concerning their personal worthlessness, and they may be consumed by guilt at what may seem to others imaginary misdemeanours. However, like the anxious person who 'hangs' his or her feelings on the most likely-looking peg available (even if, as in the case of some of the more outlandish 'phobias', it doesn't look very likely to others), the depressed person may simply try to find *something* to account for how terrible s/he feels.

Mercifully, depression lifts after a time, though not necessarily for any more obvious reason than its original descent. Sometimes it is replaced by a state of unusual energy and optimism. In its more extreme form ('hypomania'), this swing of mood can contain a degree of aggressive self-assertion and insensitive ebullience which can be more distressing to others (though not to the 'sufferer') than the previous state of abject depression.

There are, of course, other ways in which people's feelings can run out of control. These may or may not be associated with elements of anxiety or depression of the kind already discussed.

There is, for example, a form of guilt which haunts a lot of people's lives and is by no means always linked to depression. It may seem to be more an aspect of personality, a way in which the person characteristically responds to the implied, maybe even nonexistent, demand of others. In many larger families there seems to be at least one person who takes on the cares of the rest, whose superconscientiousness contrasts, perhaps, with the careless selfcentredness of at least some of the others and is constantly made use of by them without hesitation or scruple. Furthermore, what started in the family often becomes extended to every other social situation the person occupies, including work. Even though people in this kind of role may be able to see perfectly well that they are being exploited by others, any attempt they make not to respond in the customary manner is likely to cause them unbearable guilt until they once again conform to expectations.

Jealousy can be a distressingly out-of-control emotion capable of wreaking havoc in the individual's personal life and relationships.

CATHERINE

Form of distress	Current predicament	Background predicament
Most of Catherine's day is taken up with watching, testing and setting traps for her boyfriend. Once she detects (as invariably she must) the slightest sign of infidelity of thought or deed (he only has to look at another woman), she works ceaselessly both to get him to admit his guilt and to reassure her that he loves her above all. Needless to say, their relationship is strained to breaking point. She has always ended her previous relationships, often out of (never well-founded) suspicion and jealousy.	It is difficult to find anything wrong in Catherine's current life. She is clever, beautiful, and very successful in her job, and though his patience is tried to the limit, her boyfriend is loving and attentive.	Catherine's father deserted her and her mother when she was two. Her mother was an air hostess, who spent a lot of time away from home. First Catherine was looked after principally by her grandmother, who died when she was three. She then had a nanny whom her mother sacked when she was five. When she was eight, her mother married a rich businessman, and she was promptly sent to boarding school, where she remained, apart from sometimes exotic holidays with her parents, sometimes lonely ones without them, until she was eighteen. She hated school.

Once again, it is the lack of visible justification that turns 'normal' jealousy into a supposedly 'pathological' condition needing professional attention. It is easy enough to empathise with, say, the jealous anger of a young woman whose boyfriend is flirting ostentatiously with someone else, but our imagination seems to fail us when, in the absence of such behaviour on his part, she harangues him for hours about his past relationships, ransacks his possessions in search of letters or photographs, and plunges into despair at what she is convinced is his disdain for her. In the first case, we are ready without hesitation to endorse the legitimacy of the emotion in relation to an event in the external world giving rise to it. In the second, we attribute her problem with almost equal conviction to a hypothetical internal pathology for which we actually have no evidence at all. It does not seem to occur to us to search her world a little more carefully and thoroughly. The banal assumptions of our culture, it seems, have made it more and more difficult for us to take an interest in each other's lives.

Loss of control of thoughts

For most people, most of the time, it seems that what they are thinking about is what they have chosen to think about. If invited to switch our attention from one line of thought to another, we can probably do so without too much difficulty, and even if we are not necessarily conscious of choosing to think this or that, the usual drift of our musings and associations – our 'stream of consciousness' – does not as a rule seem uncomfortably out of control.

There are times in everyone's life when, quite clearly, we are preoccupied with issues – or more likely an issue – that come to mind unbidden and are hard to shift out of. All of us know the feeling of not being able to stop worrying about a particularly pressing difficulty, or of not being able to concentrate at such a time on things we want to concentrate on, like reading a book.

Having thoughts or ideas imposed upon us without the involvement of our own will is also a common experience – it happens to us every night in our dreams. Again, the activity of writing frequently seems to generate ideas or narratives of which the writer had no conscious awareness – they seem to write themselves. On the whole, though, with the exception perhaps of nightmares, such experiences as these do not cause us any particular distress.

The kind of thinking that has come to be called 'obsessional', on the other hand, is most definitely distressing. This is not so much because obsessional thoughts seem to be imposed upon us as because they are bound up with feelings of tension and anxiety. They are also frequently bound up with a compulsion to do something – some repetitive or ritual action, perhaps – but since this is by no means always the case, I shall reserve discussion of compulsions for the next section.

CRAIG

Form of distress	Current predicament	Background predicament
Craig is afraid he's going mad. At times when he should be concentrating on his work as a printer, he finds himself urgently preoccupied with 'silly thoughts' about who he would be if he were not himself, or about why a particular object in the room is where it is and not somewhere else. Such thoughts also seem to invade his mind unpredictably at other times of the day. Craig is also very worried that he may have contracted a fatal and contagious disease that he could pass on to his family.	There is a threat of redundancies at work, and though Craig is the most conscientious of his colleagues, he feels he is not 'one of the boys' and they may take the opportunity to get rid of him. He seems also to be under pressure from his rather possessive girlfriend whom he has known since schooldays, but from whom he is perhaps becoming a little distant now.	Craig's parents never got on particularly well, though they are still together. His father was a well-meaning but distant man, completely absorbed in running the small family business. His mother was an anxious, rather fussy and intrusive woman, ambitious for her son but somehow not entirely in sympathy with him. An only child, Craig had always been 'a bit of a loner' at school, though he had done well academically.

Sometimes, as is the case with Craig to a considerable extent, the distress associated with obsessional thoughts seems to arise more from an uncertainty about how 'normal' they are (or, more strongly, a conviction that they are crazy) than from any direct association with anxiety-laden issues in the person's life. Especially for young people, it is not always easy to tell whether the thoughts and fantasies they find themselves engaged in are indicative of some kind of mental abnormality, quite possibly serious. It is rather as if we suddenly came to question the significance of our dreams for the state of our mental health – does their bizarre irrationality indicate that we are mad?

It is very hard to convince Craig, for example, that his speculations about existence have been the legitimate preoccupation of philosophers throughout their lifetime, and I have encountered many other young people who are disturbed by being unable to shake themselves free of thoughts or fantasies which, perhaps, contain elements of violence or other unacceptable impulses they fear may get out of control.

The intensity and frequency of obsessional thinking does often seem to fluctuate with the degree of stress in people's lives, though this may not always be obvious to them: as, again, with some forms of 'phobia', the thoughts become a focus for anxieties which have their origin elsewhere. Indeed, the content of obsessional thoughts is often, though by no means always, linked to a dread that some feared event is about to take place or to a feeling – clearly recognised as irrational – that thinking about it systematically and intensely enough will somehow prevent its happening. There may in this way be a superstitious element in obsessional thinking (as there is more often and very markedly in the case of compulsive behaviour). On the whole, however, though there is undoubtedly *meaning* in obsessional thinking (it happens for perfectly good reasons, as I hope will become clear in the course of subsequent discussion), in the majority of cases the person concerned is not aware of what the meaning is. This is not because of some failure of insight or intelligence on his or her part, but because there are no adequate cultural tools with which to get to grips with issues of this kind.

It is not only in 'obsessional states' that people may become painfully unable to direct the mind where they want it to go. This is also a feature of acute self-consciousness. If you become intensely aware of yourself as the object of the gaze of others, you may become locked into a kind of desperate self-monitoring which allows you to take account of practically nothing else in your social environment. It is almost as if you float above yourself, observing yourself going through the motions of talking to others, but excruciatingly aware as well that you can barely attend to what they say, and certain that they are as aware as you of your social incompetence. For shy people, something like this is a pretty common experience, and they may in time come to accept it as a more or less normal part of their lives, but the more shamefully inadequate people feel, the less they can forget themselves in their social encounters, and the more desperately fixed their attention seems to become on themselves.

One of the chief difficulties with all forms of loss of control over the direction of your attention is, of course, that the more you try to concentrate on something else, the more riveted you seem to become by the very preoccupation you are trying to escape.[10] This phenomenon in itself is a considerable cause of distress.

Loss of control of actions

Finding yourself unable to control your actions can be particularly distressing and alarming, not least because other people may become almost as involved in the problem as you are. This is particularly the case with the more serious addictions to drugs or alcohol, the results of which can at times be more devastating to families than to sufferers themselves,[11] but even with less dramatic forms of loss of control, it may be impossible for people to disguise from others the struggles they are going through, and the apparent irrationality of their conduct may become painfully exposed to bafflement or even ridicule. People who find themselves subject to so-called compulsive behaviour do their best to hide their difficulties from others, suffering agonies of shame as they perform their rituals in secret.

DAVE

Form of distress	Current predicament	Background predicament
Before leaving his room in the morning, Dave feels compelled to perform a number of safety checks on gas, water and electricity. These have become rituals which have to be performed absolutely precisely, and if any element is neglected (say, the order in which gas taps are checked), the whole procedure has to be started over again. If he doesn't do these things, he suffers unbearable tension and anxiety.	Dave is doing quite well on a postgraduate media-studies course, though, because of his rituals, he finds it difficult to get to college on time. A couple of relationships with girls have ended rather messily and painfully, and he doesn't make friends easily, but otherwise there seem to be no great problems in his life.	Dave and his two younger sisters were brought up, as he sees it, lovingly and attentively by highly committed parents. They were devout, almost fanatical Methodists who laid enormous stress on conventional morality, any slight departure from which was punished by deep – almost shattering – disapproval. Both parents tried to protect their children from the evils of the outside world, and his mother in particular relied heavily on religious ritual to ward off threat.

'Obsessive-compulsive' behaviour can take a variety of forms, ranging from rituals of washing and cleaning to elaborate checking that some careless action, for example while driving, has not resulted in catastrophe. Almost always the conduct is aimed at the prevention of damage or injury, frequently to other people (Dave's worst nightmare was that, because of his carelessness, he would return home to find the house where he lived, and everyone in it, consumed by fire), or at reassurance that no such damage has already been incurred.

What is most puzzling and distressing for the sufferers is, of course, that the need for care or reassurance seems to go far beyond what is rational. The highly intelligent woman who takes fifteen minutes to select a packet of cereal in the supermarket so that she can be sure of not poisoning her family knows perfectly well that her infinitely tiresome precautions have no effect on the reality of the situation, but she knows also that she feels terrible if she doesn't take them.

Compulsive rituals are in this way acts of superstition, a form of magically controlling possible eventualities which are in fact uncontrollable. It is as if people in the grip of this kind of conduct find their lives dedicated to solving insoluble problems; the more insoluble the problem, apparently, the fiercer (and more exhausting) the effort put into solving it. It is often also the case that, if a problem does seem to be 'solved', it is almost immediately replaced by others even more difficult, until eventually a challenge is found that admits of no conceivable solution. Can you, for example, make absolutely sure by endless scrubbing and vacuuming that there is not a trace of asbestos dust in your house? Might it not have been introduced by someone's shoes or blown in on the wind? I remember a man in the town where I grew up, an inmate of one of the local asylums, who spent his waking life running between two clocks, perhaps 150 yards apart in the high street, trying to establish that they told the same time.

Difficulties associated with eating – 'anorexia nervosa' (self-starvation) and 'bulimia' (binge eating followed by self-induced vomiting) – are further examples of conduct over which the person is unable to exercise control. Most people who have ever tried to diet can understand how difficult it is deliberately to lose weight (though even here we are often unaware of the lengths we'll apparently go to in order 'not to notice' how much we're consuming), but it is less easy to empathise with the person who has starved herself to the point of death while passionately not wanting to die and trying all she can to eat. We can understand what we take to be weakness in the face of greed, but not, as with anorexia, when the reverse seems to be the case: involuntary abstinence from pleasure.

ELIZABETH

Form of distress	Current predicament	Background predicament
An intelligent and attractive woman, Elizabeth is painfully preoccupied with diet and exercise, petrified of becoming overweight. Every so often she binges secretly on very large quantities of, in particular, bread and butter spread with sugar, and chocolate. After each bingeing session she has to make herself sick to prevent digestion of the food.	Elizabeth feels pressured at work by new supervisory duties, particularly in respect of one or two women, previously equals, who she knows don't like her. Trying her best to be fair, she feels they take advantage of her. Her social life is limited, and her husband a little remote and lost in his own work problems.	Elizabeth's father was a clerical officer for the electricity board and her mother a socially ambitious teacher, not very happy with her lot or her husband's status. Both parents were remote, critical and rather stern, favouring both her older and younger brothers.

As with obsessive-compulsive behaviour, the preoccupations of people with eating problems often bear little relation to reality. 'Anorexics' seem, usually, literally unable to see the extent of their terrible emaciation, while 'bulimics' remain convinced of and anguished by their 'obesity' even though to an objective observer they are conventionally slim and attractive. Once again, it is the apparent irrationality, the clash with our normal understanding, that brings such phenomena into the field of psychiatry. Fat people, after all, though they may struggle with their diets, at least *know* that they are fat, and are trying to do something about it, while people with eating disorders seem to be trying to do something about imaginary difficulties. However, rather than concluding that there is something the matter with the sufferers themselves, it is more fruitful in my view (as will be elaborated in later chapters) to question the adequacy of our normal understanding and to begin to see that our everyday conceptions of rationality and will power are exposed as lacking rather than confirmed by the so-called pathology of compulsive behaviour.

Sufferers from these kinds of difficulties are not a race apart from the rest of us, but are as puzzled and pained as anyone else by the apparent inconsistencies of their conduct. They are neither unconscious schemers nor wilful architects of artful plans to seek attention or manipulate relations with others, but find themselves enacting, often with excruciating shame, patterns of behaviour which are as mysterious to them as they are irresistible.

FRANCES

Form of distress	Current predicament	Background predicament
Every so often Frances finds the tensions and stresses of her life escalating to a point where they seem unbearable. The only way she has found to relieve these is to cut her arms and thighs with a razor blade. The sight of blood welling up through the cut calms her. Her arms and legs are criss-crossed with scars. Sometimes she has to get a cut stitched, but usually she hides her handiwork, and she has no suicidal intent.	Frances survives on casual waitressing jobs and has little social life. She has had a number of usually disastrous relationships with men, some of whom have been violent towards her. She tends to drink more than is good for her.	Frances comes from a large family where both money and parental interest were in short supply. Her mother had a vicious temper, and seemingly a particular dislike of Frances, whom she battered from time to time. For a couple of years she was sexually abused by one of her older brothers.

Nothing could throw these issues into sharper relief than the predicament of the 'self-mutilator'. Beyond the immediate sense of relief it brings her, there is no secret satisfaction or manipulative intent, no 'secondary gain' for Frances in cutting herself. She understands no more than anyone else why she does it, and, though in many ways as ready as others (including the professionals) to accuse herself of various kinds of duplicity, she knows in her heart that it is not to be explained by the more obvious conventional hypotheses: it is not merely a question of 'attention-seeking' (for she does her best to hide it) or 'punishing herself' (it is a relief more than a pain).

For those fortunate enough not to have found themselves in the kind of situation outlined in this section, the best approximation to understanding how it feels from the inside to be compelled to do something one desperately wants not to do may be to reflect on what it's like to be in a state of conflict over something. The problems facing the dieter have already been mentioned; there are other common experiences, like trying to give up smoking, in which the mind and the body seem to take different directions, with the body coming out on top. And yet it is not just a question of failure of mind over matter, of 'weak will', for the will is involved in achieving the body's bidding: the planning involved in buying a packet of cigarettes when we have vowed not to do so can be quite considerable. We get no further in trying to understand these dilemmas by moralising, by making them the conscious or unconscious responsibility of the sufferer. Instead, the role played by our notion of 'will' in the relation of mind to body will be considered in Chapter Six.

Current predicaments

Whatever the form in which distress makes itself felt, it occurs for a reason or, more often perhaps, a constellation of reasons. It is never the case that 'symptoms' simply erupt from within the person unbidden by events in the outside world. If someone has previously been leading a relatively untroubled life, feeling reasonably confident and optimistic, the onset of feelings of anxiety, depression etc. is an indication that something has become not right with his or her world.

People can seldom immediately identify the reasons for the distress they are experiencing, and there is a school of thought which claims that it doesn't particularly matter whether they do – it is more important, it is felt, to 'cure' the distress than to understand it. This is not as crass as it might sound, since there is certainly no logical connection between knowing why something is wrong and being able to do anything about it. The therapeutic assumption – that knowledge of cause, or 'insight', leads automatically to cure – has led to some oversimplified ideas about how to tackle emotional distress. However, rather than knowledge of cause being unnecessary for cure, it is more the case, I think, that cure may be impossible however much we know about the cause. Apart from relieving uncertainty, realising what the factors are in the outside world that are giving you pain is potentially 'curative' only if it is in your power to do something about those factors.

In what follows, then, it is important to remember that identifying factors in your environment that are giving rise to difficulty does not necessarily lead to a diminution of the resulting distress. But, for a whole host of reasons (not least to absolve yourself from 'responsibility' for your pain), it is probably better to know than not to know what they are.

Typical factors which lurk behind the development of distress can be viewed from two broad perspectives: the personal and the societal. Sufferers themselves are likely to be principally, and often solely, aware of the 'proximal' causes of their distress – the ones they experience, so to speak, up against themselves, in their immediate relations with the persons and events of their everyday lives. Viewed from the societal perspective, on the other hand, it becomes possible to discern the operation of 'distal' (remote) causes of which the protagonists may be completely unaware. In practice, it is impossible to discuss the kinds of predicaments people have to cope with in their daily lives without referring to both their personal, proximal perspective and the more distal factors affecting them. The significance of distinguishing between proximal and distal causes will be elaborated in Chapter Four.

The commonest causes of emotional distress and unhappiness are to be found, obviously enough, in the spheres of home, work and social relationships. Indeed, the most obvious are often overlooked by the professionals simply because they form such a familiar part of the experience of all of us. Financial deprivation and insecurity, unemployment (both actual and threatened), perpetual indebtedness – such factors as these form a backdrop of misery for a large, and increasing, proportion of the population, and their ubiquity should in no way detract from our recognition of the psychological damage they cause.

Sometimes precisely because of such material deprivations, people often also live in bitter and abusive relationships with others – most often women with men, children with parents – from which escape is for practical reasons virtually impossible. Loneliness and loss are also a familiar part of the lives of all too many people, especially of course the elderly.

Little would be achieved by earnestly constructing examples of difficulties such as these. Their effects are obvious to anyone of averagely human sensibilities, and the only surprise – or perhaps rather absurdity – is that politicians, media people and social scientists should find it necessary to dwell on such questions as *whether*, for instance, unemployment causes depression. Only a rogue, a fool or someone with an *interest* in asking the question could, it would seem, possibly claim not to know the answer in advance.[12]

There are, however, many people who consult doctors and other experts in 'mental health' in genuine puzzlement about the causes of their distress, although their lives are blighted by deprivation and/or oppression of the kinds mentioned above to an extent which accounts easily for their feelings, often many times over. People seem to think that they should be able to bear such privations not only without complaining, but even without suffering, and if this proves not to be the case, they assume that something must be wrong with them. The notion that we should in all circumstances be able to smile through adversity is one of the mystifications that keep the mental-health industry alive.

For many, if not most, of us, reality has in any case a distinctly adverse bias, and this sometimes makes it difficult to recognise that there are reasons outside ourselves for what seem to be our purely psychological troubles. It becomes hard to pick out from the general run of our experience anything that seems more than usually difficult to cope with; so used are we to struggling that we no longer recognise it as struggle, and are able to set no limits on what we think we should be able to cope with.

GINA

Form of distress	Current predicament	Background predicament
Quite confident and outgoing as a teenager, Gina has become increasingly 'agoraphobic' over the years of her mid-twenties, and, though she pushes herself to go out, feels extremely uncomfortable in shops, on public transport and at social occasions where she doesn't know people.	Gina has two young school-age children for whom she bears the main responsibility. She married at eighteen a man who has become increasingly caustic and undermining of her, and occasionally violent. He is now out of work, while Gina does evening shifts cleaning at a local office complex.	Gina was one of four children. Her father drank heavily and rowed constantly, and often violently, with her mother. Neither parent was particularly occupied with the children, though Gina, as the only girl, was called upon to help in the home while her mother went out to work. She missed a great deal of schooling and obtained no qualifications, though she is very bright.

At the time when Gina married the first man who was kind to her, she had no conception of herself as an unusually intelligent and pretty young woman, nor did she recognise the disparity between herself and her husband in these respects; she was just glad to get away from home and to start building her own life.

Her husband, however, was always uncomfortably aware that he could have difficulty keeping up with Gina, and so he welcomed her basic lack of confidence in herself and lost no opportunity of increasing her awareness of the extent to which she depended on him to deal with the outside world (for example, because of her lack of schooling, Gina's literacy was not of the highest order). He was intensely threatened by her impatience with his relative slow-wittedness, and when they rowed he would occasionally hit her as the only counter he could find to her greater argumentative skill. Sexual attraction had not played a part in Gina's decision to marry, and her increasing distaste for sex became a bitter bone of contention between them. All this, plus the principal responsibility for their children, who she was determined should not feel as emotionally isolated as she had done, and the added strain of having to work in the evenings, stretched her beyond the limits of her (very considerable) ability to cope, and the resulting loss of confidence in herself announced itself as anxiety: she herself could see her predicament only in terms of personal failure.

Some women still find as they start to enter middle age that their world as wife and mother is coming to a conclusion without any apparent alternative on the horizon, though changes over the last twenty years in child-rearing and the typical division of labour within the home have probably made this plight less frequent than it was. But, with Heather as with Gina, the dependency of women on men (regardless of whether the men abuse their position to become oppressors, about which there is no inevitability) remains an issue which causes a great deal of difficulty, surfacing usually as loss of confidence and consequent anxiety.

Having been a 'housewife' for fifteen years can be tantamount to spending time in a 'total institution', cut off from the changes and developments taking place in the outside world, gradually losing confidence in one's ability to cope with them. However sensitive to the situation the male partner may be, his greater access to and freedom in the outside world are almost certain to inject into the relationship elements of isolation, envy and

HEATHER

Form of distress	Current predicament	Background predicament
At forty-five, Heather has become virtually house-bound. Although always shy and sensitive, she had until a year or two ago been able to cope perfectly adequately in her role as wife and mother, but now she is overcome with crippling panic attacks at the prospect of having to leave the safety of the home for virtually any reason.	The third of Heather's children is about to take her A levels; the older two have already left home. Her husband, a self-employed businessman, works long hours and is impatient with Heather's difficulties. They seem to have grown apart over the years. Five years ago a brief affair with his secretary came to light.	Heather's mother was, and is, a vain, self-absorbed woman, openly contemptuous of her policeman husband, now dead, to whom Heather had been closer. Heather and her brother did not receive a great deal of attention from either parent, though their father did the best he could until he died when Heather was sixteen.

resentment on the one side and frustration, impatience and incomprehension on the other. What is in fact the inevitable consequence of occupancy of different worlds (a pattern imposed by distal socio-economic factors well beyond individuals' control) is likely to be proximally interpreted by those involved as a purely personal predicament.

Difficulties of relationship confronting younger men and women who wish to form a settled partnership, combining companionship, sexual fulfilment and the building of a family, have undoubtedly been multiplied and complicated by social and economic developments over the past couple of decades. Not the least problem is how to maintain personal independence and freedom from the oppression of one sex by the other in a setting where the (frequently unequal) resources of both have to be pooled to maintain even basic standards within the family. Further, the competitiveness generated by at least an ideal of equality in the 'marketplace' has to be combined with the give-and-take of forms of sexual expression which are still deeply rooted in the traditions of earlier times (e.g. what it is to be male or female).

In these circumstances, it is proving difficult for many partnerships to achieve the desired goals within one relationship, which seems to have become a task no easier than squaring the circle. Attempts to solve the problem mostly seem to involve separating in some way the functions of sex and companionship. For example, a couple may form a childless liaison in order to embellish a home and fill it with consumer goods which establish an acceptable social image and 'state' an appropriate 'lifestyle', while conducting more or less casual sexual liaisons with third parties. Or a woman may marry a man she knows to be gay and who is therefore less likely to make 'selfish' demands upon her. Or couples with children may agree to live apart, though still sleeping together when the man visits, maybe quite regularly.

Again, it is obviously easier for a woman to play a breadwinning role more equal to her husband's (as likely, of course, to be a necessity as a matter of choice) if she can divest herself of some of the major responsibilities of traditional motherhood; these in turn have to be taken over by someone else, usually a childminder or nanny in a less advantageous social position.

Not infrequently, these 'solutions' are achieved only with a degree of pain, confusion or guilt which those involved tend to interpret proximally as the result either of their own inadequacy and incompetence, or as the intransigence, malice or brutality of their partner.

Ian simply cannot understand why he should find himself becoming almost uncontrollably angry with June when he can't 'fault her' in any respect. She is clever, attractive, successful, a 'wonderful mother' and – so far – an extremely tolerant and affectionate wife. He has dredged his past, without success, for psychological traumata which might account for his 'illness'. Maybe, he thinks, it's a question of some kind of dietary allergy. He's consulted a hypnotherapist, with only temporary relief, and he now feels at his wits' end.

IAN

Form of distress	Current predicament	Background predicament
Ian has been off work for two months with mild depression. He is unable to concentrate on anything and has panic attacks when driving. He complains of irritability which he is afraid might get out of control, especially with his wife June, a 'lovely girl' who he is afraid will leave him if he doesn't get a grip on himself. Their sex life has come to a virtual standstill.	Ian is a middle manager in an insurance office. He met June as her supervisor when she was a management trainee. Since then she has joined another firm, becoming its marketing manager. She is often away from home on business, and now earns nearly twice Ian's salary. They have one little girl, whom Ian has been looking after since he's been off work.	Ian comes from a traditional working-class background. He feels close to his parents, though sees less of them than he used to, and he has grown a little apart from his brother and sister, though without animosity.

The high rate of divorce leading to the formation of second relationships involving children from the first introduces another set of pressures on all concerned. The absence of rules or established social patterns of conduct in such circumstances means that people have to invent for themselves ways of handling the inevitable difficulties. They are thrown back on purely personal resources to support conduct whose justification has to be constantly argued for, often in increasingly bitter family quarrels: there is no external criterion of what is or is not reasonable or acceptable in such situations, and the protagonists may end up frustrated and isolated behind a defensive wall of righteous indignation.

Jill feels that she has already put her children through enough without Kevin's nagging them, even though it is Jill's welfare he's concerned for. She feels he has no right to intrude in this way into her relationship with her daughter. Further, though she sees that

JILL

Form of distress	Current predicament	Background predicament
Jill was always an overconscientious 'worrier', but serious panic attacks started only after she had met her second husband, Kevin, and they have got worse now that they are in the fifth year of their marriage. Jill is riddled with guilt over having, as she sees it, deprived her two teenage children (a girl and a boy) of their father, and she encourages them to see him regularly.	Kevin is a much kinder, more tolerant and reliable man than Jill's first husband, and Jill also contrasts strongly with his first wife, who was extremely selfish and somewhat promiscuous. Jill can't stand Kevin's nineteen-year-old son, who is periodically thrown out of the house by his mother and so has to live with Jill and Kevin. Kevin is also, as Jill sees it, much too strict with her daughter, who he feels abuses her mother's good nature.	Jill's mother was an anxious, self-concerned woman whose husband devoted his life to ministering to her needs. Jill was left pretty much to her own devices, being also required to look after her two younger brothers when her mother was too 'ill' to do so.

he has a responsibility to his son, and though she is ashamed of her feeling, she finds the latter's presence in their already crowded house as practically intolerable – he is noisy, dirty and disrespectful, and she can't understand why Kevin, so ready to criticise her daughter, doesn't take a stronger line with his own son. In his turn, Kevin is similarly guilty about having deserted the boy in his teens, and does not feel it appropriate to 'go on at him' too much when he is already having such a rough time with his unstable mother. Jill's children, though they have little respect for him, feel torn in their loyalties to their father, who uses them as message bearers to his former wife, and to Kevin, whom they see as the more responsible and concerned of the two. They are puzzled and distressed by their mother's confusion and vacillation in disciplinary matters and by the tensions generated in the household. They quite like their stepbrother.

The difficulties of young people too are given a distinctive shape by the times in which they grew up. The social revolution which took place in the 1980s[13] seems to have distracted a significant proportion of the 'parent generation' of the period (by which I mean all those having care of the young, not just their biological parents) from attending to the psychological needs of those engaged principally with the task of learning how to live. Furthermore, the social conditions of the 1990s do little to welcome the young into the adult world. Especially perhaps for young men, there is virtually no assurance that they have a social value, that the world has need of them – a state of affairs reflected clearly enough in the dramatic increase in the suicide rate for this group.[14] Whatever one might think of its desirability, young women at least still have the option of fulfilling their biological function.

Keith appears to be profoundly uncertain not only about what he feels about himself and his life, but also about whether he feels anything much at all. It is difficult to trace within him any element of desire. He finds it literally impossible to think of things he would like to taste, to see, to feel, and there seems to be no particular gusto even with sex. The world contains nothing he wants, and it appears to want nothing of him other than that he should have a satisfactory 'lifestyle'. He is puzzled about how to conduct his life in the directed way other people appear to. He only knows how to measure things as it seems to him his parents did – according to material success. For example, he is far more comfortable with choosing food on a menu according to how expensive it is than to what he feels like eating. It is as if nobody while he was growing up tried to elucidate or explain to him what it is to *experience* the world, to make preferences in terms of pleasure and pain, good and bad.

Luke can see only one form of social existence open to him, which is to join the macho, petty-criminal network of socially, educationally, materially and vocationally disadvantaged young

KEITH

Form of distress	Current predicament	Background predicament
Keith feels depressed and without 'motivation'. He also has periods of quite extreme, anxious agitation when he can concentrate on nothing except a feeling that something terrible is about to happen. He quarrels a lot with his family and worries about 'not getting on' with people his own age, girls and boys.	A 22-year-old graduate, Keith got a good degree. He feels alienated from and irritated by his parents, both successful solicitors. He has no idea what he wants to do, at present taking occasional casual jobs. He has girlfriends, but does not feel involved with them – they tend to 'get on his nerves'. In relation to other young people, he 'doesn't feel real' – they seem somehow to have substance in a way he doesn't.	Both Keith's parents were preoccupied with building their careers as he grew up, and when they were at home together spent most of their time sniping at each other. From working-class backgrounds themselves, they were concerned that Keith and his brother should have a good education, and sent them as day boys to the local public school.

people whose only possibility to 'be something' is to develop the, so to speak, unofficial spaces left by a world totally preoccupied with individual success and survival and utterly indifferent to them. And yet the prospect is totally distasteful to him. Though incapable of seeing himself in this light (because nobody has ever given him the slightest indication that it is so), Luke has a kind of reflective intelligence and a sensitive appreciation of reality which set him apart from most of his peers and – perhaps unfortunately – make it impossible for him to ignore an ideal of how he would like life to be.

Mary wanted a baby. She didn't particularly want to be a single parent, but she did want to become independent of the difficult and claustrophobic situation in her mother and stepfather's home, to live her own life and to have 'someone to love'. With very little

LUKE

Form of distress	Current predicament	Background predicament
Luke took an overdose when his girlfriend returned to her husband. He feels completely alienated from his social peers and workmates, is deeply in debt and is about to get evicted from his flat. He is cut off from his family and feels very isolated. Luke feels unlike anyone he knows; only his girlfriend seemed to understand what goes on inside him.	Luke left school with no qualifications, but subsequently got a diploma in catering. He has a very low-paid, part-time job which runs from week to week. Even so, he is in charge of kitchen staff who resent and tease him (he is unusually tall and thin). Luke has an acute, original mind, but finds no one to share his perceptions. He would like to 'go to college' but has no financial support and very little confidence.	Luke's parents separated early in his life, which was spent mainly with his father and seven years older sister. His father drank and gambled and his sister moved as soon as she could to another part of the country with a man now in prison. After leaving school Luke went through a difficult period involving drink, drugs and trouble with the police.

money, a lot of parental criticism and disapproval, no social life, harassment from her baby's father's family and intrusive surveillance from the social-service department, she nevertheless managed to care for her child competently and devotedly.

Background predicaments

As soon as it enters the world, the infant has to start learning to deal with the immediate set of circumstances which fate has assigned it. Our successes and failures in this enterprise will during the course of the first decade or so of our lives form what we may choose to call, in shorthand, our character.

It is important to realise that there is a lot more to character than just the idiosyncratic personal foibles which make it possible

MARY

Form of distress	Current predicament	Background predicament
Gradually increasing loss of confidence in herself has led to Mary's developing panic attacks, especially when out shopping on her own.	Mary is a single parent of eighteen. She has a mixed-race baby two years old whose father deserted her after living with Mary for six months. Her mother is supportive, but 'interfering', and Mary is reluctant to leave her baby with her because she 'spoils her' and makes it more difficult for Mary to cope afterwards. Social services are involved, and though of some material help are also, she feels, 'on her back', not least in insisting that she concern herself with the baby's racial identity through attending classes, etc. She is also harassed by the father's family.	Mary's parents separated when she was thirteen and her mother remarried shortly afterwards. Mary hated her father and didn't particularly like her stepfather either, though she remains attached to, and slightly in awe of, her mother. To the disapproval of all concerned, she got pregnant and left to live with the father of her baby as soon as she could.

for us to recognise each other as individuals. 'Character' also embodies the knowledge we have acquired of the world and the expectations this has led us to develop about how it is likely to treat us.

We do not invent these expectations – they are, more or less, imposed upon us by our experience of a real world. If, therefore, we wish to achieve a full understanding of why and how we react as we do to events in the present, we need to take into account, among other things, the influence of the past. The past, in other words, forms part of the *reality* of the present and is not lightly to be dismissed.

Issues concerning the influence of the past will surface several times in the course of subsequent chapters. For the moment, I want only to consider some of the more frequently encountered types of predicament shaping the characters – the knowledge and expectations of the world – of people whose later distress may lead them to contemplate seeking professional help. As indicated earlier, the constellations of early influence set out below are as seen from the perspective of the sufferer, and are not intended as 'the explanation' of their suffering. My concern here is, then, with the individual's proximal world, and does not stretch far beyond his or her view of it. The inevitability of that view's being distorted does not mean that it is 'wrong'; we may say, rather, that we are speaking of a limited truth – the truth for the individual concerned.

It is, of course, the family that looms largest in most people's consideration of their early lives, and it is with family – in particular parental – influence that we shall be mainly concerned in what follows. For the sake of convenience, I have once again divided what may be seen as damaging forms of family influence into a number of subcategories; as before, these are not intended to have special scientific validity, nor indeed to exhaust all the possibilities.

Oppression and indifference

Straightforward cruelty and physical abuse blight the lives of many children, and leave scars of various kinds – particularly, perhaps, an entirely understandable mistrust of people in later life and difficulty in forming close relationships with them. The child may, for example, become a kind of expert in violence – either in vigilantly detecting it so that it can be dodged in time (a kind of 'early warning' approach to relationships) or in learning its rules and applying it as vigorously as once it was suffered.

Violent abuse often does have the single advantage, if such it can be called, that it is easily recognisable and clearly attributable to its source. The drunken child-beater, for all the fear he instils and damage he does, can at least also be hated. Siblings who can form some kind of solidarity against their oppressor, perhaps also with their mother, experience a more benign world than do, for example, people who could not escape violence in their childhood, either because they were alone with their tormentor, or because violence was endemic within the family as a whole.

MICK

Form of distress	Current predicament	Background predicament
In his mid-thirties and recently married with a small son, Mick has suddenly succumbed to panic attacks, especially at work. He also worries about his temper at home: though not violent, he often shouts alarmingly, and is very strict with his little boy.	Mick is under threat of redundancy at work, and stretches himself beyond his limits in trying to comply with the unreasonable demands of his job. He finds settling to the responsibilities of husband and father difficult, having previously led an extremely free single existence.	Mick was a gifted and sensitive child, but his mother couldn't stand him, and regularly vented her rage upon him as a little boy, hitting him, pulling his hair, beating him with anything that lay to hand. Once she broke his arm. His father was not violent, but a cold, hard, narrow-minded martinet, whom, however, Mick respects as a 'fair' disciplinarian. His father viewed Mick's sensitivity with alarm, and made him join the army to 'make a man' of him.

Mick's intelligence and sensitivity made it possible, certainly, for him to criticise his experience as he grew up, but he was not lucky enough to encounter any real alternative to his world. His schools were in the deprived area where the family lived, with most teachers too harassed and demoralised to notice and encourage his talents – one who did was dismissed as 'a nancy' by his father. Mick knew that he wanted things to be different, and to be different himself, but he didn't know how, and veered between a compliant desperation to be liked and sudden flashes of violent anger.

The damage done by sexual abuse also includes the model of relationship it impresses on the victim, and at its most prolonged and violent simply wrecks, among other things, the possibility of the person being able to develop later trusting and tender sexual relations with others. Usually, however, it is more complicated than this, and its peculiar mixture of oppression and threat, guilty secrecy, mysterious (from the child's point of view) sexuality, and affection – the inappropriate crossing of family and generational boundaries – may have all kinds of consequences which, even though they may not prove catastrophic, are certainly likely to affect later life and relationships.

It is common for people to experience some form of 'sexual abuse' as they grow up, whether at the hands of other children, being groped by strangers on buses or being invited to view the equipment of local flashers. It is certainly possible to get unnecessarily strident and alarmist about such experiences as these, as also relatively transient and minor forms of abuse that might be committed by a dementing elderly relative or a drunken neighbour. But where the abuse persists, or occurs in an atmosphere of secrecy (often with the frightened complicity of other family members), in such a way that children cannot place their experience against a standard of what is socially acceptable or receive the support and validation of those close to them, their only recourse is to see themselves as responsible for what is happening (for that is the way we are taught to view pretty well all our conduct). This is the start of the feelings of guilt, dirtiness and self-loathing that are the well-known consequences of abuse.

The lack of security and failure of confidence which creates the kind of 'basic anxiety' so well described by Karen Horney[15] is often the result of forms of oppression or indifference less spectacular, but not necessarily less damaging, than those described so far. Rejection, abandonment, oppressive parental control and rigidity, may all serve to undermine the child's sense of itself as a character of substance or value, as may his or her awareness of having a favoured sibling.

Parents' actions may amount to rejection of their children even where this is the last thing they intend. Fathers or mothers feeling driven to desert the family because they can no longer bear the bitterness and frustration of living with a spouse they've come to loathe can easily forget that from the child's point of view it is *s/he* who is being abandoned. Such was the case with Ann, above. Her father's desertion of her at the age of fourteen served only to reinforce a view of herself (not, let it be noted, a *mistaken* view) that she was not the kind of person even a father would particularly want to stay with.

In the far from subtle way that psychoanalysis has of shifting the burden of responsibility from the more to the less powerful, the notion of 'sibling rivalry' suggests that difficulties involving brothers and sisters are due mainly to some kind of selfish struggle between them. In my experience it is more often the case that children defend themselves as long as they can from the painful recognition that a brother or a sister brings a light to parental eyes which go dull when they themselves come into view. Again, the conclusion such children arrive at is not that they are discriminated against, whether unfortunately or unfairly, but that they are unlovable in some way that their brother or sister isn't. An even more impossible situation to have to cope with – and one which seems to arise quite often – is where an older sibling died in infancy only to become for the parents a kind of idealised paragon with whom no living mortal could hope to contend.

The provision of love that is strictly conditional – powerful when present but desolating when withdrawn – presents the child with a world which has to be carefully watched, placated or manipulated. This was part of Dave's difficulties. The world he grew up in could go horribly wrong, not always predictably, though if he got it right, it was not without its rewards. His development of a kind of extreme superstitious caution may have looked pretty crazy at first sight, but it made a good deal more sense once one understood how he had spent his childhood and youth tiptoeing through a minefield.

Parental indifference towards children, simple lack of interest in them (which may come about for a hundred reasons – at this point it is not our purpose to understand them), is probably the commonest cause of a level of self-confidence always vulnerable to erosion; there are several examples in the brief stories offered above. The feeling that you *matter* is not the innate heritage of every human being, but, if you are lucky, a gift from the social and familial world into which you are thrown at birth. In the absence of that gift, in circumstances, that is, where you did not particularly matter to those on whom you were most dependent, almost every social situation becomes laden with the threat that others will detect your fundamental lack of worth. As suggested earlier, becoming nothing *is* the experience of panic.

Intrusion and distortion

Abuse, neglect and indifference, whatever the evils they create, do not necessarily interfere directly with the child's perception of reality, though of course they might. They may *constitute* his or her reality, but they do not on the whole serve to distort the very processes through which s/he seeks to understand the world.

It has long been recognised by a thoughtful minority in psychology and psychiatry that one of the most difficult things for children to have to deal with is a situation where they are forced to abandon their own view of reality in order to conform to the emotional needs of the more powerful people around them, usually of course their parents.[16]

Some of the most damaging forms of intrusion on the child's ability to make *accurate* sense of the world are carried out in the name of love, though it is probably more correctly understood as anxiety. Many an anxious mother, driven by her own profound insecurity, has fussed over her child, imposing upon it a kind of fearful surveillance which inhibits, eventually, its every independent step. Parental anxiety of this kind, which is never acknowledged as such but presented to the child as a necessary protection from a terribly dangerous world, can prove quite crippling in later life. However, sufferers from anxiety who are able to acknowledge that their fears are a property of *their* world rather than of *the* world need not worry that they may somehow infect their children (perhaps genetically) with their own difficulties; it is only when parental anxiety focuses on the child, or else so dominates the family that everyone has, without drawing direct attention to it, to order their lives around it, that it is likely to create a real problem for others (Jill's mother was like this). I have known many very severely anxious and 'agoraphobic' women who have raised extremely self-confident and successful children.

Parental (again, usually maternal) anxiety about the world's darker aspect – its brutality, depravity, degradation – can lead to a superstitious censoring of reality and a prohibition of the expression of inevitable human feelings like anger which make it impossible for the child to face directly aspects of life that are in fact inescapable and to recognise and cultivate features of its character and experience that are part of every human being. This kind of background constellation seems often to lie behind the later development of 'obsessive-compulsive' strategies for dealing with the less acceptable sides not only of life but, more particularly, perhaps, of one's own character. Dave's example is again a case in point: unable to recognise, let alone openly acknowledge, perfectly normal feelings of anger and resentment, he experienced them as a potential danger lurking in the world around him which he had somehow to control and protect people from, for reasons he didn't at all understand.

Nadine had been taught by her parents' example to believe that love and duty were indistinguishable (even though her sister's

NADINE

Form of distress	Current predicament	Background predicament
Nadine is extremely worried about her inability to concentrate on her job as supervisor of a large secretarial agency; she is depressed, unable to remember things, and comfort eating has led to her becoming overweight, about which she feels very guilty. Having lost contact with her friends, she also feels isolated and lonely.	Nadine's job is demanding but unrewarding: she carries a lot of responsibility but gets very little thanks for her efforts. Her aged parents make very heavy demands on her spare time. She has recently divorced her rather feckless husband of fifteen years, who had been more like a spoilt child than a partner. She has no children.	Nadine's parents had never really been able to love her as they had her clever, pretty older sister who had gone to university and realised all their ambitions. Instead, they had discharged their duty towards her. From Nadine's point of view this meant that she had for as long as she could remember been subjected to a kind of strict moral supervision aimed, presumably, at turning her general conduct into something of which her parents could approve. They never ceased to treat her as a rather stupid and irresponsible child.

relatively carefree situation seemed a puzzling exception to the rule). Though she tried her best to apply her considerable abilities scrupulously in every department of her life – her job, her role as wife and daughter – she never seemed fully to succeed, and her existence as a whole seemed always sadly lacking in satisfaction. The harder she tried, the more empty she felt. Her mission in life seemed to be to please, in particular, her implacable father. It never even occurred to her that she could try pleasing herself.

The inappropriate crossing of generational roles is another way in which parents may intrude on the lives of their children to shape their character for life. In some cases parents may draw a child as ally or accomplice into battles they are having with their spouse; in others they may become like dependent children themselves so that their offspring are forced into a parental role. Ann, Gina and Jill are all examples of this latter predicament. Possession by the kind of superconscientiousness discussed above is frequently the result of having imposed upon one at an inappropriately early age responsibilities of parental proportions, usually for the care of younger siblings, but quite often also of parents themselves. Because the boundaries of responsibility are extended so enormously for a child placed in this position, s/he may never learn where the limits of his or her capacity to respond to demand lie, and in later life may continue to acquire duties and responsibilities to the point of breakdown (this theme will reappear in Chapter Five).

Parents may also compete with their children. Freud made the 'Oedipal' competition between son and father central to his theory of neurosis, but true to form, he saw the child as the instigator of the struggle for the love of the mother/wife. In fact, it is far more often the case that an essentially insecure and anxious parent feels compelled to ensure that s/he is not surpassed in any respect by a son or daughter. Brenda's mother, for example, could not allow her daughter to compare with her either morally or intellectually, so that there was a whole range of ways in which Brenda simply could not *be*. Daughters are also more easily undermined and rendered vulnerable to later anxiety by tyrannical fathers who do not allow their arbitrary (though not necessarily violent) rule over their timid wives and cowed children to be questioned. Boys in this situation may eventually grow big and rebellious enough to challenge the tyranny, or simply to leave.

Parental favour can sometimes be as damaging in the long run as disfavour. The blindly benevolent but nevertheless inflexible rule Norman's mother exercised over him prevented his developing any sense of having an independent will. Always in the back of his mind was the feeling that he could rely on her more than on himself, and so he was unable to develop any consistent direction

NORMAN

Form of distress	Current predicament	Background predicament
Mildly depressed and unable to motivate himself, Norman is also having difficulty controlling his drinking. He gambles compulsively and is squandering what little money the family has, mostly in secret. He is losing his temper at home more than he would like.	Norman was made redundant from his job as area sales manager for a furnishing business a year ago, and is still out of work. His third marriage, of eight years, is rocky, mainly because of his wife's discovery of his drinking and gambling.	In the eyes of his strong, domineering mother, Norman could do no wrong; she regarded his two older sisters with contempt. His father was a reasonably benign but distant figure who absented himself from the household as much as possible and consoled himself with other women.

in his life. In addition, any desires of his own which he did experience (but of which she would have disapproved) had to be indulged in secret and quickly became out of his control.

Parents' power to determine the nature of reality for their children may be used to represent indifference as love, neglect as solicitude, truth as wilful misconception. A child may, for example, quite easily be persuaded that its innocent perception of reality is a function of its own naughtiness, even wickedness. For there is nothing like the innocent perception of reality to rock the familial boat in situations where sources of pain or discord have to be denied and suppressed if the boat is to stay afloat. A comment on Heather's part, for example, that her mother seemed to have a particularly close understanding with the male neighbour who gave them lifts to swimming lessons, drew immediate outraged condemnation and punishment from both her parents in a way she couldn't possibly understand at the time and this contributed to a lifelong lack of confidence in her own judgement. Catherine, bombarded throughout her childhood, first by her mother and later by her stepfather as well, with messages about the sacrifices that were being made in her interest and guilty assurances about how much she was adored, took some time to see that the pain she felt at the loss of those who had loved her (her grandmother and a nanny), the bitter isolation of boarding school and the hollowness of parental assurances of love, were not somehow indications of her own social inadequacy and ingratitude, but sources of an entirely justifiable resentment and an all too well-founded anticipation of the likelihood of betrayal.

The single-minded concentration on material betterment in the 1980s, combined with a susceptibility to the dominant make-believe ideology of business, seems to have resulted in some, particularly middle-class, parents having failed to nurture in their children any sense of what human beings are really like. Keith's parents were ambitious for him, certainly, and it was important that he should be a credit to them, but beyond that they had little time for or interest in him, so preoccupied were they with the construction of their largely separate images. From them as well as from the wider culture, he gleaned a knowledge only of the smooth outer surface of things. Under this surface was a world of quite bitter competition – his parents bickered almost continually – but the bitterness was always glossed over and denied, never dealt with directly in a language which could be used to take its measure. For Keith, it was as if the only true reality was that reflected in the world of advertising, and when internal experience failed to match up to external pretence, its rawness and untidiness, the inarticulateness of feeling, seemed chaotically alien, overwhelming and frightening.

Social disadvantages

Some factors of the social background work to erode the individual's self-confidence independently of specific figures such as parents. Social class is one such factor, and in my view probably still the most important. I have written about the phenomenon of 'class injury' in detail in *The Origins of Unhappiness* and I do not, therefore, want to repeat those observations here, but it is important to point out that a 'sense of worth' is not simply a matter of personal psychology and immediate family relations, but may also be an objective valuation which is placed on us at birth, and, if negative, escaped only infrequently and with the greatest difficulty.

The feeling of not being as good as some notional standard of, presumably, middle-class respectability may not only haunt individuals, but also set in train parental efforts to 'better' their children which, while unquestionably carried out with the best intentions, lead to damaging distortions of their reality. For example, the Methodism of Dave's parents had in part originated as a means of surmounting what was seen as the social degradation of the urban proletariat, but its principal effect was to render the family more or less incapable of acknowledging and dealing competently with the darker sides of life.

Although society is as riven by inequality as ever, and preoccupation with status was never more acute, it does seem that, towards the end of the twentieth century, traditional class divisions are less easy to discern than they were only fifteen to twenty years ago. But it is still the case that for many people class is a significant factor of identity, and confusion over one's class background can lead to a kind of personal 'statelessness' not unlike confusion over nationality. Many middle-aged men who were able to realise their intellectual potential via a school system that operated across class barriers, but whose background was in the deferential working class which 'knew its place', have found themselves in jobs where they have both to compete and to socialise with middle-class colleagues who seem to move instinctively in a world which they themselves can never experience as other than essentially alien. The resultant feeling of being a stranger in what is in every other sense their own world can give rise to a considerable amount of anxiety.

The factor of *embodiment*, taken in a social context which fixes the body with an evaluative gaze, is again one that may profoundly

OLIVIA

Form of distress	Current predicament	Background predicament
For some time Olivia has been feeling uncharacteristically depressed, weepy and irritable with her three daughters. She has lost all interest in things, and gets anxious and panicky if she has to go out.	Married and with her first child at seventeen, Olivia has devoted her life to her children and her husband Tony. Now she is only in her mid-thirties, but her children are almost grown-up. Tony is a rock of dependability, though not as lively and bright as Olivia. Some of his family, she knows, abuse her racially behind her back. Tony is now out of work and the responsibility for managing the household falls on her. She enjoyed working part-time as a waitress in a local café, but the manager made constant allusions to her colour (e.g. 'You work pretty well for a coon'), and every so often she'd have to take racist abuse from customers.	One of several children from her mother's three relationships, Olivia was the only one of mixed race, her father being Ethiopian and her mother white. In looks, Olivia takes after him more than her mother. She is strikingly beautiful, tall and graceful. She never felt at ease with her step-relatives, most of whom made it clear that she was 'different'. Her mother, however, supported her lovingly throughout.

affect the individual's emotional wellbeing. Being fat, tall, short, or even having red hair, can for all too many children be a torment which makes their school life a misery of shame and isolation. There can be little doubt, too, that a commercially exploited male sexuality which fetishises the female body and makes it the object of relentless pornographic scrutiny, turns the simple fact of being a woman into a *problem* which cannot be evaded, even by the strategy of 'anorexia nervosa'. Men too, of course, worry a great deal about their personal attractiveness, and are by no means able to disown their bodies, but the difficulty for (particularly) young women is to be able to be *anything but* their bodies, and, whether beautiful or ugly, it is almost impossible for them to escape the awareness of embodiment.

Being black is of course another feature of embodiment that may render the individual socially vulnerable. Having lived with that vulnerability all their lives, and unable to escape a social background where racist attitudes are pervasive, many black people themselves find it difficult completely to shake off the idea that there is something inherently inferior about being black. Of all social injuries, this is the deepest and most cruel. Olivia, for example, for all her considerable intelligence and perceptiveness, felt that if she was kind enough to people she could 'make them forget' that she was black. In her mid-thirties, it came as a real surprise (and enlightenment) to her when a white friend pointed out that people abused her about her colour at least partly out of envy, precisely because they could find nothing else about her to criticise.

Background predicaments of all kinds, whether mediated within the family or imposed through more general social disadvantage, shape character and attitudes in a way that makes them a virtually ineradicable part of the person. We believe what we learn about ourselves, however unjust the lesson. The difficulty for psychology and psychotherapy (so far largely unrecognised) is that we cannot change our beliefs at will. The implications of this will form the substance of much of the rest of this book.

CHAPTER THREE

The Tyranny of 'Normality'

Many people (including many of its accredited students) come to psychology out of a desire to understand themselves or those around them better, assuming that psychology will provide well-founded and reliable keys to the complexities and mysteries of human mental and emotional functioning. This, sad though it may seem, implies a very naive view of the nature not only of psychology, but of knowledge in general.

Psychology is not simply a disinterested enquiry into 'what makes people tick'. Like every other branch of knowledge, psychology has aims and purposes that cannot be detached from the fundamental interests of the society that defines, supports and furthers it.[1] Human enquiry is not pursued through a gaze of wide-eyed innocence, simply gathering 'facts', sorting and storing them until a complete account of the nature of things has been achieved. Our gaze is, on the contrary, always directed by our needs and our wishes and the social powers which, in turn, seek to control them. Absolutely 'disinterested' enquiry is not just difficult to achieve, it is an impossibility, if only because being human is inextricably bound up with having interests.

There is of course not just *one* psychology, and psychology could presumably have taken many turns. Sadly, any expectation that it should consist principally in a kind of Socratic quest to 'know ourselves' in order to make our living together in sympathy and solidarity more achievable – the expectation that, perhaps, attracts so many people to it in the first place – is quickly disappointed. What psychology did principally become is revealed with telling clarity in the standard definition of it which held sway during its formative decades in twentieth century: 'the prediction and control of behaviour'.

It is not at all difficult to detect the kind of concern underlying this definition: it is obvious enough from the very meaning of the words. The behaviour to be predicted and controlled is of course that of people other than psychologists themselves. Psychologists stand apart from the subjects of their experimental investigations and observe them with lofty detachment. It betrays surprising philosophical naivety that behavioural psychology should have presented itself, as it so insistently did, as 'value-free', since the values implicit in this kind of 'objective expert' stance are so obvious: the psychologist becomes an instrument of social discipline, observing, reporting and advising on the ways in which the behaviour of others may be 'predicted and controlled'. At times these values became explicit (though still unacknowledged as values), as for example in a paper by H. J. Eysenck, the most influential psychologist in Britain in the 1950s and 1960s. He wrote of a 'technology of consent'

> which will make people behave in a socially adapted, law-abiding fashion, which will not lead to a breakdown of the intricately interwoven fabric of social life . . . a generally applicable method of inculcating suitable habits of socialized conduct into the citizens (and particularly the future citizens) of the country in question – or preferably the whole world.[2]

Psychology becomes revealed, not as a disinterested science trying to penetrate and unlock the secrets of the human psyche, but as a would-be technique of systematised power driven by aspirations of megalomaniac proportions. Of course, any programme as blatantly grandiose and unrealistic as that articulated by Eysenck could scarcely be taken seriously and in fact presents no great threat to human freedom, but the theme it overstates lies much more subtly at the heart of a whole range of psychological approaches, including most of those dealing with therapy and treatment.

As much as anything, the game is given away by the way in which the psychological expert is so often to be located apart from the objects of his or her interest. In many other branches of knowledge, the human enquirer's aims, interests and personal and social make-up are (almost) completely detachable from the object of study, but psychology cannot be like that.[3] Psychologists being of the same order of psychological complexity as their so-called subjects, their 'discoveries' must apply as much to themselves as to anyone else: they unavoidably become objects of their own study, and any attempt to escape this complication through a pretence that they can, by virtue of a kind of exclusive, esoteric knowledge, set themselves apart from the rest of humanity betrays a sociopolitical more than a scientific programme. It shows that what they are involved in is not so much knowledge about people as power over them.

It was above all Michel Foucault who exposed the essentially disciplinary nature of so much of psychology, psychiatry and psychotherapy.[4] It is of course not the case that mental-health programmes and procedures for the psychological measurement and classification of particular 'disorders' and 'deficits' openly proclaim any socially repressive intent; indeed, there is no reason why those who carry them out should be conscious of any such intent, and the majority are probably not. To be successful, programmes and procedures of this kind must be conceived and executed within an ideology of *care*. It was Foucault's particular achievement to reveal how much of this care (of course not all of it) is really about control.[5]

When it comes to the specifically 'therapeutic' aspect of psychological approaches, one does not have to read far into the literature before becoming aware of their 'conquistadorial' concerns.[6] This is evidenced in, for example, the patronising superiority of the language used to describe patients; the obsession with 'diagnoses' which, inevitably, place a kind of moral distance between therapist and patient; the almost paranoid concern with exclusivity, in which an attempt is made to establish and, so to speak, patent a system which only a select few can practise.

The stance taken by the system-builders of therapy towards patients is in this way almost always one of omniscient superiority, the language, if not positively hostile, at best condescending. Where people are not sorted and labelled according to the essentially meaningless categories of psychiatric diagnosis, they tend to be characterised as 'neurotic', 'infantile', 'immature', 'inadequate', 'maladjusted', 'manipulative', 'attention-seeking' and so on. Patients are people who are incomplete or damaged in some way, therapists people who have the (exclusive and protected) knowledge and power to identify and make good the patients' personal deficits and render them worthy once again of the company of their fellow human beings.

Lying right at the centre of the psychological enterprise, the tacit if not explicit focus of everyone's concern, is the concept of normality. Establishing what is 'normal' has been the business of a huge investment in 'psychometry' as well as the core of the diagnostic programme in psychological approaches to treatment. 'Psychometric tests' have been developed and standardised on a vast range of human characteristics. Intellectual abilities (including, of course, IQ), 'traits' of personality, vocational interest and abilities, diagnostic factors, have all been identified and turned into measurable aspects of personal functioning, all of which in turn compare the individual with a statistically established norm. Even where no such systematic approach to measurement exists, the essential psychological judgement is one that pronounces on the degree of the individual's departure from the average.

Psychology has become the instrument of conformity, not the appreciation of uniqueness. Difference is interpreted as deviance. Although, in the 'clinical' area, it is probably 'better' to be 'normal', there are, of course, deviations from the norm that are regarded in a positive light. It is 'better', for instance, to have an unusually high than an unusually low IQ, but even in cases like this the dimensions along which we may vary are established according to the characteristics of a 'population'.[7] There is no room for uniqueness: whatever characteristic psychology is measuring in you, you have, if you are not 'normal', either more or less of it than the average.

The principal consequence of all this is that social life becomes a process of comparison, usually invidious, and to consult a psychologist or psychiatrist is like coming before a judge. Psychologists, as the arbiters of 'normal' behaviour and experience, function precisely as judges, and the majority make little attempt to disguise it (though many of them are not aware that this is their principal role).

Psychological judgement can be very comprehensive: not only may individuals' status be assessed from the material and moral aspect, but it is quite likely also to be considered from an aesthetic standpoint. 'Psychometry', for example, may place the individual relative to the norm on a whole range of abilities and aptitudes which are regarded as more or less unalterable and quasi-biological, IQ being the most obvious example. I have already noted how moralistic some approaches to psychotherapy (particularly psychoanalysis) can be: a judgement is made of the extent to which people are conceived to be driven by 'unacceptable' impulses of aggression and sexuality, possessed by 'guilty fantasies' and 'infantile desires', etc., and even though therapists may, through their 'interpretations', convey that their intent is neither to reprove nor punish, patients can scarcely help concluding that these are moral imperfections.

The aesthetic judgement nestling apparently innocently at the heart of so many 'humanistic' approaches to psychotherapy and counselling may in some ways be the most difficult to cope with. For, although the hope is held out that through 'personal growth', 'self-actualisation', etc., forms of experience and relationship far from the dreary norm may be achieved, the fact is that the clients of these particular brands of therapy are likely to find that, despite their investment, life continues to run along much as it always has, and may conclude therefore that they must be lacking in some vital respect. Most 'humanistic' therapies enshrine in this way an exalted notion of the potential of human 'being' which is beyond all but the most self-deceiving of ordinary mortals and which, if taken seriously, can only lead to a sense of personal disappointment and failure.[8]

In view of all this it is not surprising that so many people approach their first consultation with a psychiatrist or psychologist with trepidation, for trepidation is indeed the appropriate emotion for a situation in which such comprehensive judgements can be passed, where so much seems to hang in the balance.[9] For although in one sense people 'know' that the professional they have come to consult is there 'for their own good' and to help them with their difficulties (that is to say, they accept the ideology of care), they know also that they are likely to be on the receiving end of a 'clinical assessment' which will place them, very possibly unfavourably, in relation to a range of norms concerning their mental adjustment and their personal and social adequacy. And they are not wrong, for behind the ideology of care lies a much broader, if less articulated, concern to maintain a culture that lays the blame for psychological and emotional suffering squarely at the door of those who suffer.

But it doesn't have to be, and isn't always, like this. There are other ways of understanding distress than merely as deviance, and it is possible to think about personal suffering without its being interpreted as personal failure.

Rather than an apprehension of self, informed at its core by invidious comparison (where the best that can be said of one's self is, as H. S. Sullivan put it, 'at least I'm not as bad as the other swine'[10]), what is needed is an understanding of how personhood comes about, freed of all the moralistic under- and overtones which a century of psychology has managed to create. We need to abandon our fixation on the 'normal' and consider who we are, and how we came to be so.

The making of persons

The first thing that it is important to establish is that one does not *choose* to be the person one is. The issues of choice, freedom and responsibility are complicated and difficult, and our popular as well as our 'official' psychological understanding of them are probably more harmfully misleading than almost any other (we shall be considering these issues more directly in later chapters), but only the most wishful and unreflective thinking (of which, unfortunately, there is no shortage) could conceive of the individual person as self-creating. We cannot be held responsible for who we are, and the shame and blame of invidious comparison are therefore simply inappropriate.

We need to understand how 'the person' comes to be constituted not so much because we can necessarily do very much about our 'selves' but because we need to know what we can reasonably expect of ourselves and how we can influence the factors that shape personhood – if not for our own good, then at least for the good of others yet to become persons. Indeed, perhaps the most important thing to understand is precisely that we cannot do very much about our 'selves'.

Although psychology has been very much concerned with what it calls 'individual differences', the individuality concerned is always in relation to a norm, which leaves no room at all for individuality in the true sense. Indeed, individuality is a vexed question not only for psychology, but for philosophy and politics as well, and the way most systems of thought seem to try to solve it is to focus on one particular aspect of human nature in order to suggest, for example, that human beings are either *all* individuals or *all* part of a virtually indistinguishable mass. The thing is, we are both.

Embodiment

The very foundation of our nature as human beings is the way we are made – our embodiment. Everything we come, through the process of socialisation, to know, to think, feel, perceive, believe, imagine and desire, is conditioned by the kind of physical organism we are. Our interest in the world, the ways we approach, sense, handle and move within it, are given to us through the structures and capacities of our bodily organs. There is no experience, no passion, no *mind* without body.

We do not earn our embodiment, it is just given, and however much factions within society may attempt to colonise the body with power by endowing its superficial characteristics (e.g. skin colour) with indices of worth or by claiming that blood can be blue, in the end only fools and knaves can fail to acknowledge that in this fundamental respect we are all equal. Prick us, and we bleed. Cut us open, and we all look the same. There are, it is true, superficial differences between us in height, weight, colouring, and more important distinctions to be made in respect of sex and degree of maturity, but apart from these we are pretty well identical. In my view, it is our shared embodiment that lays the ground of our *community* and establishes thereby the fundamentally ethical nature of the relation between us.

For, being built the same way and sharing identical organs of sensation and expression, we cannot escape a knowledge of how we *feel*: knowing how *I* feel tells me also how the other feels. In this respect, and stripped of our social pretensions, we are all incontrovertibly equal. We cannot ignore the sympathy that gives us knowledge of each other's pain (though we can, and do, abuse it without mercy) because my nervous system stirs at the very sight – even the idea – of your injury.

Our embodiment determines our feelings of pleasure and pain, and makes it possible for us to read in each other the joys and sufferings which form the most essential stuff of our lives. There is no 'nobility' of suffering, no 'refinement' of feeling which would permit one person to claim greater value than others for his or her physical 'sensibility'. Raw sensation is the same for us all, and we can ignore its significance for others only by conceptually removing ourselves from the human race in the most basic act of bad faith. When it comes to the experience of pain, the most socially privileged are placed instantly on the same plane with the most deprived (this fact makes any kind of socially differentiated provision of health care fundamentally immoral).

Experience

In another respect, we are all absolutely unique. It is useful to reflect from time to time that, even on a globe teeming with animals outwardly distinguishable from each other in only the most superficial ways, absolutely nobody has been where you have been at the time you've been there and with the same people.

One of the greatest difficulties facing a 'scientific psychology' which can consider individuality only as different degrees of conformity is that no two people do share the same experience. Assumptions important for research in normative psychology – for example about people sharing 'the same kind of background' – have to overlook the fact that, as far as people are concerned, there's no such thing as the same background. Many social scientists would no doubt see this as hair-splitting, probably claiming that people's backgrounds may be sufficiently similar for valid comparisons and generalisations to be made (e.g. that siblings share 'the same' familial environment). When it comes down to the individual trying to make sense of his or her own experience, however, the shortcomings of the normative approach become obvious. John and Jane's experience of 'the same' family background can be radically different, if only because John had Jane for a sister and Jane had John for a brother.[11]

This is no trivial matter. Only you know what your life has been like, what demands you have had to meet, what pains you have had to suffer. Throughout your life, only you have been occupying that space in the world which has been yours, and the angle from which you have experienced the world and the other people in it is utterly unique. Your relations with others have been shared with absolutely nobody else. Nonsense to pretend, to pursue the example above, that siblings share the same world or the same relations with their parents. Parental favouritism is a huge factor in shaping the experience of children, and just think, for instance, how different are the worlds of John and Jane where he has been bullying or sexually abusing her for years of her youth.

There can be no question of 'normality' when it comes to considering the significance of your private experience; there is no average to be calculated from a sample of one. There is in this way, at the heart of our existence, an aloneness of singularity, the terrible vulnerability of one against all, which (because we have all known it, all our lives) is easy to overlook but which we read easily enough in the faces of small children when they become doubtful of their safety in the society of others. Because of this, we depend for our wellbeing on the sympathetic support of at least some of those around us; we need to know the boat is shared at least with one or two, that we are not the only ones to be alone.

Right from the very start, the world is presented to you to organise and evaluate from a perspective which you share with no one. Your view of what is real and true, and your experience of pleasure and pain, are established from judgements only you can make. Those judgements may be supported, and indeed facilitated, by others, but ultimately you take your stand up against the world in utter solitude. Where you do get the help and encouragement of others, you are likely to develop a good degree of confidence in your own judgement, to feel that you have a secure understanding of the realities of the world, that you can move towards and within it without fear of unforeseen catastrophe or massive social rejection. For this, the help you get from others (particularly, of course, parents) needs to be centred on a knowledge of the uniqueness of your situation, to recognise that it is your shoes you're standing in, and not theirs.

There must be, I think, a crucial period of infancy where a competence to judge the world may become established, and no doubt a much more prolonged period of early life in which that competence may be extended and elaborated, or else threatened and undermined. The *courage* needed for a tiny, powerless organism to take a chance on the nature of its reality, to venture a first hesitant transaction with the all-powerful beings it encounters, must be colossal, and can only be acquired through a process of *encouragement*, in which a loving recognition of the uniqueness of the baby's perspective is central to the nurture and instruction offered.

Where this does not happen, where the infant is bullied or indoctrinated into a view of the world which has no basis in its own feelings and perceptions, it simply has to abandon any idea of its own competence to judge, to submerge its autonomy in a blind and ultimately inescapable obedience to the authority of others. (We shall return to this theme in the next chapter.)

Babies of course need the powerful support of their parents – they cannot simply be left to their own devices to create a world for themselves. But the parental attitude needs to be one of, so to speak, informed tentativeness, as if the parent were to say: 'I think it may help you in the task I take you to be struggling with to conceive of it this way, to handle it like that. Let me know if I'm wrong.' This, of course, is what many parents do instinctively without the slightest self-consciousness. But not always, and where a parental view of the world is simply imposed, the baby is robbed of the very foundation of its capacity for autonomous thought and action, and becomes incapable of interpreting independently its own experience.

In this way, we need from the very earliest moment to become equipped with the means of making sense of a world in which there is no absolute confirmation of our judgement simply because there is no one able completely to share our experience. When it comes to assessing the significance of your experience, you are, ultimately, on your own. Rather like the 'good' parents, others can do no more than make suggestions which may help you articulate a feeling or intuition, or invite you to consider possibilities you may have overlooked. This is why the normative approach does such violence to the experience of the individual: by being compared to an average he or she is instantly dislocated from a personal biography, and the joys and sorrows of a unique lifetime are swept aside as irrelevant.

Culture

The fact that the location from which you have experienced your world is uniquely your own does not mean, however, that everyone's 'psychology' is totally different from everyone else's. As well as a private aspect, we have a shared, public one. Nobody else can have experienced what you have experienced because only you have been where you have been, but the ways in which you understand and interpret your experience are likely to be shared with a very large number of other people. These are the ways given by the culture into which you are born and bred; they are not chosen and developed by you as, so to speak, your personal creations or acquisitions, but impressed upon you impersonally.

Most obviously, the language you speak is not something you invent for yourself, but is culturally imposed. And language contains, of course, many of the tools of understanding and interpretation; it sets the limits on what you can talk about and establishes the concepts with which you make sense of the world. Furthermore, what you can talk about determines in its turn what you can think about. Language shapes and articulates our primitive, felt conceptions, and makes them manifest not only to others, but first and foremost to ourselves. We feel, of course, as if our thoughts are entirely our own, and in the sense that only we are having them at a particular time and place, that is indeed so, but the form in which we have them is shared with everyone else: we can think only in terms of meanings and assumptions we have in common with all those who share our culture, and we have no choice in the matter.

Culture imposes on its members far more than merely the language they speak and the way they think. Although our experience may be unique, culture defines its meaning. Just about all the evaluations we make of ourselves and others are shaped by the culture in which we live: we cannot step outside the network of common meanings which defines our very existence somehow to create a personal world (or, if we do, we will certainly be regarded by others as mad). For example, what it is to be male or female, adult or child, competent or incompetent, acceptable or unacceptable, good or bad in all the thousands of ways these judgements can be made, is determined always by reference to cultural standards over which the individual has no control at all – any more than s/he has control over the language s/he learns as an infant. In this way, our ideas about ourselves and our satisfaction or otherwise with the way we are will often depend heavily on cultural norms and standards which are far beyond the reach of any individual to change.

One important implication of this is that, contrary to what a lot of the psychotherapy and counselling industry would like us to believe, we cannot be self-creating, but can manoeuvre only in the room our culture allows us. We cannot create for ourselves alternative realities that liberate us from cultural constraints, perhaps by replacing them with more desirable inventions of our own. 'Stone walls do not a prison make' is a fine piece of wishful thinking, but in fact illustrates no more than the possibility of escaping *reality* into the *imagination*. Stone walls are precisely what make a prison, and if you're behind them you're a prisoner, however much you may fantasise about sunning yourself on a desert island.

A second important implication of the defining property of

culture is that our sense of ourselves as persons is dependent on the integrity of the cultural forms of 'personhood'. If, for example, a particular cultural form starts to disintegrate – say the form 'masculinity/femininity' – individual people will begin to feel personally disintegrated in this respect. What is in fact a social phenomenon comes to be experienced by ordinary people as a personal problem.

Exactly this kind of thing has come about quite pervasively since the 1970s as, in the industrialised world at least, the amoral culture of business and the market has re-established the grip on society which was for a moment loosened by, in particular, the events surrounding the Second World War. Not only have conventional roles such as those of 'husband' and 'wife' changed radically, but the very conception of what it is to be a valuable and competent contributor to society has changed practically out of all recognition. This has meant that, quite apart from the bewildering redefinition of sex and gender roles many have found themselves struggling with, whole swathes of the middle-aged population, in particular, have experienced themselves as inadequate failures, anxiously grabbing at the opportunity trailed before them for early retirement.[12]

Because we do not have a popular psychology that recognises the dependency of the subjective experience of 'being a person' on cultural 'forms', the pain people feel in these kinds of circumstances is nearly always experienced in isolation, as a problem of personal inadequacy or 'relationship' difficulties. The example of Ian, in the previous chapter, shows how a man from a background where quite set and stable ideas of 'gender roles' were and to an extent still are the norm, becomes completely demoralised when he finds himself in a competitive 'market' of marital relations in which his wife not only challenges his traditional role but actually takes it over. Ian had no conception that society had changed, but just thought of himself as 'ill'. It took him a while to see that the pain he suffered was in fact not a form of illness, but a result of the experience of cultural disintegration. In other words, that's how people feel when an aspect of the culture on which they depend for their sense of self starts to disintegrate.

Jill's problems, similarly, had as much to do with the absence of any cultural norms about the proper conduct of second marriages (involving children from the first) as with any personal shortcomings of her own. Although her own background had no doubt to an extent sapped her confidence in herself and left her with a pretty punitive conscience, she was in fact a very able and perceptive woman, as sensitive as anyone could be to attending to the needs and wishes of others as a basis for social harmony; it was not knowing what the 'rules' were that made her life so difficult and potentiated her panic attacks.

In Keith's case the failure to acquire a workable idea of the relationship of inner experience to outer social behaviour seemed to be the result of having been brought up at a time, and in a particular class context of 'upward social mobility', where the principal cultural preoccupation was with the construction of an 'image' in which only the outer featured, and that in a particularly oversimplified and superficial form. One thing Keith had certainly not realised was that, among all those young people around him who he assumed were so much more 'together', there were many feeling exactly as disturbed and alienated.

In pointing out that the culture determines aspects of people that they cannot change – aspects usually regarded as 'personal' and 'psychological' – I am not arguing that they are unchangeable. The point is, rather, that they cannot usually be changed just by the individual in whose interest it may be to change them. They can certainly be changed through the operation of social power on a larger scale, as the examples above illustrate. It is also possible to negotiate cultural change politically. There seems little doubt that the women's movement has been influential in redefining gender roles, at least within some social strata, to an extent that has been concretely manifested in the lives of individuals (not always with their awareness, of course, and not necessarily either with their approval).

In relation to culture, we don't have much of a choice about whether we are 'normal' or not. If we are not 'normal', it may be either because we have for some reason been exposed to realities unlike those of others, or because the norms themselves are losing their integrity. Either way, there's not a great deal we can do about it as individuals, and to see 'abnormality' as some kind of personal lack or failing, perhaps to be put right by 'psychological intervention', sets up an entirely inappropriate framework in which to try to understand our subjective experience of ourselves and any emotional distress which may attach to it.

The appreciation of character

A particularly damaging effect of the obsession with normality which conventional psychology and psychiatry do so much to reinforce is to make us doubt the validity of our own experience. Many people, rather than being able to exist confidently at the centre of their own world, find themselves agonisingly conflicted over whether what they perceive, feel and conclude about things in their everyday dealings with others constitute *legitimate* perceptions, feelings and conclusions, or whether they are somehow reprehensibly unusual. 'Do other people feel, think, see things like me?' can become a question constantly posed to oneself in a kind of unremitting state of anxiety. Life may be lived in the secret dread that at any moment an unguarded comment will reveal the crazy eccentricity of one's perspective on life and/or relations with others.

This is, when one thinks about it, a very strange, not to say unfortunate, state of affairs. For the only certain knowledge you have of how human beings work is given to you through your own experience. Rather than asking yourself, via an apprehensive comparison with a mythical norm, 'What is it like to be human, and do I fit the description?', you could be realising through your own experience: 'So *this* is what it's like to be human.'

Confidence to believe one's own experience consists of a kind of boldness in which the individual takes himself or herself as the 'standard' of humanity and trusts his or her own subjectivity. This is not to suggest that everything one thinks or feels is necessarily true and real and genuine, but that the validity of thoughts and feelings, their acceptability, the claim they may have on the respectful attention of others, are *not* established in relation to their 'usualness' or 'normality'.

Anyone who abandons his or her own standpoint in order to reflect what s/he takes to be the 'normal' view (and all of us do this at least sometimes) risks losing the principal means s/he has for interpreting reality accurately and dependably (not, I should emphasise again, infallibly). Where this happens, people's ability to make judgements about the significance of their experience, to act spontaneously in their relations with others, etc., becomes tentative and vacillating, even paralysed, and decisions await the anxious, and quite possibly fruitless, reference to what is 'normal'.

We discover how it feels to be human by attending carefully to our own experience, and indeed (recognising that each person's experience is in one important respect unique) to the experience of others. To insist that only some kinds of supposedly 'normal' experience are in some sense valid or permissible is to commit an act of violence on all of us, since none of us is 'normal' in the singularity of our experience of life.

Breaking the anxious silence which dread of 'normality' tends to impose on people's revelation of their own experience can be tremendously reassuring. To discover that others are as eccentric as we are, that they too have unorthodox and unconventional thoughts and feelings, can be a huge relief, liberating us to think and feel what we like.[13] Great artists can perform this function. Listen to Tolstoy's account of his mother's death in his largely autobiographical *Childhood, Boyhood and Youth*:

> I stopped at the door and looked but my eyes were too swollen with weeping and my nerves so unstrung that I could distinguish

> nothing. The light, the gold brocade, the velvet, the tall candlesticks, the pink lace-trimmed pillow . . . , the cap with ribbons, and something else of a transparent wax-like colour – all ran together in a strange blur. I climbed on to a chair to look at her face but there in its place I again saw the same pale-yellow translucent object. I could not believe that this was her face. I began to stare hard at it and gradually began to recognize the dear familiar features. I shuddered with horror when I realized that this was she. But why were the closed eyes so sunken? Why that dreadful pallor, and the blackish spot under the transparent skin on one cheek?

And later,

> Having slept soundly and peacefully all that night, as is always the case after great distress, I awoke with my eyes dry and my nerves soothed. At ten o'clock we were called to the service which was celebrated before the body was borne away. The room was filled with weeping servants and peasants who had come in to take leave of their mistress. During the service I wept as befitted the occasion, crossed myself and bowed to the ground, but I did not pray in spirit and was more or less unmoved: I was more concerned with the fact that the new jacket they had dressed me in was too tight under the arms; I thought about how not to dirty the knees of my trousers when I knelt down, and kept stealthily observing all the people who were present. My father stood at the head of the coffin. He was as white as a sheet and obviously had difficulty in restraining his tears. His tall figure in a black frock-coat, his pale expressive face and his movements, graceful and assured as ever when he crossed himself, bowed, touching the floor with his fingers, took a candle from the priest's hand or approached the coffin were extremely effective; but, I don't know why, I did not like him being able to show himself off so effectively at that moment . . .[14]

Tolstoy was not a man to be terrorised by the norm. He does not ask himself what he ought to have been thinking and feeling as he viewed his mother's corpse, whether others' attention would, like his, have been drawn to the blackish spot under her skin. He knew well enough that his show of grief at the ceremony was merely outward and formal, and he does not hesitate to reveal his preoccupation with the tightness of his jacket or his reservations about his father's demeanour. In recounting with such candour what was after all his unique experience, he does not shock us with his eccentricity but reminds us what it is to be human.

What we know about the world is given to us through our unique experience of it. Even though we can only formulate and express that knowledge in terms shared with all the other members of our culture, nobody else can claim to know better than we what we saw, felt or thought about at any particular time. Nobody can judge our reality as somehow being less or more adequate than some notion of what is 'normal'. It is not our place to *judge* each other's realities, but rather to enquire into them sympathetically and respectfully.

Even where somebody's knowledge of reality seems to depart radically from our own, it makes no sense to conclude that somehow their experience is invalid or that the world they occupy is in some sense not as real as the average. People can, of course, misinterpret their experience, make mistakes or lie about it, but its *normality* is not the measure of its validity.

The fact that we share the same bodily structure is the grounding of our sympathy with each other and this in turn the basis of a morality which makes treating others as we would wish to be treated ourselves axiomatic.[15] Sharing a common culture, as well as providing much of the fabric of what we take to be our 'personality', is what makes it possible to understand, communicate and share our knowledge with each other. Our experience of life, on the other hand, is what gives us our knowledge and makes us the unique characters we are.

Rather than engaging in a continuous, fearful self-assessment to establish how far we deviate from what is 'normal', we would do well to regard ourselves as characters with an experience of life and a unique knowledge of the world which, far from hiding it in shamed silence, we should be ready to impart to those less expert than we. Only you have been where you have been and only you know what it felt like: you are indeed the expert in your own existence and it may well be the case that there are things others could usefully know which only you could tell them.

Catherine, for example (see Chapter Two), was an expert in betrayal and, having experienced it in various forms throughout her early life, spent much of her time trying to ensure that it didn't happen again. In this, it should be noted, she was remarkably successful: her vigilance meant that all her relationships were ended by her before any man got the chance to inflict on her the kind of pain she had experienced as a child. Normality and abnormality are irrelevant to an understanding of her predicament: she was, for very good reasons, a jealous character. She anticipated life in line with the lessons it had taught her, and though those lessons may have been uncommon, they were certainly not 'wrong'.[16] No doubt it was necessary for her to learn new and different lessons, but that did not mean that she could or should repudiate the old. Experience such as hers has a great deal to tell us about the injuries we do each other, often in the name of love; paradoxical as it may seem, her knowledge is actually valuable.

We seem to find it easier to pay attention to and learn from characters in novels than we do from characters in real life. *Madame Bovary*, for example, is no doubt a wonderful study of sexual passion and betrayal from which a huge amount may be learned by those whose lives have followed more pedestrian paths; but why dismiss similar insights as 'pathological' or 'abnormal' when they are afforded by the living characters we encounter in the course of our everyday existence?

Your knowledge of the world is hard won, carved in blood and bone and nervous tissue. Your character is in many respects the history of your embodiment. Perhaps it is because modern life is lived so much in the context of electronic technology on the one hand and pure fantasy, fuelled and exploited by commercial interests, on the other, that we pay so little heed to our embodiment. We like to think that painful experience can be erased and replaced like a magnetic recording or that, if we really, really want to, we can summon up the will to live in accordance with our wishes, unbound by the realities of our too solid flesh. But it is not so; the world imprints itself on our bodies and our bodies constitute the living, material record of our path through worldly space and time.

In the rawness of our experience, the chaotic jumble of our impressions, impulses and dreams, we are all eccentrics. Whatever the lessons of your life, there is nothing to be ashamed of or to fear about them. Fear and shame are introduced only through the process of invidious comparison set up by a mythical 'normality' and used in particular to disqualify the experience of those whose knowledge of the world suggests that all is not well with the organisation of our society. As the character you are, the embodied product of your times and places, you have a right to be taken seriously, for your knowledge to count. Truly shameful are those (usually more powerful) others who sit in judgement of your character and your knowledge and loftily discount them – perhaps by giving you a 'diagnosis'.

For the normalising eye – whether of the professional diagnostician or merely the everyday, defensive scrutiny of invidious comparison – is cynical, suspicious and unsympathetic. It looks past the patent reality of the individual person in search of inadequacy and duplicity. In contrast, the loving regard of the connoisseur of character – Charles Dickens is the supreme example – believes what it sees, wonders at and positively savours the diversity and complexity of our embodied efforts to solve the often tragic riddles life sets us.

Take, for example, the woman who, brought up as an orphan correctly but without love in a family of her dead parents' relatives, spends her adult life trying to please implacable men. She has no sense of herself as important, but uses all her gifts and all her (not inconsiderable) moral strength to try to make her successive marriages to two men (the first died) work. Both men are weak and abusive towards her; one of them verbally extremely cruel. How easy it would be for the therapist whose efforts to 'normalise' her she steadfastly resists, to talk about 'personality disorder', 'masochistic needs' etc. and to dismiss her endurance of unhappiness as a form of weakness. But to do that one would simply have to ignore the reality of her sweetly tolerant, vulnerable courage. Her existence is in many ways a kind of lived enquiry into the mysterious nature of love, pursued with a gentle but inflexible stubbornness which, though one can see that it is doomed to eternal disappointment, is none the less moving and admirable for that. Hers is a character to be appreciated, not scorned.

It is above all important that you take *your own* character and experience seriously. It is the only firm anchorage you have in the world. This is, of course, not to say that you have nothing to learn from others, nor that everything you think and believe is right – far from it – but it is to say that the ultimate test of truth must, for you, be against your knowledge of the world. Sticking by what you know, maintaining respect for the lessons of your life, can be uncomfortable, and it is easy to be seduced by the blandishments of magical wishfulness or the security of authority. But in the end what is important is staying sensitively in touch with the real world of your experience, because that's the only way you will be able to influence the events that determine what happens to you and to others. It is essential to know when the emperor is clothed and when he is not, even though people will not always thank you for telling them.

The proper attitude of those seeking to help people in distress is one of appreciation and respect. The experience of suffering is not invalid, but has, as well as its reasons, its lessons. There is a great deal to be learned from people who know how a life can be derailed by misfortune or tragedy, and the lesson has usually very little to do with their own personal culpability. Denigration, probably the most widespread professional attitude (however subtly 'clinical' its packaging), has absolutely no place in any kind of psychiatric or psychological help. But neither, more surprisingly perhaps, has blanket approval.

I have already indicated, in the discussion of therapeutic comfort in Chapter One, that there seem to me to be difficulties with the idea that therapists can or should dispense a kind of loving concern for their patients. I do not mean that this does not sometimes happen, nor that it is necessarily wrong when it does; the point is that the provision of love cannot be professionally guaranteed. To undertake to love somebody for a fee must involve a form of deception if only because love cannot be willed.[17]

The same is true of the more technical-sounding 'unconditional positive regard' ('warmth' for short) of Rogerian counselling. Whether or not a therapist approves unconditionally of a patient is, even if it is something s/he can choose to do, irrelevant to their transaction. It is not the therapist's business either to approve or disapprove, but it is his or her business to treat people politely, kindly and with respect. As a matter of fact it is easy for therapists to *like* patients because of the balance of power between them: the commonest reason for disliking someone is being threatened by them, and the situation in which therapist and patient find themselves is one that protects the therapist from threat. But the fact that this is very often the case doesn't mean that it has to be. Psychotherapists would be very strange animals if at times they did not find themselves disapproving of someone they are trying to help.

The point is not how therapists should *feel* about people (for over that they have no control), but how they should *treat* them. I see no reason why you should not expect and require from your psychiatrist, psychologist or psychotherapist the same minimum standards of politeness and respect you would expect from any other professional person. Given that patients are, at the time of consulting professional helpers, often in considerable distress, we might further hope that they would be treated with kindness and compassion beyond the average.

It is, as well, a tremendous privilege to be taken into the confidence of so many different characters whose experience of life can be so revealing of the way the world looks. An element of gratitude, even humility, would not be misplaced in the professional response.

CHAPTER FOUR

Troublesome Worlds – People and Power

Emotional distress is not simply a personal matter. To understand why you are suffering – and to establish from that whether there is anything you can do about it – it is necessary to extend your enquiry far beyond the boundaries of your personal experience and relationships. Most conventional approaches to psychotherapy, certainly the best known, have not only failed to recognise the importance of this point but have actually made it more difficult to grasp.

For, as was pointed out in Chapter One, the claustrophobic setting of the therapeutic relationship naturally confines the gaze of the participants to the psychological dynamics of the consulting room. The therapist examines the patient for signs of personal pathology and the patient looks to the therapist for techniques of cure. The raw material of therapy becomes what the patient can express, remember, imagine or dream, and the main means of cure is limited to the influence the therapist can exert over the patient's mental and emotional life merely by talking and 'interpreting'.

To be fair, many psychotherapists have recognised that outcome in psychotherapy is restricted to what can be achieved through the nonspecific factors involved in an essentially personal relationship between patient and therapist, and that evidence of profound, lasting improvement from psychotherapy is weak.[1] However, this (no doubt for sound commercial reasons) has on the whole not led psychologists and psychotherapists to modify their theories about the causes and cures of emotional distress, but rather to unleash ever more sophisticated and intense research effort on the consulting room and its beleaguered occupants in the illusion that the holy grail of therapeutic effectiveness will at last lie revealed.[2]

The consulting-room model of human psychology which has developed over the last hundred years or so has had a profound effect on our idea of ourselves, reinforcing an emphasis within our culture on personal responsibility and autonomy in relation to psychological suffering. The effect of this has been to lift us out of the social environment and attribute to us not only a distinctly moral role in the acquisition of our own troubles but also the power to better our lot principally through our own devices (though perhaps needing a therapist to act as a kind of midwife to our efforts). The rest of this book will be taken up with an attempt to suggest alternatives to this model which are less illusory, and hence ultimately less damaging to our ability to cope with distress.

What the consulting-room model does above all is to inflate enormously, and grossly misleadingly, the power of individuals to take charge of their own fate. Rather than being one of two essentially autonomous agents able to negotiate profound personal change through consulting-room transactions, we are in fact infinitessimal social atoms caught in a vast and complex web of power which, among other things, permeates the consulting room through and through. Not only can we not choose our place in society, but neither can we select our personal experience, decide how to feel about it, nor determine the quality of our relationships through acts of will. It is not, as we shall see later in this book, that we are power*less*, but our powers are very strictly limited by the social environment in which we live, much more so than is envisaged by almost any approach to psychotherapy.

The issue of 'free will versus determinism' has tended to polarise opinion between those who take the view that human beings are entirely free to fashion their own fate and those who believe that every human action, no matter how minute, is determined by the inexorable play of cause and effect in a universe where everything is foreordained by the iron laws of science. In the field of the psychological therapies this split separates some of the wilder humanistic and existentialist therapists on one side from the hard-nosed, 'scientific' behaviourists on the other.

As I hope will become clear later (Chapter Six), I think this dispute is so difficult to resolve mainly because it poses the wrong question. It is not the case that *either* we are free *or* we are determined; some of us are a lot more free than others. The interesting question to ask is: *How* free are we in any particular situation to obtain what we want or need? Another way to approach this is to enquire into the amount of power available to a person to change things and the nature and extent of the powers that bear down on him or her to impede change, or indeed to change his or her circumstances disadvantageously.

What makes it possible to live a comfortable life, psychologically as much as materially, depends very heavily on the influences that impinge upon us at any given time within the social environment. Our freedom to change depends on the extent to which we can modify these influences. Much of the time, we may be able to do very little. Most approaches to psychotherapy take very little account of this limitation on our freedom – not surprisingly, perhaps, in view of the vested interest therapy has in the promise of change.

When you think about it, the language of therapy and the principal concepts it concerns itself with are extraordinarily unlike the main preoccupations of your everyday life. Whereas almost before you wake in the morning you are likely to be worrying about the rent or the mortgage, whether you'll keep your job or pass your exam, therapeutic language seems to have a lofty – at times almost contemptuous – disregard for such matters, as if they were merely distractions from the really important issues of your unconscious desires and fantasies and the ways in which, through them, you are supposedly creating your own problems.[3]

Therapy has to take this line, of course, because it has to concentrate on aspects of your 'psyche' and 'personality' which could plausibly be altered by you. The difficulty is, though, that once outside the consulting room the real world very quickly makes clear what it is and is not going to let you do. What 'makes us tick' (and loudly, at that) is not the ideas, wishes and plans inside our heads, but the pushes and pulls of the all too material forces which structure the social environment. The ideas, wishes and plans inside our heads are, to be sure, how we *experience* the material forces which press down upon us, but they are not identical with them, and in fact, taken on their own, have no power at all to alter anything.

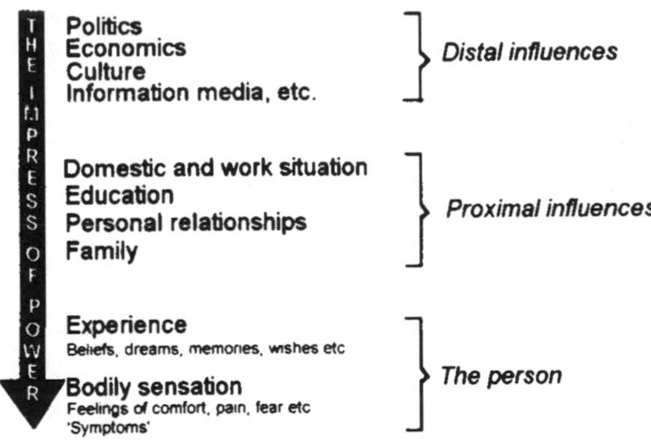

Figure 1: influence of the social environment

The structure of power

As suggested in Figure 1, what we most immediately *feel* is the influences of a world which stretches far beyond the individual person. These influences are mediated by our experience, filtered through our interpretations of the past and anticipations of the future as well as shaped and made sense of by all the cultural equipment we have acquired. The credibility of most approaches to psychotherapy hangs on the idea that we can work directly on our experience in order to change how we feel. But much of this experience – what one might call our psychological meaning-systems – is itself the result of external influence and has little, if any, power to change itself. There is no independent dynamic of experience that would allow us to detach *meaning* from the material reality which creates it and somehow mould it into an alternative reality where we can live more comfortably. We can try to live in our imagination, but the imaginary is precisely not real.

Our experience is acquired through the most proximal influences upon us: those which are transmitted by the people and things we encounter directly in everyday life. We are always, so to speak, up against a world which impinges directly on our senses, and anything at all that comes to be part of our experience does so via immediate personal contact. But this does not mean that the most proximal influences are necessarily the most powerful. For proximal influences are in turn shaped and held in place in the social structure by higher-order powers which act on them.

There is no great measure of agreement among sociologists on the definition of 'power', though pretty well all seem to agree that it is about getting other people to do things. For present purposes power could be defined as the means of obtaining security or advantage. Such means come in a variety of forms. Coercive, economic and ideological power seem to be the commonest types to be distinguished, most frequently encountered within such societies as ours in the form of military might, wealth and the ability to manipulate information and meaning. Different kinds of power often go together, but this need not always be the case – any adult, however poor and bereft of other forms of influence, has an ultimate recourse to brute force in some circumstances (probably exercised most frequently over children, unfortunately).

It is infrequent for really great power to be possessed by individuals, and even billionaires depend on large numbers of other people if they are actually to make their wealth count in the world to any significant extent. For most 'ordinary' people, what power they have usually stems from their association with others – being part, that is, of a relatively powerful organisation or group. But power certainly operates to the greater advantage of the few rather than the many: though the tyrant or dictator will be dependent on an army for the maintenance of his power, he will almost certainly be living a more comfortable life than his soldiers.

Although the levers of power are likely to be concentrated in the hands of a relatively small number of groups and individuals, its actual operation does not have to be a particularly conscious or self-conscious process. Like the working of Adam Smith's 'invisible hand', the distribution of power throughout society takes place without any need for deliberate, meticulous planning on anybody's part.

The principal medium of transmission of power in present-day Western societies is probably via the manipulation of self-interest. This is largely an automatic process, in which all the various official and unofficial institutions within society play their part, from big business, government and the media at one end to the black economy, the family and the school playground at the other. In order to 'hold people in place' by manipulating their interests, it is not necessary, as I have written elsewhere,

> to maintain a very highly explicit, precision-engineered system; rather, the application of power would be a bit like tipping a bucket of water down the side of a hillock – by one route or another it will find its way to the bottom, facilitated by (and so deepening) available channels, cutting some new ones, swamping small obstructions, flowing round (and thereby isolating) little islands of resistance, and so on.[4]

The experience of power

What all this means is that the proximal events and relationships that loom largest in your experience of life, though they are certainly of the greatest significance as far as you are concerned, are not necessarily the most important causes of your joys and sorrows. The teacher who instructs you badly and fails your exam, the boss who makes you redundant, the husband who doesn't listen when you want to talk, the father who lashes out unpredictably, all have a pretty powerful effect on you, but a longer perspective might show that, because of the influences pressing down on them, they have very little choice in how they conduct themselves. The teacher may be following a politically determined curriculum, the boss transmitting the policy of a newly merged company, and so on. It may of course be in some theoretical sense that they *could* act otherwise, it's just that to do so they would have to act irrationally.

This is easily enough understood by most adults, but even so we rarely see beyond the actions of those who trespass against us to the reasons that might argue their forgiveness: emotionally, we live very much in the proximal world. For children, whose power is so minuscule in relation to that of their parents, it is even more difficult to get an objective perspective on what is happening. To a small child, it is likely to seem that power starts and stops with its parents, that they have absolute freedom to shape the world as they wish. Planted in the infant's head from the word go is a philosophy of which some aspects stay with most of us for the rest of our lives: the belief that beings with absolute power must have reasons for their actions which they have freely chosen.

A particularly poignant result of this philosophy for small children is that they are virtually bound to attribute parental displeasure, or even cruelty and hatred, to their own moral or material shortcomings – for what other reason could such powerful beings possibly have for behaving the way they do? 'If my mother hates me, it can only be because I am, in some respect at least, hateful.' Many are the fifty- and sixty-year-olds who seek still to earn the love of a parent who abused them throughout their childhood, as if they might still be able to uncover and make up for the faults or blemishes which so displeased.

The aspect of this philosophy that lodges stubbornly with pretty well all of us is the idea that the *causes* of actions reside in the *intentions* of those who carry them out. Even after we achieve a degree of sophistication which permits us to see that there may be reasons for what we do over which we have no control, we still habitually look first at the supposed intention – we still tend to blame others and ourselves as if they and we could have done otherwise.

I do not by any means wish to argue that we are all the victims of an inexorable determinism and that none of us can help what we are doing. The point is rather that we need to get sufficient distance from the immediate impact of our proximal experience and the passions it engenders to see that accurate explanations of our own and others' conduct involve much more than just intentions. And the point of doing this is so that we may achieve a more accurate understanding of ourselves. For example, my mother may have had other reasons for hating me than simply my hatefulness.

The way we experience and deal with the difficulties and pressures of life will always depend to some extent on lessons we have learned from the past, and our perspective on those lessons is always proximal. Enquiring into past experience, perhaps attempting to extend our perspective a little into the more distal causes of it, is often a good idea not because it leads to insights inspiring instant change, but because it can correct conceptual errors which obscure our view of reality. Realisation that, after all, the cause of my mother's hatred was not my hatefulness, though it won't lead instantaneously to my feeling better about myself, will at least perhaps give me reasons for believing that hatefulness is not just an inevitable and ineradicable part of my nature, and this may clear the path for action which I would not otherwise have been able to take. (There will be more to say about these issues in Chapter Seven.)

The impress of power, then, though in all probability originating at considerable distance from individuals, is inevitably experienced by them proximally, through the mediation of those with whom they are in daily contact. The infant's experience is impressed upon it bodily – 'wired in' – at least as soon as it emerges from the womb. Experience is not provisional or hypothetical, it cannot be picked over so that some parts can be selected and others rejected: it is, so to speak, stamped on the child's body as the indelible imprint of reality.

From the child's perspective, then, what all-powerful adults around it do is of the first importance for its understanding of the way the world is. The baby is thrown at birth (if not before) into a predicament from which there is no escape and the conclusions it draws from the experience are likely to stay with it lifelong.

At first, the child has no words with which to organise and think about what is happening to it; for the first year or two its experience will be recorded in the form of feelings (and anticipations) of pleasure, pain, apprehension and excitement, and, no doubt, various kinds of images associated with them. Only gradually, with the increasing availability of language, will these become differentiated into coherent ideas and thoughts. Furthermore, the feelings and images in which our earliest experiences are registered are not simply replaced or supplanted by more 'rational', language-based modes, but rather provide the foundation for them. Lying beneath the articulate ideas, thoughts and descriptions we may have of our experience are always inexpressible aspects of them which are simply felt or pictured.

Nor is it just in early childhood that experience may be recorded nonverbally – there are all kinds of circumstances in later life (varying from simple unfamiliarity to extreme threat) when words fail us not only in the expression but also in the acquisition of experience.[5] It is again important to emphasise that there is no question of choice over the impress of experiences such as these: we cannot choose not to undergo them, nor can we opt for them to be different once we have undergone them.

The absence or unavailability of language is probably what explains the frightening quality of 'uncanniness'[6] that sometimes accompanies feelings, experiences or 'compulsive' actions in later life that seem to the individual involved profoundly irrational. What enables us to 'know' what we're doing is being able to rehearse our actions in words. Where words fail us, it may seem to us that we are losing our minds.

Both pleasure and pain experienced at a time before we could successfully attach words to them may well have a lot to do with, for example, difficulties such as 'eating disorders', in which sufferers find themselves quite unable to resist impulses to conduct which they know perfectly well to be self-destructive. Again, 'uncanny' anxiety may surround particular circumstances or activities in a way that strongly suggests the return of feelings, and sometimes indistinct images, from a time when they were simply raw, literally inexpressible, experiences of the imposition of adult power. The sexual abuse of small children before they have had the opportunity to develop a vocabulary which could make sense of what is happening to them seems often to leave them in later life with a painfully intangible sense of 'something' distressing pervading areas of their experience without their being able to say exactly what, but perhaps in the form of vague, dreamlike images.

Even though the acquisition of language may help make it possible for us to register events in a way we can subsequently make sense of, it still does not permit us, as children, to step back from our experience and criticise it. The child is locked into the perspective of its immediate environment – usually its family – and has no way of knowing, at least until it goes to school, that there are other perspectives. Moreover, it takes an exceptionally reflective person to question in later life whether the impressions of reality s/he received at various points throughout childhood were in any way unusual – and even if it is realised that they were, it doesn't make them any the less real.

Parental power can operate in all sorts of ways to shape experience, to reinforce autonomy or to undermine confidence. We have already seen in Chapter Two how Heather's observation of her mother's flirtation with a neighbour was greeted with immediate, punitive disconfirmation from the two people on whom she most depended for accurate information about the world. This event – no doubt the only one of its kind in her experience – significantly weakened Heather's confidence in what was, after all, a perfectly sound grasp of reality. She could neither abandon her view nor entirely trust it, and if she became aware of being oppressed or abused by others (as for example with her husband's affair) she could never quite believe in the validity of her judgement enough to take any kind of definite action.

Elizabeth's 'bulimia', experienced by her as simply a shameful, not to say very puzzling, form of greed, was in fact a fairly obvious extension of conduct she could scarcely have failed to acquire as a child. Sandwiched between two siblings favoured by her rather stern, ascetic parents, she could only by stealth obtain quite ordinary pleasures of life. Just as Heather hung admirably but fearfully on to her accurate view of her mother's sexual adventure, so Elizabeth had enough sense of self-preservation to acquire for herself the odd treat. But she could do so only in secrecy and with the ever present threat of the betrayal of her brothers and inevitable parental disapproval. This pattern became a way of life, an embodied part of Elizabeth's character, and she could not simply divest herself of it, even when she could see how she had come to acquire it.

The impress of parental disapproval is extraordinarily difficult to shift. Almost all Heather's often extremely insightful comments about others are prefaced by 'I expect it's me' or 'I know I must be wrong'. Elizabeth has not been able to sympathise with or approve of her healthy childhood stubbornness: her parents' imputation of badness (in the form of 'greed' etc.) has become part of her own in-built make-up, and she is now the first to be disgusted with herself.

The whole of our lives can be shaped by the authorisation of parental power – what has and has not been permitted us during our formative years. Norman, for example, has throughout his somewhat erratic life always had an almost superstitious sense that something would turn up in times of trouble to bail him out of difficulty. In fact, something always has – in the shape of his mother. As a child he could have had no more powerful ally – even his father quailed before her – and he would have had to be extraordinarily self-denying (even had such a course been open to him) to turn down her support. But the alliance was not without its costs as far as Norman was concerned. He knew as a boy that some of his desires and activities would have to be concealed from his mother if he was not to test her loyalty too far, and so he developed the kind of double life which resulted eventually in his drinking and gambling running out of control. In fact, he had very little autonomy: while the conduct of his 'open' life was licensed by his mother, it was not underpinned by his own desire, and so periodically ran out of steam. The secret life of his desire, on the other hand, because it was not authorised, could not be given any kind of direction, nor be directly acknowledged even by himself.

The reality of power

There is nothing mysterious about the potency of parental influence: it is derived simply from the fact that, relative to their children, parents are so powerful. They hold all the levers that control the child's material as well as psychological development: not only is the infant dependent on its parents for its physical survival, the most basic sensations of pleasure and pain, but they also mediate its very access to reality through the discriminations of *meaning* which they encourage or discourage, permit or forbid. It is via parental influence that the embodied foundations of character are laid.

The irony is, of course, that though parents set the boundaries of the child's universe, they may in the wider scheme of things have extremely little power themselves. The less power available to parents, the less their room for manoeuvre in a possibly far from benign world, the narrower will be the options they are able to give their children (and the more uncomfortable the child's life will probably become). Indeed, relatively powerless though they are, children can in some circumstances become an outright threat to their parents.

For example, where a child starts to observe or conceptualise things that introduce elements of uncontrollability into the parents' world, issues they simply cannot, for one reason or another, handle, the parental response may be extremely – sometimes horrifically – punitive. It is likely, for instance, that Mick's mother's excesses were sparked at least in part by her gifted and sensitive son's ability to confront her with aspects of her own reality that were simply unbearable. I have certainly encountered people who were quite literally tortured as children (one with a flaming gas cigarette lighter) because they would not deny seeing things that threatened to destroy a parent's fragile hold on family life. The familiar phenomenon of a mother's silent complicity in her husband's sexual abuse of their child no doubt also has a lot to do with the necessities of the life in which she is caught.

For the most part, however, parental power is not exercised deliberately; indeed, because parents are often themselves so powerless, they may not have the slightest idea that they are wielding any influence at all. But parents are powerful in relation to their children simply because they are there, occupying the role society has accorded them. Nobody, for instance, could have felt less powerful than Jill's mother, whose whole adult life seemed to consist of one long demonstration of her incapacity and reliance on others (including her own children). And yet her anxiety constituted the controlling force around which the entire family had to arrange itself, shaping a reality from which Jill will probably never entirely escape.

It is necessary to dwell on the issue of parental power because of its importance for the formation of character. The physical machinery underpinning our relations with the world around us – the embodiment of our psychological meaning-systems – is unavoidably established under the shadow of parental influence. But this does not mean that early family life is the only, or necessarily the principal, source of later distress. Parental influence can be for good as well as for ill, and in any case we live our lives under the impress of powers that are mediated in many ways other than simply through the family.

I have already suggested in the discussion of 'current predicaments' in Chapter Two how much our emotional suffering comes about as the result of pressures in our everyday lives. If these are to be properly understood, it is important once again to emphasise that strains and stresses that seem to be a matter of essentially personal relations are likely in fact to originate in far more distal regions of the social environment. We experience them as personal merely because that is the only way in which they can be mediated – social influence is only ever transmitted by *people*, and it is the people we encounter in everyday life whom we tend to blame for the ills that befall us.

It would for example be very easy to see Gina's predicament as stemming almost solely from her relationship with her husband. This, certainly, was the way she experienced it herself, and it would have been hard for anyone listening to her story not to become indignant about the treatment she received at his hands. And yet her very attempts to 'solve' the problem, most of which eventually consisted of abortive alliances with other men (one or two of whom were indeed generous and kind), only served to demonstrate how much more complicated her situation was. Her lack of education and very low self-confidence rendered her both ashamed and dependent in a way which introduced painful complications into her relationships with any man, no matter how tolerant he might be, and yet the possibilities open to her of making good her deficits – for example, by 'going back to school' – were limited by all kinds of real material constraints. Similarly, the need for her to learn independence from men simply as protectors and providers was greatly hampered by the necessity of caring for her two children during out-of-school hours and holidays. She had very little money, and virtually all her family were out of work. Even while her marriage lasted it was so embedded in material privation that virtually any relationship would have been strained to breaking point.

'Society' does not consist of individual men and women picking and choosing what they would like to do and whom they would like to be with, constrained only by the amount of wealth they can scrape together through their own enterprise. Were things really like this, Margaret Thatcher would be right – there would be no society, just a terrifying 'state of nature' in which everyone would be out for him- or herself. As social beings, we inhabit an environment structured by powers that *hold us in place*. How much room we have for manoeuvre will depend upon the extent of the powers available to us. For most of us, these are extremely limited.

Most of the time we cannot even see where the influences that we experience proximally come from. All we can see is what we take to be the intentions of others, and all we feel we can do is to resolve to alter our circumstances, get on our bikes. But the uncovering of intentions and the making of resolutions doesn't seem to get us very far; and not surprisingly, because all the resolution in the world is quite useless without power, and even the kinds of power that may be available to individuals are usually puny in comparison with the higher-order, distal powers which determine the social structure and our place within it.

One of the most disheartening experiences of 'doing psychotherapy' is to observe the tremendous courage with which people can tackle their problems and *still* fail to solve them. Gina, for example, was brave to the point of self-destruction in setting out to do something about her predicament, but the world which she came up against in the process was just too harshly unyielding, and over and over again her only recourse was to fall back on her one 'asset' – her attractiveness to men – to save herself and her children from complete destitution. And even that path was doomed, because she could not *choose* a man from the position of independence she lacked the powers to achieve; she had to persuade herself each time that 'this is the one' just as her original 'choice' of husband, though far from suitable, offered her just about the only way out of an intolerable situation.

Luke, similarly, resolved to lift himself out of the trough he found himself in by trying to repair the damage that had been done to his education when in his teens. There is no doubt that he had the necessary intellectual resources: he was very bright and had an original, perceptive mind which, in other circumstances, could have brought him considerable academic success. But nobody can act simply under their own steam, and the material and psychological hurdles were just too great for Luke. He had to support himself on a pitifully low income and he was deeply in debt. The insecurity of his job was a constant worry. In order to achieve his aim of studying social sciences at university, he would have first had to apply himself to the grind of preliminary qualifications. He received absolutely no support within the social stratum he occupied, which was geared to quite other means of survival: family members as well as acquaintances simply laughed at what they saw as his pretentiousness. Luke almost fell apart trying to keep his nerve long enough to get started on evening classes, but, inevitably, starved of any material and almost all emotional sustenance, it failed him.

It is in my experience not the case that people do not wish or do not try to tackle the difficulties, past and present, that beset them. Neither is it the case that when their efforts fail it can be put down to their 'resistance', their psychological weakness or their personal 'inadequacy'. It is because they lack the powers to make a difference. Sadly, however, this is rarely the way they see it themselves: having battled long and hard against impossible odds, even the bravest and most stoical souls are likely to berate themselves for what they see as *moral* failure. How well we have been schooled into blaming ourselves for our deprivation!

The inadequacy of the consulting-room model

Psychotherapy, of course, has been absolutely no help in this predicament. Although often very accurately establishing through a lengthy process of clarification exactly how past and present relationship problems and material difficulties have contributed to individuals' distress, psychotherapy proceeds then to burden them with the responsibility for their own 'cure', as if feeling and acting in new ways depended solely on their personal will. But though we may well come, or be brought therapeutically, to *see* the truth – even the error of our ways – putting matters right is not simply a matter of seeing things differently. Things happen to us in a real world structured by real powers, and though there may be some variability in the way we experience this process, we can*not* experience it any way we like. Psychologically as well as bodily, we are held in place by influences over which, for the most part, we have absolutely no control.

Conditioned as we are by the consulting-room model and entrenched cultural ideas of personal responsibility and will power, this is likely to seem a bitter pill to swallow. Can I really be saying that very often nothing can be done about the kinds of emotional distress addressed by psychotherapy? Of course I am not saying that. What I am saying is that the types of solution offered by most approaches to psychotherapy are illusory. The first thing we have to do is understand and face up to the nature of our predicament, to take seriously the fact that the origins of our troubles lie not in the way we see things, nor even in the intentions of those with whom our lives intersect, but often in the distal powers which shape our social environment. If that involves disillusionment, so much the better. There is no virtue in labouring under illusions.

At the heart of human experience there lies a paradox which, as well as causing us endless difficulty, is a perpetual source of illusion and mystification. This is that what seem to us *subjectively* to be the most powerful influences on our lives are *objectively* the weakest. The fact that we can only directly experience life proximally means that we are constantly overwhelmed by the impress of power at the point where, just about literally, it impacts on our bodies. The evidence of our senses tells us what is causing us pain. It is very nearly impossible to doubt that what offends our eyes or ears, what stabs directly into our nervous system, is the cause of our problems. Seeing, hearing, feeling are believing.

The child who reels under his father's fist can have little doubt about who is the cause of his problems, and in a sense, of course, he is right. Talk to his remorseful father, though, and you are likely to find that he is aware of a whole host of pressures which led to his 'just not being able to stop' himself. Our difficulty is that we cannot by nature easily detach experience from explanation. What impinges most powerfully on our bodies looks incontrovertibly like the reason for our pain. But of course it is not so. The white snooker ball hitting a red can only narrowly be said to be 'the cause' of its movement, and hardly at all 'the reason' for it. If we are to understand why we feel as we do, we have to look beyond the people and things that simply mediate the distal powers which set things in motion.

But it is difficult to look beyond, if only often for the simple reason that we cannot see. It is as if there stretches around us a power horizon beyond which the chains of cause and effect mediating influential powers are hidden from our view. Our private experience, far from giving us privileged information about the reasons for our troubles, is actually misleading, for, overwhelming as it is, we are likely to attribute to it explanatory power it doesn't actually have. Certainly, only we can say *what* we are feeling (wherein, as we have seen, lies the source of our uniqueness), but when it comes to saying *why* we are feeling it, matters are very different.

For when it comes to the explanation of experience, the experiencing individual is in no stronger position than anyone else – indeed, it could well be weaker. This is obvious in the case of children. A child's power horizon is very close indeed, and, as has already been suggested, children are likely to attribute a degree of freedom to adults far greater than they really have; an adult observer of the child's predicament is, if reasonably unbiased, likely to have a much more accurate explanation of it than the child itself.

How far you are able to identify the reasons for what is happening to you will depend on the distance to your power horizon; that is, on the amount of accurate information available to you about the chains of influence that end up ultimately impressing themselves directly upon you. It is perfectly possible in any given situation that there will be others with a better view. People sharing a proximal world will be more or less in the same boat and so surrounded by the same horizon. Like children, we frequently attribute to each other more power than we actually have. It often happens, for example, that superiors at work, or bureaucratic officials of one kind or another, are thought by those dealing with them to have far more power than is actually the case to inflict difficulties or solve problems. A friendly word from the boss can carry a degree of reassurance out of all proportion to his actual power: however sincerely he delivers it, the board may at that very moment be planning to 'restructure' your job out of existence.

The difficulty that confronts us as we try to make sense of our lives and order our relationships is, then, that we are necessarily in ignorance of many of the factors that bear down upon us to influence our conduct. What we tend to do in this situation is search ourselves and each other for intentions and motives which might explain our actions. On the whole, I think, we are not very clear about what intentions and motives are exactly, nor about what is the difference between them. Motives are perhaps regarded as slightly more suspect than intentions – slightly dishonourable, often 'ulterior' aims which we are aware of but want to keep quiet about. Intentions are more upfront – the things we are trying honourably to achieve, though not necessarily always with success.

Motives, certainly, are at a slightly greater distance from us than intentions. Intentions seem personal, private, things that move us from the inside. Whether you could, plausibly, have the right to tell me what my intentions are is open to question – maybe you could suggest what they are, negotiate a view of them, so to speak, but not just *tell* me. Motives are a bit different, often seen as more external. My *Shorter OED* defines 'motive' as 'that which moves or induces a person to act in a certain way; a desire, fear, reason, etc., which influences a person's volition'. So motives are not just personal, internal things. It would be perfectly plausible for you to tell me what my motives are because what moves or induces me to act may be just as open to your inspection as to mine – quite possibly more so at times.

'Motives' fit in better than 'intentions' with the idea of our being moved by distal forces over which we have little, if any, control, but still there is a suggestion, even in the dictionary definition of 'motive', that what *really* causes our behaviour is 'a person's volition', and the examples of motives given ('desire, fear, reason') are on the whole also very internal things. Once again, it seems to me, we are having trouble escaping the immediacy (what I have called the proximality) of our experience. We are, I believe, confusing *the experience of being influenced* with *the cause of our conduct*: we *feel* ourselves doing things, and then take that feeling to be the cause of what we are doing.

Because of its central importance to our whole understanding of therapeutic change and how we can alter our conduct, I shall be returning to these issues in greater detail in Chapter Six, where I shall also give more concrete examples of how they affect us. For the moment I want just to underline the paucity of our understanding of what 'makes us tick', the inadequacy of the consulting-room model, and the severe restriction on the depth of our vision of the causes of our conduct. As we try to understand the reasons for what we do to each other, we are all for the most part relatively in the dark, unable to penetrate the gloom of motivation beyond the confused ideas and feelings we and those closest to us are able to divine and articulate.

As long as we limit the search for the wellsprings of action to the 'person's volition' and assume also that it is only through personal volition that changes can be made and human distress relieved, we shall continue to be confused. We have to shake ourselves free of the intense sense of conviction that the almost overpowering immediacy of our personal experience gives us about our motivation and see that, like children, we have only the vaguest notions of why we act as we do. Like the red snooker ball, all we register, most of the time, is that we have been hit by the white, and we have no idea of what the general strategy of the game might be – or even that we are in a game at all.

The role of societal power

It is not just our ignorance of distal power that makes it so difficult to resolve the 'paradox of experience' we have been considering – the subjective attribution of importance to events in inverse proportion to their actual, objective importance. Many of the more powerful elements in society have a strong interest in our continuing to believe in the consulting-room model. This must be so in a society that distributes power (and therefore advantage) pyramidally, with the most powerful being at the apex and the least at the base. The powerful few can only preserve their advantage over (i.e. exploit) the relatively powerless many through the use of, among other things, mystification. As long as the many believe that their greater privations are the result solely of their own actions and of those with whom they are immediately in contact (also members of 'the many'), the question of the distribution of power itself is not going to arise.

Already well prepared by our experience as infants of the impress of power in the family to conceive of ourselves as personally responsible for the errors of our ways, we do not take much persuading in later life that the troubles which beset us are largely of our own making. When, therefore, government ministers (actual or would-be) talk of 'irresponsibility', failure of 'duty' and lack of 'values' as *causes* of joblessness or homelessness or general social disintegration, or of 'criminality' as a cause of crime, they are using a language that we are already more than half inclined to accept. Similarly, almost all media comment on the sometimes desperate actions of the most deprived and despairing members of our society ('sex-crazed monsters' etc.), all the revelations of 'evil' in the tabloids, the musings of television pundits and weekend-supplement feature writers on how we might tackle the discomforts of our lives, are couched in terms of what we as individuals are guilty of, or should have resolved or might yet resolve to do.

What this completely diverts attention from, of course, is the apparatus of power (so well analysed by Foucault) through which our conduct is held in place and which controls the possibilities and choices open to us to better our lot (and which, for example, government ministers are in a far better position to influence than we). Rather than extending our gaze distally – out into public space – to try to discern the operation of the forces that serve to constrain our freedom and blight our lives, the cultural trend is increasingly to persuade us to turn it inwards into that private domain where, supposedly, we examine our motives, form our intentions and make resolutions (even if, to do so successfully, we are advised to have a 'counsellor' at our side).

Apart from anything else, the consulting-room model simply doesn't work. The comforting warmth of the therapeutic presence soon wears off once the patient leaves the consulting room and re-enters the chilling embrace of all those influences that caused distress in the first place. Just as New Year resolutions start getting difficult to keep on 2 January, so the simple realisation that something needs to be done, no matter how convincingly it is made, is not enough to undo the past or reconstruct the future. The same character walks out of the consulting room as walked into it, and the same world awaits him or her as was there before. Therapists are not sorcerers with magical powers to transform either the person or the world; their influence is minimal, limited for the most part to the simple solidarity they can offer to people in distress.

In order to escape all the distortions of our understanding that the paradox of subjectivity/objectivity brings about, it is necessary to remind ourselves constantly that neither we nor the vast majority of the people who occupy our proximal world have anything like the power we think to make significant differences to our circumstances. There is therefore very little point in our berating ourselves for our lack of courage or failure of will, or in imputing 'evil' to others, or even in blaming them particularly strongly for the wrongs they seem to do us. Much more to the point is to try to get as clear a view as possible of the intricate networks of power which press down upon us all, to unravel as far as we can the infinite complexity of the ways in which they entangle us, and to use whatever powers may be available to us to free ourselves of their grip.

Certainly in the long run, but possibly also in the short, this is not so much a 'therapeutic' as a political undertaking. The conditions of our lives are determined by the state of the world we live in – in particular, of course, its social organization.[7] We will not bring about real improvements in the former until we address ourselves seriously to the latter. It is no accident that the political role of ordinary people has dwindled almost to vanishing point and that the function of citizen has collapsed into that of consumer of counselling – it is in the interests of the powerful and privileged minority that this should be so. In order to rebuild the possibility of citizenship (which is in part to see that the principal form of power available to those of us at the base of the social pyramid is *solidarity*), we may first have to become clear what is and is not possible for individuals to do to minimise the distressing effects of the world they live in. It would be hard to do without psychotherapy if we did not first disabuse ourselves of the illusions that the consulting-room model creates.

CHAPTER FIVE

What Should We Do? Moral Demands

A large component of the felt suffering associated with psychological distress has to do with 'feeling bad' – not in the sense of feeling ill (though that may of course be present as well) so much as in the sense of feeling unworthy. Feeling ashamed, feeling guilty, feeling 'different', feeling undeserving of the love and respect of others, form a significant part of most of those 'conditions' that tend to get labelled anxiety, depression and so on, and indeed for many people are experienced as the cause of their suffering.

As we saw in Chapter Three, patients frequently approach their doctor or therapists with apprehension, expecting to be found 'abnormal' in a way that places them outside the company of ordinary, decent people. This may well be more than just a fear of statistical abnormality and may encompass an expectation of *moral* condemnation. You're not merely unusual, you are *bad*.

This phenomenon is not limited to the area of psychological distress. The social life of all of us is inescapably bound up with moralistic judgement. We all spend a great deal of time in the moral evaluation of our performance in relation to others and theirs in relation to us. Eavesdrop on any reasonably intimate conversation and it won't be long before you encounter justifications of self and accusations of others. We need, it seems, to maintain a good opinion of ourselves and to make sure that this is reflected in the eyes of others. It is comfortable to be in the right, painful to be in the wrong. We all worry about what people think of us, and the attribution of blame is one of our principal social concerns.

So preoccupied are we as a society with blame that we often overlook the importance of explanation, even where it would be particularly important to maintain the distinction between the two. Whether we're dealing with the actions of individuals, with collective problems like poverty or urban rioting, or with tragic accidents like aeroplane crashes or other public disasters, the first question we ask is: Who's to blame? We are not happy, it seems, until we have located the reasons for events such as these *inside* a person or a group in the form of an intention for which they can be held morally responsible. We watch each other with a kind of unremitting vigilance, ready to pounce with a damning accusation at the first available opportunity.

However, though they seem to have become fused in our minds as equivalent, blame and explanation are clearly not the same thing. Blame is about apportioning moral responsibility; explanation is about finding the reasons for things. Blame and self-justification are, perhaps, necessary features of a proximal existence in which we have to negotiate our relations with each other on the basis of what we can see (which, as suggested in the previous chapter, is not very much). Explanation, on the other hand, reaches further out to the causes of things, operating within a distal perspective which renders the intentions of individuals largely irrelevant.

The difficulty facing the person who is wrestling with feelings of shame, guilt and unworthiness is that the conceptual framework, the whole vocabulary of thought and understanding available to him or her, offers no escape from the 'blame dimension'. It seems that the only way to absolve ourselves of moral condemnation is to shift the blame elsewhere, most likely onto the shoulders of somebody else. This is exactly what happens in the acrimonious debates about who is to blame for so-called mental illnesses like 'schizophrenia'. Practitioners and research workers who point out that family relations and communications may result in the acute disturbance of more vulnerable members (particularly of course children) are immediately pilloried for 'blaming the parents'.

We seem in fact to have made for ourselves a world in which we move in a kind of minefield of recrimination, where we scrutinise each other constantly for indications of culpability, gingerly tossing each other unpinned hand grenades of 'responsibility' as in general we become more and more suspicious and defensive. It is scarcely surprising in circumstances such as these that guilt and shame – 'feeling bad' – should constitute so central a part of the more pronounced forms of distress. This is pretty well bound to be the case so long as we remain incapable of separating blame from explanation.

I would certainly not want to maintain that the apportionment of moral responsibility – 'blame' – has no valid part to play in the conduct of human affairs. In the proximal sphere in which we are fated to play out our lives there is almost certainly no way we can escape moral judgement, and indeed moral judgement may be an essential way of ordering our relations with each other in some respects. But we do allow it to spread beyond the confines of its proper field of application, and we need to be more aware than we are of where blame is appropriate and where it is not.

One place where blame is certainly not appropriate is in the psychological process of trying to understand why people feel and act as they do. Even in posing these questions, the importance of explanation as opposed to blame immediately becomes apparent. For a psychologist to assert that someone is unhappy because 'it's her own fault' would be transparently inadequate. What one requires from a psychologist is an explanation that transcends banal accusations and imputations of blame and reaches out to the chains of social cause and effect in which the person is entangled. When it comes, therefore, to your understanding the reasons for your own distress, it is important to remember that *you are your own psychologist.*[1] Although it may well be impossible to resist feelings of guilt, of 'being different' and so on, there is no way in which such feelings could conceivably contribute to an explanation of your problems, and in this latter respect they have simply to be ignored.

Although very obviously aware of the problem of moralistic judgmentalism, therapeutic psychology has not really itself succeeded in escaping the 'proximal' prejudices of our culture, and its most significant failure in my view is not to have developed a language that avoids our common moral assumptions, our habitual concern with issues of responsibility and blame. For while it is true that most therapists, from psychoanalysts to Rogerian counsellors, stress the importance precisely of *not* blaming patients and clients for the psychological predicaments they find themselves in, this is achieved largely through a suspension of moral judgement rather than through a recognition of its irrelevance.

Indeed, as already noted, psychoanalysis constitutes a quite extraordinarily moralistic approach to 'neurotic' suffering in which all kinds of 'badness' are attributed to the personal unconscious of people who can be redeemed only through a kind of morally cleansing process of rational rebirth ('where id was, there shall ego be'). The whole language of the 'humanistic' approaches to therapy positively drips with uplifting precepts and blueprints for life on a higher moral plane,[2] and even Carl Rogers's advocacy that therapists maintain 'unconditional positive regard' for their clients avoids blame only by prescribing its opposite.

But it is in my view utterly inappropriate for people in distress to have to approach their therapists as, so to speak, penitents whose best hope is for tolerance or forgiveness. It is not just the case that therapists should forbear from moral judgement, but that we should see that psychological explanation has nothing to do with moral judgement at all. Occasionally one hears therapists agonising over their moral sensibilities in relation to, say, sex offenders or abusers of children, as if they might be tainted, corrupted or somehow emotionally damaged by professional contact with such people. This seems to me a particularly silly form of preciousness. The point is that trying to understand people's predicaments simply has nothing to do with judging them. I have heard people say, for example, that they would draw the line at trying to 'treat' Adolf Hitler. I don't see why. Hitler and a potential therapist might not have got very far even had he felt like consulting one, but the attempt to understand him would have harmed nobody.[3]

The origins of shame

Those who suffer from feelings of moral inferiority, which may at their worst constitute a bitterly pervasive self-loathing, do not as a rule find it difficult to see that such feelings cannot have any real justification. Even those who experience themselves as irredeemably culpable because of their difference from others in some respect, are usually quite ready to acknowledge that this would not be a reasonable way to evaluate anyone else – what is felt so strongly to apply to the self does not extend to the judging of others. This is frequently the case, for instance, with people who suffer from shyness: if you stand in a corner at a party 'not knowing what to say' to people, you feel yourself to be an object of contempt, but the last thing you would do is feel contemptuous of a fellow sufferer. In the place of the person who you feel must despise you, your heart would actually go out to yourself!

In trying to understand how we could be possessed of apparently unshakeable feelings of unworthiness which are at the same time so obviously undeserved from any objective standpoint, we need to consider once again the impress of power under which they are acquired.

It is impossible to overemphasise the vulnerability of the small child to the power of the social environment into which it is launched. Every tentative step it takes in trying to understand its world, every judgement it makes about the nature of things, every interchange through which it negotiates its relations with the all-powerful adults around it, is fraught with terrible possibilities of rejection and derision, if not worse. Even the most fortunate child whose courage is consistently built up through the loving approval of others is certain at times to come painfully unstuck.

For most of us, the route to gaining some kind of influence within our childhood world is through the love and approval of our parents: the main powers we can acquire are those which are accorded us. It is the conditional nature of this approval that presents us with the problem of shame. This is not a bad thing: it would be no worthy pedagogical aim to try to bring up children who are shame*less*, and children who are so brought up – either because they received no love at all or because they were 'spoilt' with a kind of blanket approval disguising indifference – tend not to make the most attractive adults (even if they are free of the curses of shyness and self-doubt).

Shame, then, arises from the experience of being denied (temporarily) the love or approval of people in whose good opinion one depends in order to maintain an emotional, intellectual and social grip on the world. As children, we have no way of telling whether the suspension of approval we suffer at any given time is justifiable or not (we are almost bound to believe that it is), and the manipulation of shame in children is a weapon which adults can all too easily abuse. An experience that may come about in inevitable but small doses as part of a necessary process of socialisation may also come in massive overdoses where parents (and possibly others) use it as the principal way of controlling their offspring. But the child knows nothing of the injustice of this: it will conclude simply that, instead of being 'out of order' some of the time, it is being really bad most of the time, and its movement around the emotional minefield of its life will become increasingly uncertain and expectant of sudden pain.

It is, then, a central aspect of the child's powerlessness that it cannot see into injustice: it is quite likely that the only source of information available to it concerning the validity of the actions and views of those who oppress it comes from the oppressors themselves. As Alice Miller so compellingly shows, there is likely to be no ground from which the child can question whether the emotional torture it endures really is 'for its own good'.[4]

Sometimes escape is possible. One of the bravest women I've met had throughout her childhood and adolescence been abused physically, mentally and sexually, almost unremittingly, by whole ranges of adults in and outside her family. As far as I could see, the only reason she had not been psychologically destroyed by her experience of life was the fact that she was one of a large group of sisters and stepsisters who maintained an inspiring solidarity (for example, two of her sisters came physically to the rescue when she was being abused sexually by a neighbour). As I have already noted, consistent ill treatment is in some ways easier to cope with than the capricious use of punishment or shame: I can think of another utterly admirable woman whose early life was so terrible that she was actually rescued in part by Hollywood – she learned 'from the films' that people actually could love each other (one could scarcely say that her adult life has been 'normal', but her courage and her totally uncompromising honesty make her an extraordinarily positive force in the world).

But where parents don't, so to speak, blow their cover by being just so awful that the child concludes there *must* be a better world outside the family, the only logical conclusion available to it is that the cause of their displeasure must be its own badness. Being excluded from parental love or approval is the first, prototypical experience of feeling 'outside the pale' – which is the form in which it is likely to recur in later life.

Parents do not usually tyrannise their children for the pure sadistic fun of it. Children have powers of which they themselves have no knowledge, particularly the ability to spot the emperor's nakedness, and it is frequently out of fear of these that parents feel, consciously or unconsciously, that they have to exercise 'control'. Children do not realise that the adults around them are also still children inside, and that they too live apprehensively under the critical moral gaze of a society obsessed with blame. Quite apart from anything else, the child's very innocence in relation to the social pitfalls of life make it a danger to those around it who are struggling in more ways than one to 'keep up appearances'. The trouble starts for the child once parents' anxieties get out of control and they can no longer use the art of shaming in the child's interest, but instead as a weapon with which to defend their own self-image.

Truthfulness and trust

It is hard not to conclude from listening to the accounts people give of their childhood that, far from being (as in fact they are) spectacularly powerless in relation to adults, children are often perceived as dangerous. Certainly, much of the activity of parents and others charged with the care and instruction of children seems to be concerned with finding ways of limiting what little power they have got. Children quickly learn, for example, that truthfulness is an essential component of their claim on love. It seems that, in order to earn the affection and respect of the adults around them, children are discouraged from developing a truly private life: their thoughts, feelings and motives must be open to the inspection of adults at all times, and they should be ready at any occasion of cross-examination to give as honest an account of themselves as they possibly can.

This heavy emphasis on truthfulness in childhood translates later into our extraordinarily self-contradictory notion of 'sincerity', in which a profound knowledge of the treachery of words is matched in intensity by a kind of desperate need to *believe in* sincerity. The whole of political and commercial life, for example, is pervaded by a vast enterprise dedicated to manufacturing the appearance of sincerity in circumstances that virtually ensure its impossibility. All of us know this, and yet hardly any of us can credit the irrationality of it all, so strong is the yearning for true 'credibility' which has been stamped upon us at our most impressionable age.

But whatever the later societal consequences may be, we are certainly likely to learn as children that it is shameful to have a private life which we are not willing to expose on demand to the most powerful people around us. Since the development of a private life, a personal world of thoughts, feelings, ideas and images, is an absolute inevitability – is indeed something over which we have not the tiniest element of choice – and since there are certain to be elements of that private life which we are unwilling to discuss with others, we are almost bound to carry round with us from our earliest moments of self-reflection a sense of shame which is literally in-built.

There probably are cases where a child does feel able to share with an unusually indulgent (not to say intrusive) parent absolutely everything that courses through its head (a circumstance no doubt boding ill for later relationships), but most of us need to be able to cast a decent reticence over much of what we detect buzzing around inside us, and the adult demand that this be open to inspection is likely to cause us continuous difficulty as children. We all of us feel that we have things inside us that would make us unlovable if only people knew.

As with truthfulness, so, often, with 'trust'. Instead of constituting a loving, liberating belief in someone, 'trust' can become the anxious parent's way of extending control into the very heads of their children. Truly to trust someone is to credit them with having good reasons for what they do even if we cannot see or understand what they are. In the biblical story, Abraham trusted God to have good reasons for insisting that he sacrifice his son Isaac.[5] It would be asking a lot of the rest of us to take risks on quite this scale, but it is a necessary risk of parents' love that they do not always use their power to prevent their children from doing things that seem incomprehensible, reprehensible or even dangerous. However, for parents unable (usually because of the extent of their own anxieties) to take such necessary risks, trust becomes something quite different: a form of remote control.

For example, for Nadine's father, unable to get out of his head that, unlike her (in his view) prettier and more talented sister, Nadine could not be *trusted* to conduct her life sensibly and productively, his measure of 'trust' as she grew up became the extent to which she conformed to his wishes when out of his sight. Whereas he and her mother would spectate passively and approvingly as her clever sister surprised them with her talent and her boldness, opening up for them worlds of which they had no previous conception, they could scarcely bear to let Nadine think a single thought for herself, and when she did escape their attention for any length of time, they would set little traps for her to see if she was toeing the line.

It was not until much later in her life that Nadine was able to grasp what had been (and still was) going on. As a child, she had perforce to interpret her father's intense concern with her every move as love, and her own repeated inability to meet his requirements as a kind of congenital stupidity or moral weakness which made it all the more remarkable that anybody could love her at all. Even long after she had moved away from home, her life, far from being liberated, was almost completely controlled by her father's 'trust'. Almost her every action was determined not by what she herself wanted, but by whether her father, if he knew, would approve. 'Trust' was a kind of leash which prevented her from living any kind of life truly her own, or from developing any needs or wishes of her own which she could satisfy or enjoy.

Nadine's life, like the lives of so many people whose childhoods were characterised by the anxious moral supervision of at least one parent, was lived conscientiously, indeed selflessly. She accumulated duties at work and, having married a man who had an almost limitless need to be looked after, also at home (she divorced her husband only after his third bout of infidelity). She paid endless attention to the needs of her ageing parents. She was unable to say no to almost any demand made on her and so became involved in a whole range of out-of-work community and charitable activities. None of these gave her any pleasure; indeed, she had no clear idea of what pleasure was. Even her comfort eating was no healthily enjoyable greed, but rather the secret and guilty snatching of a little illicit sustenance (and she always made sure that when she did binge it was on basic foodstuffs which could in no way be seen as luxurious – no boxes of chocolates for her).

Where the best approximation to love a parent can provide is supervision, insistence on truthfulness and the use of 'trust' as remote control, it is common for people's lives subsequently to be dutiful but empty, for the notion of 'want' to be totally submerged in the insistence of 'should'. People who have had to shoulder inordinate responsibility (for their siblings, for a parent) at an early age have a similar problem. Frequently not knowing how to refuse others' demands, combined with the inability to acknowledge or even recognise their own wishes and needs, means that people from this kind of background go on shouldering responsibility to the point where they simply collapse under the strain. This is not because they are 'inadequate' – they are most often superadequate – and the 'depression' to which they may eventually succumb is probably best understood as the mute rebellion of an abused nervous system.

For most of us, the impress of parental power in childhood, in the form in particular of moral control, is neither so great nor so relentless as to result in a near-total loss of self, but rather leaves us vulnerable to the conviction that there are inside us wishes and impulses, feelings and thoughts, that are uniquely shameful. If we have bought the parental line that it is wrong to tell lies, that to be 'trusted' means to act only in ways of which the powerful would approve, we are quite likely to have an uncomfortable feeling that we are the possessors of guilty secrets which make us people who should not be trusted, that our outer aspect is a sham which people would quickly see through if they caught a glimpse of our 'real selves'.

The 'need to please', 'need to be liked', which people so often sense as a particularly contemptible part of their make-up, is something that virtually all of us share, and it has a great deal to do with the necessity of, so to speak, shoring up the external impression we make on others in order to render the penetration of our defences, the discovery of our shameful interiors, a little more difficult. Though the contrast between how we feel inside and how we wish to appear to others is universal and causes most of us many an uneasy moment, the extent to which we suffer in this way depends probably on the degree to which we were allowed as children to develop private lives without the threat of adult censure.

'Feeling a fake'

People who are truly at ease with themselves, if they exist at all, are extremely rare, but there may be more who are lucky enough to be able to avoid, most of the time at least, the kind of precariousness of subjectivity – the uncertainty about one's private 'self' – that leads one to think of oneself as a fake. 'Feeling a fake', feeling more or less perpetually 'to blame' for anything and everything of which one could conceivably be accused, is, even so, a common experience, and a frequent accompaniment of social anxiety. It arises, of course, from the awareness, which surely cannot entirely escape any of us, that our private selves are very different from our public personas. Where the anxious or disapproving surveillance of power has stamped upon us as children a conviction that privacy is almost by definition 'wrong' (but not gone so far as to prevent our developing any), we will as adults always carry an awareness that the face we present to the world is not really 'telling the truth'.

It is quite easy for people to live an entire life of moral impeccability and high achievement, earning the respect and affection of nearly all those they encounter, while convinced subjectively that the whole thing has been a sham. Their excellent exam results were achieved because their teachers did not realise that their ideas were not their own or that they had just been 'lucky with the questions'. Their success at work came from a series of fortunate accidents or from their having been unfairly privileged by superiors who hadn't been clever enough to see their faults. Their personal relationships, despite every indication to the contrary, were really hollow, and nobody who could see behind the mask could possibly like, let alone love, them. The only possible circumstance that could redeem such a person, s/he feels, would be if outside appearance and subjective sense of self were to match perfectly.

The official psychologies and philosophies of the twentieth century have, if anything, only served to increase the vulnerability of our subjectivity. Jungian psychology's disapproving assessment of the overdeveloped 'persona', Sartrean existentialism's positive valuation of 'authenticity', Freudian psychology's mistrustful vigilance for 'unconscious motivation', and so on, have all done their bit to contribute to what has become the banalised craving for 'sincerity', an urge to collapse the public into the private and to publicise the private by turning it inside out. It is as if the only person we could trust, including ourselves, would be one who is completely transparent, outside indistinguishable from inside.

But, however inconveniently complicated it may make our lives, we are three-, not two-dimensional creatures. We have depths hidden not only from each other but also from ourselves, and if the waters are at times murky, it is simply in their nature to be so.[6] Mistrust of and shame at our privacy merely turns us into cardboard cut-outs colluding in the pretence that what you see is what you get, but secretly agonised over the certain but incommunicable knowledge that there is more to us than meets the eye.

This virtually universal, in-built propensity to shame and guilt renders us ripe for exploitation by any power prepared to make cynical use of it. Any parent, colleague, competitor, boss or politician with an interest in our toeing a particular line can play on our fearful sense of our own hypocrisy to make us drop like a hot potato any objection to his or her plan we might be tempted to raise on the basis of our subjective instinct. Because our subjectivity is so precarious, to take a stand *as a subject* – to 'stick our neck out' – on any particular issue is for most of us a frighteningly risky business. The moral battle of our right to interpret the world from our own subjective standpoint is joined from the moment of our exit from the womb, and once our privacy has become infected by shame, the powers that be are well on the way to winning.

At a trivial level, it is this lack of trust in a subjective self that lies behind the phenomenon of always being in agreement with other people's arguments. Many of us will be familiar with the feeling that there seems to be a curious unassailability about the arguments of anyone with any claim to authority (seen, that is, as possessing a certain form of power), even when those arguments are quite contrary to our own beliefs, or are contradicted by other 'authoritative' arguments (which seem equally compelling!). 'Whatever he says, I always seem to agree with him' or 'I always feel there must be something wrong, but I can never think what it is' or, less drastically perhaps, 'I can only think what I should have said hours afterwards' are the common experiences of those of us who live in a subjectivity-sapping culture in which our confidence in our own judgement has been eroded from the earliest age by the intrusive moral scrutiny of power.

More seriously, our precarious subjectivity renders us vulnerable to manipulation by anyone in power who can confidently and convincingly appear to 'know best'. The entire institutional apparatus of a society that is constructed first and foremost to maintain an unequal, pyramidal distribution of security and advantage, is saturated through and through with an ideology of benign parenthood, instilling at every possible opportunity the idea that, like Mummy and Daddy, people in power are there for your own good. All too frequently, Mummy and Daddy are themselves caught up in this apparatus, dutifully reproducing the ideology at the very point that serves most effectively to maintain it.

Nearly all of us have succumbed to this ideology to some extent. We turn our faces to power with the innocent openness of sunflowers following the sun, unable to believe that our elders and betters, bosses and leaders could be motivated by anything other than an intention to do their best for us. There can in my view be no explanation other than the innocent trust of the 'sunflower mentality' for how whole societies can be turned willingly and well-meaningly into bureaucracies for the achievement of diabolical ends, as in, at one extreme, Hitler's Germany and Stalin's USSR or, at the other, Thatcher's Britain.

The point, of course, is that the intentions of those who direct us may well be benign, but we have already seen that intentions count for very little when it comes to understanding why people do things. We have not yet learned to look beyond the proximal world of intentions to the play of the more distal influences which hold us all in our place. In order to do that, we need no doubt to learn first how to arm ourselves against the exploitation of conscience in our private lives.

Countering the 'moral' impress of power

The distinction between public and private is crucial to a proper understanding of morality. Moral rules are about how we conduct ourselves in relation to each other, not about the propriety of what goes on inside our own heads. You can't *do* what you like, but you can certainly *think* what you like; social disapproval may legitimately be used to constrain your actions, but is utterly irrelevant to your feelings.

There are some unfortunate religious ideas about its being as wrong to commit a sin in imagination as in practice, but these, it seems to me, are best dismissed as attempts at extending an intrusive and illegitimate form of parental 'remote control' into the individual's private space. For the point about trying to introduce rules to control psychological processes like thoughts and feelings is that *it simply cannot be done*. Rules can apply only where there is the possibility of choice, and you can't choose what to think or to feel at any given moment.

Even the standard ideas about the nature of morality embedded in our culture, inadequate as they are in many respects, recognise that moral precepts cease to be valid in situations where the person's power to choose is for one reason or another diminished. A whole range of extenuating circumstances, from insanity to lack of knowledge of cogent facts, may be invoked to soften social condemnation in any particular case. What is important when people do something wrong is to determine whether they had the power to do otherwise: was any other course of action open to them?

If we're not careful, we stray here into notions of 'will power', which, as I shall argue in the next chapter, can be very complicated and misleading. But though we might debate in any given case whether someone could have done otherwise, or whether, for example, s/he was in the grip of powers beyond his or her control, it is clear that rules can be made that do in fact have the effect of controlling the conduct of large sections of the population (usually because they are linked to sanctions). Yellow lines on the road give me a good reason for not parking there. And if I do, it would be absurd for me to tell the traffic warden that I 'couldn't help it'. Moral rules about how we should behave, where they work, are not all that different.

The impossibility of mind control

When it comes to consideration of what's going on inside your head, the situation is very different, and in some ways much clearer. For it is not at all obvious that you can help what you're thinking and feeling. 'Whatever you do, don't imagine the colour red' is not an instruction you can reasonably be expected to obey. Similarly, admonitions that it is wrong to think about murder or sex are about as silly as telling someone not to feel cold. For, of course, there comes a point when we have no choice at all about the contents of our consciousness, and this is because we are not beings who can choose to be conscious of this, that or the other, but are beings who simply *are* conscious. There is no nonconscious part of us which can, so to speak, choose what to fill consciousness with.

Of course we can, while awake, give some direction to our mental activity, we can 'concentrate' on this or that task – make a shopping list or add up a column of figures – but even here we cannot always switch concentration on and off at will (as anyone who tries reading a book while feeling depressed will know). And in any case, in the background even of our conscious existence, there runs along a continuous process of uncontrollable mentation – thoughts, feelings, impulses, images – over which, like dreams, we have no control at all. It would be the ultimate absurdity to attempt an extension of moral control into the area of dreaming, and yet that is, in a sense, precisely what the 'privatisation' of morality tries to do.

The anxiety about what might be going on inside our heads, which powerful interests have stamped upon so many of us at an early age, has created a culture in which it seems practically impossible for people to be honest about the contents of the continuous, dreamlike stream of consciousness which accompanies our every waking, not to say sleeping, moment.[7] And for some people whose experience of censorship in childhood was particularly strong, detection of 'immoral' thoughts and feelings can become almost shatteringly worrying (we have already seen that this was the case with Dave). The same may be true for people whose subjective experience as children simply received no endorsement from respected powers, their nascent feelings and perceptions having been not so much condemned as discredited or overlooked as worthless. Large areas of Brenda's 'self', for example, were simply wordless blanks because they had been left untended, unelaborated and unarticulated as she grew up. It is often the case with people vulnerable to depression that there are large parts of themselves they feel to be 'bad' without quite being able to say what they are.

We all of us live in a profoundly eccentric private world, much of the contents of which would have us in deep trouble if acted out publicly. The fact is that not only is a good deal of our stream of consciousness completely unique, but there are also no guarantees about its moral purity. I remember a man telling me with real agitation that sometimes he felt like reaching out and touching the breasts of women who passed him in the street. The answer, of course, was that he could feel like anything at all, but if he did it, he'd end up, quite rightly, in court.

Not only can one not prevent oneself from wishing that a troublesome neighbour, a bumptious colleague, an unsympathetic teacher, would 'drop dead' at the precise moment one utters a polite 'good morning', but it is quite useful and satisfying that one has such a harmless freedom to vent one's feelings. One can indulge daydreams of murder and mayhem on quite a spectacular scale without causing the least damage, and the wildest forms of sexual fantasy, kept to oneself, cause offence to no one.

It may of course be the case that rapists and murderers spend quite a lot of time musing about rape and murder, but this is not to say that the imagination causes the act: there is no *necessary* connection between them. It is not as if our dreams, daydreams and fantasies somehow constitute an indication of what we are 'really like' or adumbrate some enduring, secret project which may eventually burst forth from us in reality. The point is that as a matter of fact we are all far, far less civilised in our private world than in public and it is absolutely not a matter of concern to find ourselves engaged, for example, in violent, vengeful fantasies, disloyal thoughts or imagined infidelity.

This is not to say that the life of the imagination is without interest. There may well be, for example, *reasons* for our imaginings which it could be useful to discover. Catching yourself in a daydream that, let us say, your spouse and children have been demolished by a mad axeman may at first be acutely disturbing, but if you can bring yourself coolly to examine the possible reasons for it (perhaps, for instance, your fantasy provides a simple solution to the burden of responsibility you are feeling for your family), you may learn quite a lot about the raw primitiveness of some of our psychological processes and the indirect way they sometimes manifest themselves. There is more to wonder at here than to worry about. At times, indeed, it might be quite important to be able to picture in the privacy of your own head scenes of rage, frustration or desire for which there can be no permissible external outlet. But in any case, the least freedom we can reasonably insist on as a right is the freedom of our imagination.

Morality, then, belongs in the real, social world in which we interact with others and where our actions can have concrete significance for the way others feel, for example whether we cause them pleasure or pain. That's why we need moral rules. The world of the imagination carries no such rewards or penalties; it really doesn't matter what goes on in the privacy of our own head. Even though speech cannot always (in fact, if we are to lead a reasonably quiet life, can hardly ever) be unconstrained, freedom of thought really is something we can claim without risking injury to someone.

When it comes to the guilt and shame which so often pervade our feelings about ourselves, what we need to do, then, is first to try to establish whether they should be taken seriously – whether, that is, they stem legitimately from our actual social relations with others, or whether they are merely the censorious echo of, for example, parental injunctions about what we should think and feel which we have internalised from the past. If the latter, we should pay them no attention (much easier to say than do, though some suggestions will be given in Chapter Seven). If the former, we need to give some thought to what *are* our obligations in relation to others.

Determining the limits of obligation

The policing of the imagination by powerful influences can lead to significant later distress, but the imposition of real responsibilities and duties can also lead to the individual's becoming overburdened to the point of breakdown. Both Ann and Jill, for example, had had to shoulder responsibility for their siblings at a time when they were only children themselves (Jill had also had to adopt a largely maternal role in relation to her own mother). Nadine had, as we have seen, been schooled from the outset in a kind of soulless obedience to duty. Many children have to grow up fast in order to compensate in one way or another for the difficulties and inadequacies of their own upbringing, and in the process they frequently fail to develop any idea (a) that their own needs and wishes have any legitimacy, and (b) that there is any limit to the difficulties they can be expected to handle and the responsibilities they can take on.

In predicaments like these it is as if moral duty is an open-ended demand that can be laid on people at the whim of those who have power over them. Superconscientiousness thus grows out of a response to a *personal* power, as though to a jealous and demanding authority able to make seemingly arbitrary rules and impose any conditions it requires (this, of course, is exactly how an unreasonably and unreflectingly demanding parent will appear to a child).

In fact, moral rules are not simply the creation of the personal authority of powerful individuals. What you should do is not determined capriciously by what God or your father think you should do at any particular time. Morality is evolved by the social community of which you are a part. Moral rules are not particularly clearly stated, codified or written down, but nevertheless we have a general understanding of what it is and is not reasonable to expect in particular situations. This understanding is precisely what the superconscientious have been prevented from developing, usually because it was not in the interests of those who had power over them that they should.

The particular mark of superconscientiousness is that it is underpinned by a nonreciprocal moral law. 'Do as you would be done by' informs every action of the superconscientious person, but it never seems to occur to him or her that this is a rule which should apply to anyone else, so that 'others should treat me as I treat them' simply doesn't enter the frame.[8] This is not a reasonable or practicable basis upon which one can lead one's life, which is why it becomes very important to establish the limits of our obligations to those among whom we live our day-to-day lives.

Where the matter of obligation gets so far out of hand as to cause persistent distress and perhaps breakdown (by which I mean not 'mental illness', but literal collapse under an impossible load), it is usually because the common-sense moral rules attaching to particular social roles are being overlooked, if not grossly flouted. Typical examples are where parents come to expect a daughter (less often a son) to devote herself to their welfare almost from the moment she leaves school (if not before); husbands expect their wives to wait on them as their mothers did even when both are working full time; older relatives, or superiors at work, abuse their power in pursuit of sexual gratification. Even in less obviously dramatic and abusive cases, superconscientious people are almost bound to become chronically overburdened, if only because they make such wonderfully easy targets for others (that is most of us) who find it hard to resist the opportunity of exploiting a willing slave.

In any case, the important questions to raise are usually those concerning what are the normal rights and duties attaching to the role of parent, child, spouse, lover, employer and employee, and so on. For example, parents (except in old age) are expected to look after children and not vice versa; married partners should share responsibility equally for most tasks and difficulties that arise in the domestic sphere; employment should be governed by some form of explicit contract; sexual interest should be expressed only in situations free of any significant duress.

Most important of all, where one party fails to deliver their side of the bargain, the other may legitimately be expected no longer to regard themselves as bound by the moral conventions of *their* role. Obedience is not owed to an unjust or repressive authority; children cannot be expected to submit to parents as well as look after them; sexuality forms a legitimate component of some types of relationship but not others; women no longer defer to men by virtue of their sex alone.

In fact, of course, we all of us know that the operation of moral rules should be marked by reciprocity and fairness. Even those who habitually find themselves being exploited have some awareness that it shouldn't be happening, but their sense of injustice, the resentment which simmers in the background, hardly ever boils up to the point of being expressed openly. There seems in many situations to be far more at work than simple transgressions of the moral code which could, presumably, be settled easily enough through normal procedures of argument and debate.

What makes the difference is the impress of power. Exploitation is probably only rarely carried out mistakenly, to be corrected as soon as the error of the exploiter's ways are pointed out. On the contrary, exploiters usually have an important stake in the success of their exploitation, which means that it is backed with all the persuasive force they can muster. Whether the exploiters are, for example, parents who need for the preservation of their own self-esteem to prevent a child from seeing their feet of clay, or perhaps a husband whose masculine pride would be destroyed by his wife's being seen as cleverer than he, the pressure brought to bear is likely to be ruthless. In personal relationships, this usually includes heavy doses of emotional blackmail and too often the threat of violence.

What this tends to mean, especially for people who have learned their obedience to unreasonable power as children, is that any challenge to authority in later life is likely to be overshadowed by a dread of retribution which, though once entirely justified, is now out of all proportion to the reality of the situation. In the adult world (at least of the Western democracies), any legal challenge we make to authority is unlikely to be met with such terrifying punishment as that risked by the rebellious child, and even the father whose rage could once be a shattering experience has probably become an arthritic old man who couldn't hurt a fly. But the painful reality of powerlessness becomes embodied in the child who, once oppressed by parental violence, disapproval or anxiety, later finds it very difficult indeed to be able simply to act on the recognition that, as an adult, all s/he has to do is 'stand up for' his or her rights. And even the now powerless parent may still find ways of intimidating a potentially disobedient offspring into submission (by 'getting upset', becoming ill or even, *in extremis*, dropping dead).

'Love,' 'loyalty' and duty

The mixture of oppression, dependency and emotional blackmail – a lethal cocktail usually referred to as 'love' or 'loyalty' – which too often characterises parent–child relationships is probably one of the most difficult issues to confront for those who become significantly distressed in later life. Power protects its abuses not only by insisting that they are 'for your own good', but also by mystifying the parent–child relation as necessarily one of love and insisting that the child's only proper response to all kinds of terrifying treatment is one of *loyal* acceptance. I have listened countless times to stories of quite appalling brutality and/or mental sadism which end up 'but I do love him/her; s/he is my dad/mum after all'.[9]

Whatever may once have been society's reasons for reinforcing family loyalties at all costs, there can surely no longer be any justification for people being forced to maintain within them such deep emotional schisms. For not only do some people spend pretty well all their lives trying to discover and testify to a love for a tyrannical parent they absolutely don't feel, but, convinced that a parent's failure to love them must be 'my own fault', others may devote their existence to trying, fruitlessly, to earn the love they take to be, at least potentially, the birthright of all.

Perhaps we hang so much moral weight on the apparent necessity of love and the maintenance of loyalty precisely because parenthood is such a lottery. Who your partners are is one of the very few relationships in life over which you have absolutely no choice. There is nothing about parents that entitles them to unconditional respect: anybody can be a parent, no matter how stupid, cruel, sadistic, immature, irresponsible, frightened, anxious or incompetent. Indeed, it may well be that 'good' parents are in a minority, and, whatever else may be the case, there can surely be no *shame* in having lousy parents.

Even if the kind of superstitious compulsion children seem inevitably to acquire to 'love' and respect those who have power over them is practically irresistible, at least perhaps we should try to rid ourselves of the moral complications of the parent–child relationship. Your parents did not fail to love you because you are *bad*, nor is it *bad* not to love people whose influence upon you was largely negative, if not positively damaging.

It remains true, no doubt, that love between parents and children is the most sustaining and positive force in the lives of those fortunate enough to experience it, and it is very hard to envisage what more satisfactory unit than the family could form the basis of society. Love, moreover, is demanding, and being a parent can be at least as difficult as being a child: tolerance and forgiveness must of course play a large role in the struggles of any family to maintain its integrity, and even the most loving will cause each other hurt.

In view of the immense warmth and lifelong security that can be gained from a loving family, it is extremely sad for those who did not fare well in the lottery to recognise that, for instance, they were not loved. But it is not more than sad. It does not reflect on their moral worth, and there is no obligation to love those who have failed to give love. You do not owe allegiance to tyrants, and there's no reason why a tyrannical parent should not be the object of a healthy hatred.

In the struggle against oppressive power and authority it is essential to recognise not only what is the legitimate sphere of morality, but, within it, what are and are not reasonable moral demands. Moral rules, as we have seen, simply do not apply in the realm of feelings, if only because feelings cannot be switched on and off at will. You cannot, if you do not, love somebody just because you are in some sense 'supposed to' (this is as true for parents as it is for children). Agonising about 'sincerity' or 'authenticity' is irresolvably pointless because, on the one hand, it is just not possible to force your feelings into line with how you wish to appear, and, on the other, it would be equally impossible to run a day-to-day life – let alone a society – in which honesty about your feelings was unswervingly observed.[10] Further, moral rules are not incontrovertible edicts handed down by some unquestionable authority, but can only reasonably be observed in a context of justice and fairness. The issue of 'telling the truth' is an interesting case in point.

Where respect and trust exist between equals, breaches of honesty are obviously likely to constitute a particularly malign form of betrayal. It cannot be right, for example, to manipulate the open, loving trust of someone by lying in order to obtain an advantage for oneself. On the other hand, childlike obedience to the injunction of Power always to tell the truth simply places you at the mercy of that power for all time and robs you of one of the principal means of challenging it (through being able to dissemble your motives).

This is by no means a matter of mere academic speculation. Where survival in a setting of abusive power becomes paramount, lying can become almost the only defence available to the abused. Tyrannical parents and brutal husbands are just two of the groups whose intrusions may need to be resisted by lying, but there are many other situations in which power is abused (including the unfair and illicit manoeuvres sometimes adopted by employers over employees) where the victim's only recourse is to subversion of the truth.

One of the factors which led during the 1980s to there being so many psychological casualties among the middle-aged occupants of responsible jobs, particularly but not only in the public service, was that such people had often been brought up to believe in the essential benignity of power. They simply could not conceive that the business revolution which swept through all our lives could be in the sectional interests of only a small minority towards the top of the social pyramid, and struggled unsuccessfully both to understand and implement the changes forced upon them, eventually cracking under the strain. Had they had a conception of resistance that included disguised disobedience to unjust power, they would have fared much better.

When it comes to the kinds of problems in relationships that concern so many of us in our private lives, we would do well, I think, to rehabilitate the concept of duty. Rather than drowning in guilt and shame about what we think we should – but are not able to – *feel*, we would do better to engage in a cool calculation of what is and is not required of us to *do*.

Nadine, resigned for years to 'popping in' to her parents' house almost daily and ferrying her mother (who, though old, is able-bodied and clear-headed) around the shops twice a week while feeling guilty that she could not do it with better grace, at last begins to consider what might reasonably be expected not only of her, but also of her mother. For one thing, there is not the slightest sign of gratitude from her mother or consideration of life's other demands on Nadine; on the contrary, she spends most of the time admonishing, criticising and 'advising' her. Both Nadine's parents, in fact, seem intent on maintaining the fiction that she is dependent on them, when in truth the boot has long since been on the other foot. One day, trying to absorb a diatribe from her mother while driving her and a large load of washing home (her parents have no machine of their own), she snaps, draws up outside the local launderette, dumps the washing on the pavement and tells her mother to get on with it on her own. (Unfortunately, this is only a momentary rebellion, and Nadine is racked with guilt for days afterwards; nevertheless, it is a start.)

We do not have to feign a love or loyalty we do not feel, nor, when it comes to duty, do we have to perform it willingly. It doesn't matter how you feel about your duty, as long as you do it. For example, where the balance of power between parents and children becomes reversed, and the parents develop an unavoidable dependence on their children, it may well be the case that, even where the parents discharged their own duties badly, the children may consider themselves bound by a duty of care. But that's all it is. Love is a bonus which comes unasked, and cannot be bidden.

The qualities of love and loyalty, like mercy, are not strained. Where our early relations with each other have been conducted from the loving fullness of the hearts of those involved, we may well find depths of confidence and security which stand us in good stead throughout our lives. But such happy circumstances cannot be willed, and their absence is an occasion neither for blame nor for shame. Nor is the presence of more negative emotions. You can no more banish hatred from your heart than you can summon love into it, and the wisest course is to accept that, whatever you feel, you probably have good reasons for it.

It may, of course, help to try to understand how difficulties in families arise, but that is far easier to do for someone who has not been involved in the bitter struggles for and abuses of power which are likely to have taken place. It is asking a lot – I think often too much – to expect people who have, for instance, been viciously physically and/or sexually, or indeed emotionally, abused throughout long periods of their childhood, to stand back and see that their parents had understandable reasons for acting as they did. It may sometimes be possible, and indeed comforting, to do so, but often it is more important for the individual to accept and justify his or her own hatred and resentment and to untangle the mystifications of 'loyalty' than it is to be understanding towards those who inflicted the damage.

A great deal of distress could be avoided, then, if we could learn to withdraw 'morality' from the private world of our feelings and to concentrate instead on the rights and wrongs of our *conduct*. For of course it *is* important how we use the powers available to us in our relations with each other. You may not be able to pick and choose your feelings, but there almost certainly will be choices open to you in the courses of action you can take towards those with whom you live in closest proximity, and the greater your power is relative to theirs, the more choice you are likely to have.

The calculation of duty cannot be performed according to some absolute code of proper conduct, but only in relation to what is possible. And what is possible for any given person will depend on the powers and resources afforded him or her by the social environment in which s/he lives. We can deploy only the powers we have. This is why, when trying to understand why people act in the ways they do, a psychologist must look beyond their private subjectivity, beyond even the proximal world of their immediate relationships, and examine the influences that bear down on them from much more distal regions of the social environment. What you *should* do, in other words, is utterly dependent on what you *can* do, which is what will be considered next.

CHAPTER SIX

What Can We Do? The Problem of Will Power

The idea that we *will* those of our actions that are not very obviously forced upon us by deliberate coercion or overwhelming circumstance is absolutely central to our view of what it is to be an autonomous person. It is, so it seems, through the exercise of will that we push ourselves into doing things: we survey the possible field of action, weigh up the pros and cons, 'decide' what to do and then 'will' the appropriate activity. There seems to be no problem about this; it is part of everyone's experience, and to suggest, as of course determinists have over the centuries, that actually our actions are governed by forces over which we have absolutely no control seems to be an affront to what we unquestionably *know* about ourselves.

This is all very well as long as *wanting* to do things and *willing* them go hand in hand. You identify the course of action you want to take and then you will yourself into taking it (you 'decide', 'make up your mind' to do it, and you do it through the appropriate act of will). Everything goes smoothly. Or maybe there are a few obstacles to your achieving the desired outcome: it's not quite as easy as you thought and the process takes longer than you had anticipated because people tried to divert or prevent you from reaching your goal; maybe you failed once or twice and had to persevere through adversity. But you won through in the end. A triumph of the will, perhaps: it is particularly the cases where we persist through obstructions and difficulties that convince us of the validity of the concept of will, for what else would sustain us and give us the necessary impetus to keep going?

What's more, the successful exercise of will, especially where achieving your aim has not been easy, brings with it a strong sense of satisfaction. Even if modesty forbids drawing attention to it, there is something praiseworthy about trying and trying again if at first you don't succeed. We admire Robert the Bruce for his moral fibre (forgetting, perhaps, that the source of his inspiration – the web-weaving spider – could scarcely qualify as a *moral* teacher and might in fact point up quite different lessons). It may seem to us that the strength to persevere, 'will power', is drawn from some internal moral source of which we can be quietly proud and which we should seek to inculcate in those for whose development we are responsible.

Things get rather more problematic when you find that wanting to do something is not smoothly linked with the process of willing it. You identify the desired course of action all right, but all your best efforts come to nothing, and what you find yourself doing is actually something quite different. This is a familiar part of everyone's experience. New Year resolutions, determination to give up smoking or to go on a diet, quickly demonstrate that seeing that something needs to be done, even really wanting to do it, is not enough to spark the application of the requisite amount of will.

In circumstances such as these, we would probably talk about 'failures of will', chastise ourselves for being 'weak-willed', maybe indulge ourselves with a tolerant admission that we 'just didn't have enough will power'. We can afford to be fairly lenient with ourselves because defeats such as these are the everyday experience of all of us: no one really expects us to keep New Year resolutions, and being able to stick to a diet is, as we all know, a rare achievement. It would not occur to us, simply on the basis of these apparent exceptions to the rule, to question our whole notion of 'will', nor indeed to regard ourselves as particularly morally defective.

When we come to supposedly clinical forms of distress, however, the situation becomes far more serious. For in many of these it seems that the will has broken down so badly that not only can people not perform the most ordinary volitional acts, but they seem – to themselves certainly, and very possibly to others as well – reprehensibly deficient in moral fibre.

Nothing simpler, you'd think, than going through a supermarket checkout, driving your car down the motorway (as you have hundreds of times before), taking a lift to the second floor, signing your name on a cheque, getting on a bus, looking at the view from a high building, feeding the pigeons in the city square. And yet all these simple, everyday activities, and many, many others, can be so taken over by anxiety that the exercise of 'will' becomes a complete impossibility. Anxiety, it is true, is probably most often experienced (more accurately) as a failure of confidence than a failure of will, but in any case, as many sufferers know to their chagrin, even the greatest 'effort of will' is unlikely to overcome the panic.

And what of the situations where the 'will' is insufficient to stop people from doing things they clearly don't want to do but nevertheless are unable to resist? What, for example, does the predicament of the 'obsessive-compulsive' person tell us about the nature of will? Why cannot Dave simply will himself to cut short his morning safety rituals? If this represents a failure of his will, what is maintaining the ritualistic conduct itself – is Dave willing it, secretly or unconsciously, or is it in some strange way 'unwilled' behaviour? How, similarly, can we account for the profound, bitter distress of the anorectic girl dying from starvation, unable to will herself to eat, but able, apparently, to go to elaborate lengths to avoid the ingestion of food; is she engaged in some extraordinary game of deception – of herself, of us?

So long as we can regard such cases as these as instances of 'disorder', as pathological departures from the norm, we may not feel that their predicaments should lead us to revise our notion of will. But if they are to be taken seriously as instances of the way human beings can *be* in regard to the control of their own conduct, they throw enormous doubt on our ordinary conception of 'will power'. And they are not, I think, different in kind from the dilemmas all of us may experience in situations *where we are in the grip of powers we do not ourselves control and whose influence we do not like.*

The simple concept of will is just not sufficient plausibly to account for how we come to act in any given situation, and quickly becomes incoherent as soon as we find ourselves at odds with what we're doing. Take, for example, the young wife and mother of firm moral convictions who suddenly finds herself involved in a passionate love affair with the next-door neighbour: it is likely to take her months just to get over the shock and bewilderment of finding that she has 'no will power' and trying to understand what has taken her over.

These issues need to be addressed not just because of the interesting philosophical questions they raise about the nature of will, but especially because of the distress which is attendant upon the 'breakdown of will'. People who find themselves unable to perform actions that other people seem able to do without a moment's hesitation or reflection are not only frustrated at being out of control of their own conduct, but feel humiliated and ashamed at what seems to be their deficiency in moral strength. It is in this area, in my view, that psychotherapy has failed its clientele most seriously.

Psychotherapy and 'will power'

Despite being faced with countless examples of people who are desperately struggling to will conduct over which they have no control, no brand of psychotherapy that I know of has taken up the implicit challenge to reconsider the popular notion of 'will power' which is embedded in our culture. While it is true that most are ready to recognise that sufferers can't pull themselves together by a simple act of will, it has not occurred to them to doubt the validity of the concept itself,[1] and, as far as therapy is concerned, it is in the end always up to the individual to will the necessary personal changes that will lead to an improvement in his or her condition.

Not all brands of psychotherapy refer directly to a concept of will – many never mention the word – but it is always implicit in their ideas about how change comes about. Furthermore, these ideas, where they have not been simply incoherent, have always been troublesome for psychotherapy.

The notion of 'insight', for example, is really nothing but a lightly disguised version of generally accepted ideas in our culture about how we come to decide, or 'make up our minds', to do things. We survey the options, weigh the pros and cons, decide on the course of action we most favour, and then do it. The trouble is that it is precisely in *doing* it that the clients of therapy often have their greatest difficulty. Psychotherapy has always worked focally on the *background* processes leading up, through 'insight', to a supposed act of will, and though it has not failed to notice that the problem for patients is indeed most acute at the moment of *acting*, it certainly has failed to take the implications of this seriously.

The fact that 'insight' – whether intellectual or emotional – doesn't necessarily lead to changes in conduct has long been a theoretical and practical frustration for psychotherapists of all persuasions, but that has not stopped them from persevering with the idea, albeit unexpressed, that clearing the ground for decisions to be made (the essential work of therapy) leaves it up to the individual to make them – all that is needed is the appropriate act of will, and if the patient doesn't choose to make it, that's his or her responsibility. Psychotherapy doesn't question the concept of will, it simply tries to restore the processes through which it might operate. If, having supposedly done so (by providing all the necessary 'insight'), it finds that patients still fail to take appropriate action, it is likely to change them with (precisely!) *wilful* recalcitrance, perhaps in the form of 'resistance'.

The difficulty for psychotherapy is, of course, that it literally cannot *afford* to recognise what stares it in the face every day: no matter how much people may *want* to change, despite their excellent understanding of the reasons for their previously 'maladaptive' behaviour, however simple it may seem to an outside observer for them to put the required changes into effect, desperately hard though they may strive to change, they simply cannot do it.

The answer to this conundrum is in fact relatively easy to find: it is not that people in this kind of situation are *unwilling* to change, but rather that they haven't got the *power* to change. The reason why psychotherapists cannot see this is that their practice depends for its credibility on the assumption that anyone able to become a client of therapy will be able to put into effect necessary life changes once s/he can see a good reason for doing so. If the *means* of changing conduct turn out not to be within the individual's grasp, the whole point of therapy is vitiated. In this way it is much more profitable for psychotherapy to cling on, however inexplicitly, to a notion of 'will power' than it is to countenance the idea that the powers requisite for change are likely to be beyond the patient's reach.

For 'will power', shadowy and unanalysable concept though it is, seems to be something available to any individual who has or can be given the strength to reach down inside him- or herself into a kind of interior moral space where, supposedly, the source of will resides. It seems as if all of us are born with a kind of moral fuel tank inside us containing the power we need to turn our projects into action. There seems, indeed, to be something humane and equitable about the idea that no one is entirely disqualified from being able to save themselves from adversity if they really, really want to, or if outside encouragement, exhortation or inspiration are strong enough.

If it really were like this, the psychotherapeutic enterprise would make perfect sense, for its procedures clearly are directed at smoothing the path for the successful operation of will, and there would be no obvious reason why they wouldn't work. Psychotherapy is very good at solving puzzles over and exposing the reasons for the problems people experience and the pain they feel: if there were a fuel tank within full of 'will power', psychotherapy would certainly enable them to tap it.

But the power to act is not a kind of in-built resource to which all of us, potentially, have access. It is something afforded us from outside. It may indeed be the case that we can – to pursue the metaphor – 'store' power we have acquired from external sources as in a kind of tank, but it is certainly not the case that the tank is full to start with. Whether or not we are able to realise our desires, put our plans into effect, do what we know to be right, will depend on our access to powers and resources which we need to acquire, or to have acquired, from the world around us. And this is something psychotherapy can help us with hardly at all.

The process of doing

Before going on to consider the kinds of external powers and resources we need in order to be able to realise our aims, a little more needs to be said first about why it is often so difficult to achieve goals we *do*, on the face of it, have the power to reach. Once again, this has a lot to do with our conventional assumptions about how action comes to be taken.

What could be easier, for instance, than opening the front door and walking out into the street, or, as you have done thousands of times before, going into the kitchen to prepare a simple meal? You are, let us say, healthy and in good working order and there are no new powers you need to carry out routines long practised – what's to stop you, then, from simply doing what needs to be done? Difficulties like these are, as already pointed out, the common experience of, among others, people suffering from so-called obsessive-compulsive disorders or depressive illnesses. The man who has failed to check the gas taps and electric switches at the right time and in the right order finds it simply impossible to leave the house; the woman conscious of the need to prepare the evening meal for her family suddenly finds that she just cannot bring herself even to go into the kitchen, and instead goes to bed and pulls the blankets over her head. It can easily seem here that what we have is a serious failure of 'will power' – and that is exactly how it often seems to the sufferers themselves.

This is because we normally think of the exercise of will as rather like having an executive director, or perhaps a general, somewhere inside our heads who assesses the options, marshals the troops, and then 'decides' on a particular course of action. We have a sense of, as it were, launching ourselves into action, or perhaps rather being launched into action, by an executive decision after the pros and cons have been weighed and our 'minds' have been 'made up'. For people who find themselves experiencing difficulty over doing things they were once able to do without any problem, it often seems as if it is this 'executive director' who has suddenly disappeared. They can see well enough what's needed and there seems to be no lack of desire to do the things that have suddenly become impossible. It just seems that the decision itself cannot be made – it is the will that has failed.

Failure of courage is another form in which difficulties of this kind are often experienced. 'I just haven't got the guts to . . .' is the despairing view of many people who find themselves unable to perform apparently simple everyday actions like getting on a bus or going shopping. Contempt for oneself, even self-loathing, are the frequent accompaniments of supposed failures of will, and not having the courage to do things that everyone else seems able to perform without even thinking seems particularly shameful. 'Courage' tends to be thought of as a kind of moral resource very much like 'will' – something people are responsible for dredging up from an interior source and if they cannot locate it, this reflects on their worth as human beings.

In one way or another, then, it seems that when 'will power' fails we are no longer in charge of ourselves in the ways we take to be normal. The decision maker has disappeared, courage has drained away, the internal fuel tanks have run dry, we are no longer masters of our own actions.

Not the least problem with the ideas surrounding will – that we have an executive director in our heads or that we depend for successful action on adequate inner supplies of courage – is that they are so mysterious. *Where* within us are these things? On what organs do they depend? How can we access, augment, replace them? As we have seen, the strategy of pretty well all therapeutic approaches had been to ignore the problem in the hope that this is not the part of the putting-into-action process that really matters, and that if we concentrate on the weighing-up procedures of clarifying reasons and surveying pros and cons, somehow decisions will get made automatically. So-called cognitive approaches are no exception to this: if people cannot do the things they clearly want or need to do, it is because the 'cognitions' (attitudes, assumptions etc.) on which their behaviour is based are somehow faulty – it's because they're looking at things the wrong way.

The mystery of how plans get willed into action is thus no better understood by therapists than it is by those who find themselves unable to do the willing, and indeed is actually ignored. Therapy has come up with absolutely no better ideas about how people come to be 'in charge' of themselves than those embedded in the popular culture, whose inadequacy is shown up so obviously by the very difficulties of which the clients of therapy complain. It is, therefore, high time that we began to consider the possibility that our notion of will is so mysterious mainly because it is wrong.

In fact, the difficulties experienced by people supposedly suffering from 'clinical' conditions, far from compounding the mystery, may actually be pointing the way out of it. What their experience demonstrates may not so much be that they have lost charge of themselves in some pathological manner as that *we are none of us as much in charge of ourselves as we think*. The exercise of will may be an illusion.

Will as illusion

The point is, I think, that we cannot help observing ourselves act, and it is easy to confuse observation with the execution of the act.[2] It may not so much be that we are *doing* things as that they are happening *through* us. Maybe we're not so much *willing* our actions as *witnessing* them.

As things happen to us and as we respond to them, we cannot but be consciously involved: we both *feel* the events (and our responses) as they impinge upon us, and we represent them to ourselves through the media of imagery and language – we *think* about them. All the time, we are, inescapably, intimately bound up with the constant interchange between ourselves as embodied creatures and the environment that surrounds us and the powers that flow through us from it and back into it. There is absolutely no way we can step outside this experience and view it objectively – it is our subjective experience of being in the world, and, among other things, we keep up a kind of constant running commentary to ourselves on what is going on.

This running commentary, if only because of the structures of the language in which it is necessarily couched, splits our experience up into logical stages, assigning to it sequences and causal chains which in fact have much more to do with the characteristics of thought than they do with the nature of the events they are trying to describe. As the influences that shape our actions flow through us, we commentate on them to ourselves by describing the processes they arouse in us in as orderly and comprehensible a manner as we can. For example, we characterise the process of being pushed and pulled in various directions as 'weighing the pros and cons' – indeed, we may often succeed in imposing an element of order on this process by actually looking for influences pro and con which we can submit ourselves to, in which case our conviction that we are somehow 'in control' will be heightened.

If all goes smoothly, we will experience the process of being influenced to act as 'making up our minds', and if we actually do find ourselves performing the appropriate action, we will tell ourselves that we have 'carried out the decision'. What is happening here is that the 'commentator' is attributing to the complex process through which we respond to the influences which bear down upon us a degree of subjective direction and deliberation which doesn't actually exist. It is not that, in performing an action, we are simply responding passively to some kind of coercion, but rather that the neat process we describe to ourselves – of cogitation and weighing up leading to executive decision – doesn't accurately represent the way we come to do things. This inaccuracy is likely to be revealed only when the 'commentator' is surprised to find things not turning out as neatly as expected.

Certainly *I* do what I do, but not under the guidance of some kind of inner executive director. Sometimes – most of the time, perhaps – what I do runs along in harmony with what I expect and wish to be doing, and with what other people consider is broadly all right and reasonable for me to do. At times such as these the commentator is perfectly happy and attributes to me a high degree of autonomy and 'will power'. Sometimes, however, I do things that run counter to my own or others' expectations, in which case the commentator's way of seeing things breaks down. In these latter cases the commentator wrongly attributes failures (of will, of courage, etc.) to me which are more accurately represented as inadequacies of 'his' descriptions.

Failures of will are not so much the sudden absence of the executive power as the commentator's inability to make sense of what we are doing, mainly because the theories 's/he' subscribes to are inadequate to the task. The point is precisely that I am *not* in control of my actions in the way my running commentary assumes. Rather than being able to stand apart from my activity to deliberate over and direct it, all I can really do is describe what happens. Rather than having 'intention' based on my 'will', I am really limited to finding out what my intentions were *after* the event. It would be much more accurate, though probably still far from completely adequate, if we saw will and intention as something we infer from our actions rather than as something we need to activate *before* we actually do things.

The trouble is that it seems to us that we *own* the events that take place inside us as our activity is shaped by the influences upon us – and in a perfectly good sense, of course, we do. But our subjective conviction of ownership goes far beyond a mere recognition that we are the hosts of processes over which we have but little control: almost irresistibly, we feel we own them in the sense of being responsible for them, even of inventing them. After all, we only feel them, they are only truly alive for us, when they form a part of our embodied experience. If the sunflower could speak its feelings as we do, it too would no doubt claim that it is *willing* its face to turn to the sun.

Contrary to what is popularly thought to be the case, being able to introspect on what it feels like to be engaged in one's own activity may actually be a disadvantage when it comes to trying to understand the reasons for our actions. We may in fact be less misled when trying to work out the reasons for other people's actions than when reflecting on our own. This is because when looking at others we are not so easily distracted by a 'commentator' who, so to speak, thinks 's/he' has privileged access to what is going on inside the person; all we can see is the way others respond to the events that seem to be affecting them from outside.

Certainly the whole edifice of behaviourist psychology was built on the observation that introspection is a highly untrustworthy route to accurate knowledge of the self, and 'dynamic' approaches to therapy also recognise the unreliability of the 'commentator', frequently preferring to read off people's intentions from their 'unconscious' impulses and preoccupations.[3] The fact, also, that small children cannot say why they have done things until *given* the explanation by an adult (until, that is, both action and experience have been given meaning within a culture) also suggests that being the agent doesn't necessarily give us privileged insight into the reasons for the act.[4] When we insist, especially with children but also to an extent with adults, that they 'tell us the truth' about why they did something, as if the agent's introspection is the only certain source of knowledge, we actually risk introducing distorting aspects of internal commentary which we could well do better to avoid.[5]

The two essential points that I am trying to establish in this discussion are (a) that human beings are not the initiators of conduct in a vacuum; we cannot will things out of nothing, and (b) that when trying to identify the wellsprings of our conduct we are not necessarily in any better position than anyone else (it is equally essential to note that they are also not necessarily in any better position than we); our motives are identified, if at all, from the influences upon us – quite possibly more apparent to others than to ourselves – and not from some kind of privileged inward view.

The causes of our actions are best understood as *powers* which flow through us and *resources*, existing in or originally acquired from the outside world, to which we have access. The feeling that we are in control of these powers and resources is largely illusory, and will be strongest when there is no conflict between what we do, on the one hand, and what we or others wish us to do, on the other. This does not at all mean that our conduct is, or is in danger of being, 'out of control', but merely that it is not under the control of an 'executive director' in our head. Our conduct is in fact directed and socialised by all kinds of influences, some of which will have, so to speak, become part of our personhood, and some which will be located outside our skins, possibly at distal regions of the social environment of which we need have no awareness at all. The fact that we can observe and commentate upon what goes on inside us does not enable us in any automatic manner to direct it, and is in fact more likely to mislead us about its origins.

When it comes to understanding what we are up to, then, we are probably best advised to take a stance towards ourselves as we would towards others, and to try to 'read off' from our actions what must be the nature of our intentions (or, more accurately, our motivation). Quite apart from the 'commentator' being misled by the overwhelming immediacy of experience into wrongly attributing proximal explanations to distal phenomena, 's/he' also has a moral partiality which makes 'him/her' a particularly unreliable judge of motivation. This is an assertion anyone can test for themselves: just think of the last occasion when you were in some kind of moral dispute over your conduct (with a spouse or partner, perhaps). Almost certainly you will have recounted the incident to yourself over and over again until you thought you'd arrived at 'the truth' – a truth which in all probability will put you in the most favourable moral light!

The advantage of looking at yourself as a kind of way station for external influences is that it makes sense of a whole range of phenomena, particularly many so-called clinical phenomena, which cannot be accounted for by the notion of 'will'. Far from being incomprehensible, 'pathological' or morally defective, the difficulties so commonly experienced by us when we become anxious, depressed and so on become explicable in the same terms and at the same moral level as conduct we take to be 'normal'. The disadvantage of doing away with 'will' is that it may appear to dehumanise us and render us morally unaccountable. I shall consider the advantages a little more before trying to show that no such disadvantage in fact threatens us.

The meaning of 'symptoms'

Psychological theories that lay emphasis on the importance of 'unconscious' motivation have long recognised that apparently 'irrational' conduct – the kind of thing thought to constitute 'symptoms' of 'neurosis' etc. – almost always has a *meaning* in the context of the individual's world. Such theories have, however, failed to draw the radical conclusion from this insight. People have, certainly, *reasons* for doing what they do even when their actions may seem at first sight incomprehensible to themselves and/or others. But the motive force of these reasons is not to be found in an unconscious *intention* (which simply shifts the concept of will, together with all its confusions and inconsistencies, from the conscious to the unconscious sphere) so much as in influences from which, for one reason or another, the illusion of control has been stripped. The 'commentator', being unable to describe accurately what the person is doing, is unable to maintain the fiction that s/he is 'in control' (and is thereby confronted with an uncomfortable truth about the 'self' of which more fortunate people remain in blissful ignorance).

For example, when Brenda gets depressed she experiences a total collapse of will, and it seems to her that, though she has a thousand things to do, she simply cannot summon up the energy – the 'will power' – to do any of them. And yet her conduct is still fairly clearly directed to certain ends, most of which have to do with a kind of necessary (and in the context of her life as a whole very unusual) self-protection. For a while she goes on strike – goes to bed when she 'should' be cooking her husband's meals, doesn't go to work, doesn't answer the telephone, and so on. She is unfortunately not able to enjoy her periods of rest, and indeed experiences them with an intensity of despair only too evident, but nevertheless they do constitute a form of rebellion and a break from the joyless routine of service which her life has become and without which it could not continue at all.

When she is depressed Brenda simply *hasn't the power* to go on. This is not a matter of her will, but the inevitable result of the unremitting drudgery of her life which her character (her embodied experience of the past) makes it impossible for her to criticise. The impress of power (in the form particularly of her mother) simply didn't allow her to develop an idea of herself as *counting* or as able to *please herself* and these were not concepts her 'commentator' could in any way take seriously. Thus, when the time came that she could just not go on any longer, she had no way of representing to herself what was happening other than to view it as yet another indication of her inadequacy as a wife and mother.

Dave's rituals of checking are a way of protecting the world from destructive forces that he is afraid might get out of control.

Given his experience as a child, when parental power impressed upon him that there were indeed in the world as well as in him potentially catastrophic forces of aggression and evil which could be dealt with only by a combination of denial and religious superstition, it is scarcely surprising that his 'symptoms' take the form they do. It is particularly noticeable, for instance, that Dave's rituals increase in frequency and intensity when things are happening in his life that would, if he were a different kind of person, make him angry. What this teaches us is not that he is the victim of an irrational pathology, but that the impress of parental power has real consequences in shaping our subsequent conduct. Dave knows, of course, that most people don't act like him, but that doesn't make it any easier for him not to be himself. Where such powerful influences are common to the culture, no indications of irrationality are visible: priestly rituals and conjurings are viewed with uniform equanimity by the congregation.

Failures of confidence of the kind so characteristic of 'anxiety states' demonstrate as clearly as we could wish that action may become impossible where certain essential resources are missing. Even so, the demonstration is lost on many – too often the relatives of those who have succumbed to anxiety. For it is one of the more unfortunate aspects of our popular understandings that, as well as blaming ourselves for the absence of powers over which we have no control, we also congratulate ourselves on their presence. The husband of the 'agoraphobic' trembling with terror on the threshold of the supermarket is all too likely further to undermine her with his cold impatience because he cannot conceive of not being able to do what she finds impossible: all she needs is to 'push herself', to apply some of the 'will power' which he so ably taps whenever necessary. Understanding may dawn, perhaps, when a couple of years later he suddenly finds himself sweating with fear at the prospect of having to drive his car down the motorway to a neighbouring town.

The wife's confidence runs dry as a combination of past deprivation and current difficulties. She can cope with the vulnerability created by the lack of encouragement she experienced as a child, by the fact that no one had much confidence in her, just so long as there is enough support and recognition in her current life. When this fails – because of her husband's waning interest in her, her children growing up, her friends moving away – her resources are no longer sufficient to keep anxiety at bay.

The husband's situation is a little different, less a consequence of vulnerabilities created in childhood. Like many men until recent times, he had a belief in himself sustained by having a valued role outside the home, giving him a certainty of his own worth and ability which made it particularly hard for him to understand his wife's problems. But suddenly his firm is taken over by a large overseas concern intent on 'rationalisation'. Redundancies are in the air, assets about to be stripped. His technical role is devalued in favour of marketing and image. Meetings become an ordeal of competitive scrutiny, and his reputation is on the line before people who are fundamentally unsympathetic. Powers that he had felt to be safely part of him are suddenly revealed as subject to the whim of others. He feels so weak that he no longer has the aggression and competitiveness needed to cope with motorway driving, and business trips become a nightmare.

For confidence, or 'courage', are precisely not things we can summon up from inside when we most need them, but are powers accorded us by the social environment. You gain confidence from having, or having had, people being confident in you. Courage comes from en*courage*ment. A certain quantity of confidence or courage is not the birthright of us all – we are not born with full tanks, and how much we are able to call upon will depend upon our experience as children as well as our current circumstances. We are as vulnerable to being overconfident as we are to lacking in confidence, though the latter is likely to be far more painful for the subject.

For people struggling to get to grips with the deprivations their anxieties impose upon their lives, nothing is to be gained by moral self-reproach or searching their interiors for the springs of 'will power'; something has to be done about making the social environment a less confidence-sapping place (more will be said about this in the next chapter). Confidence comes from outside.

The illusion as inescapable

If we are just the passive recipients of outside influence, reacting like snooker balls to the play of forces over which we have no control, would this not render all our views of moral conduct meaningless, reducing us to dehumanised puppets of fate? Would such a view not justify a cynical fatalism which simply claimed not to be able to prevent socially destructive and selfish behaviour on a massive scale, repudiating all sense of responsibility? Would we not be able to excuse any kind of antisocial behaviour by shrugging it off as the unavoidable result of, for example, an 'unhappy childhood'?

It is important first to emphasise that I am *not* suggesting that everything we do is simply in passive response to outside forces. After all, we ourselves are forces within the total environment, albeit often far from powerful ones. To greater or lesser extents we do have powers to make a difference to the social world of which we form a part, however minuscule. We are by no means as inert as snooker balls: there is a complexity about us which makes our direction of travel after being struck by outside influences extremely difficult to predict. My point is rather that *we are not in control of the processes of influence in the way that our popular moral understandings imply*. We are much more the hosts, mediators and witnesses of the play of power than we are the executive directors. There is indeed no such thing as 'will power', but that does not mean that our conduct is necessarily chaotic, immoral or without direction. What direction it has is, however, an *aspect of the conduct itself* rather than imposed by our 'will'. The direction is, in other words, revealed in what I do, not by what I intend, would like, or think I ought to do.[6]

If it were possible to step outside the arena of human behaviour, experience and understanding into some scientifically complete, cosmic view of cause and effect, it might indeed be possible to give the kind of total, deterministic account, able to predict every minute event and action, which has at times been so attractive to some thinkers. God, viewed as a kind of omniscient scientist possessed of all the facts, would presumably be able to tell whether you were going to buy apples or oranges, scratch your nose with your finger or with your thumb. In circumstances such as these questions of morality would become as senseless as it would be for us now to charge cabbages with the moral responsibility for their growth.

But we are not, and never will be, in such a situation. We are all, whether we like it or not (and however much 'scientific psychologists' might wish to distance themselves from the objects of their study), inescapably human. We have access to no cosmic view which could remove uncertainty and unpredictability from our dealings with each other. We can sense only with human bodies and think only with human concepts. We are necessarily involved in the processes of our own conduct in ways that make agonising about its morality absolutely inevitable.

The experience of struggling to keep control of our actions, of needing to do what is right or feeling guilty over doing what is wrong, of trying, and failing, to predict our own behaviour as well as that of others, is not something we can avoid even if we can recognise that, from the cosmic perspective, all such factors may be determined in advance.

We are indeed possessed by powers which we did not originate and which we do not direct, but that does not permit us to abandon our sense of responsibility, for our sense of responsibility *is* the sensation of being possessed by such powers. Even where our conduct is to a large extent the result of an 'unhappy childhood', to disclaim that conduct as having 'nothing to do with me' would be totally in bad faith, not only because we cannot escape the sense of responsibility which stems from being an agent, but also because the conduct itself *has* 'to do with me'. The challenge facing psychologists (among whom I count anyone who wishes to understand the origins of his or her own distress) is to show *in what sense* conduct has 'to do with me'.

I am suggesting that my conduct does not necessarily have 'to do with me' in the sense that I will it, that I am in executive control of it, or that I am to blame for it. I am responsible for my conduct in as much as it is I who do it, but that does not necessarily mean that I can 'help it'. But the fact that I may not be able to help it cannot free me from the struggles and dilemmas I experience in the course of acting, for those struggles and dilemmas are *the inescapable concomitants of being the host of powers and influences, whether or not I am in control of them.*

There is no such thing as 'will power', but the subjective conviction that we have 'free will' is inescapable, because *that is how it feels* to be an active human being. 'Will' is given in the experience of doing. We are in the grip of a necessary illusion. For the purposes of our everyday social lives, our ordinary ways of understanding these issues are probably effective enough, and it is far from my intention to suggest that we should abandon or reform our usual moral language. When it becomes important to understand how far we can be expected to control or to change ourselves, as it does in the case of emotional distress, we need, however, to be more precise. We need to see, for instance, that talk of 'will' leaves too many quite familiar phenomena of everyday experience unexplained and serves only to obscure our understanding. To turn our attention instead to the play of power upon and within us, and the availability of resources to us, proves in my view far more fruitful.

How free you are to do things depends on the powers and resources available to you. Beyond those you may have acquired from the past, some of which will have become embodied as part of your character, together with those which are available to you in your current environment, there are no further moral reserves of 'will power'. The extent to which you can do things that need to be done – and however clearly you can *see* that they need to be done – will depend on whether you have access to the requisite powers and resources. 'Freedom' is directly correlated with power. The more power you are able to wield, the more freedom will be available to you. However morally distasteful some people may find this, it is obvious from the way our society is organised as well as from our daily preoccupations that nearly all of us struggle to maximise our access to power and resources in the awareness that this will give us more room in which to move and exercise choice. Freedom is being able to choose.

How much you can do to alleviate distress depends, then, not on moral reserves of will to be called up from inside yourself, but on the extent to which you can bring influence to bear on the essentially *external* factors that are, or have been, bearing down on you. If there are no powers or resources you can call upon, there is nothing you can do about your predicament other than grin and bear it. On the other hand, there may be powers and resources of which you are unaware. Maybe, for example, it had simply never occurred to you to look at things in this light, so that vain attempts to tap a nonexistent internal reservoir of 'will power' had distracted you from looking outside yourself for the necessary motivation. We need to consider in a little more detail what kinds of external resources are important.

Powers and resources

The powers and resources that make it possible for us to choose between different courses of action in order to make some impact on the world vary greatly in the degree of their proximity to the person. Broadly speaking, the extent of their potency is correlated positively with their distance from the person: the more distal the resources to which you have access, the more powerful they are likely to be.

Resources of embodiment

Nobody is born without the potentiality of possessing in-built means of bringing influence to bear on the world in some degree, however slight. Although we are all constructed virtually identically, we are clearly not born equally in terms of the gifts nature confers upon us. Some are cleverer than others, some more beautiful; some are equipped to become athletes, some musicians; more debatably, some may be extrovert and some introvert. However much one might argue about the details, there can be little doubt that genetic differences in physical structure interact with established cultural values in numerous ways to give some people a degree of social advantage right from the outset.

None of these can be legitimately seen as *moral* advantages. You do nothing to deserve the gifts you may be born with, and you have no reason to congratulate yourself on those you have: it is merely a matter of luck. What makes the difference is not your embodiment itself, but the valuation placed upon it by society. Being unusually intelligent, for example, is as a rule an advantage, but in a social revolution where intellectual leaders are regarded with fear and suspicion, it could result in summary execution. Being black is pretty obviously a disadvantage in such societies as ours, but its irrelevance to any question of human worth is obvious to all but fools and bigots. Even though bodily resources are the only ones that can plausibly be said to be 'internal', they are thus still heavily dependent for their effectiveness on external validation.

Another important point to note about embodiment is that in most important respects it is, so far, beyond our control – out of reach of our 'will'. This is clearly something that irks us, and the importance to us of embodiment is easily discernible from the emphasis given in contemporary culture to health clubs, gyms, beauty salons, cosmetic surgery and genetic engineering. But for the most part you cannot significantly improve your IQ, turn black into white or change sex without considerably straining credulity, spending huge amounts of money and risking mutilation. The vast majority of us are stuck with the bodies we've got.

Bodily resources can be very important within the sphere of the individual's proximal world. For example, the issues of both beauty and intelligence can be deeply preoccupying, not to say intensely painful, for people who feel themselves lacking in either of these respects. Psychologists can be very nervous about facing up to the implications of people's worries in these two areas because, quite rightly, they recognise that (as much more obviously in questions of race) such considerations are easily corrupted by moral/political overtones that have a distinctly fascist flavour. By objectifying beauty or intelligence into some form of measurable trait we risk the beginnings of a morally illegitimate discrimination between people on the grounds of inherent personal worth.[7]

However, while acknowledging that no such discrimination would be legitimate, it is important to recognise that, albeit in some ways unfairly, it is possible for people to make advantageous use of embodied resources, and that sometimes they may be almost the only resources they have. Female beauty, for example (particularly though not solely), is made a commodity by our culture in a way which gives it distinct market possibilities, even if often these bring with them an oppressive element of exploitation. Muscle power may, rather similarly, give some (usually but not exclusively) men an option for violent influence where no other form is available to them. Brain power undoubtedly offers possibilities of more far-reaching influence.[8]

Money

Financial resources are of vast importance to us, and in this respect it is quite extraordinary that psychology and psychotherapy have paid them so little serious attention. With the possible exception of violent coercion, as through the use of military power, the quickest and most immediately effective way of influencing people is through controlling the means of their livelihood.

Money may not be able to purchase happiness, but it can probably buy just about everything else, including, in some circumstances, love. Worry and insecurity over finance are a familiar part of most people's lives, and the greater part of our daily activity, not to mention our sleeping nightmares, are concerned with getting enough money to stay alive and maintain a degree of social respectability. People who have a great deal of money are not only cushioned from forms of insecurity to which the rest of us are frequently prey, but they are able to exchange their wealth for practically all other forms of influence.

No doubt it is because of its absolutely fundamental importance to our lives that money – income – has become, so to speak, the ultimate repressed in our social intercourse. It is no longer indecent to discuss our sexual activities in public – even members of the royal family show little reticence in this regard – but it would not be regarded as proper to enquire into the extent of someone's financial resources. The heir to the throne as well as his spouse, happy enough to reveal marital indiscretions to television interviewers, would no doubt be utterly affronted if asked to display to the camera the balance sheets of their estates. As we saw in Chapter Four (see note 3), even the great architect of repression himself seemed blithely unaware of the extent to which his own professional preoccupations were guided by financial considerations. Psychology has more to do with money than with sex.

No doubt our vulnerability to financial power is precisely what leads to our being, on the whole, so secretive about how much money we have. There is a strategic element to the manipulation of power which makes it only prudent to keep your cards close to your chest, but when it comes to considering the choices you have in being able to influence your circumstances, there is no shame in acknowledging, at least to yourself, that financial resources are of the first importance.

Education, class and cultural capital

Education, of course, provides very real access to distal forms of power which make it possible for people to obtain social and financial advantage as well as an understanding of – and hence an ability to manipulate – the way the social structure around them works. At the very lowest level, literacy confers enormous advantages over those who have not achieved basic skill in reading and writing (life can be a torment of confusion and shame for the illiterate); at higher levels education is one of the most important resources for acquiring vocational or professional security and status as well as giving the possessor a purchase upon the apparatus of social influence.

Throughout the scale of educational achievement people may seek to differentiate themselves from each other, for example on the grounds of taste, in ways that establish social advantage. The French sociologist Pierre Bourdieu has documented the importance of various kinds of 'cultural capital' to the establishment and preservation of social power.[9] These are forms of power that, though not necessarily directly related to financial resources, may be possessed by people who are themselves quite unaware that they have acquired them from outside – they may, for example, experience them as personal qualities or marks of distinction that are somehow in-bred. The markers of class membership are closely bound up with various forms of cultural capital.

Although Bourdieu's work has particular relevance to French society, where intellectual and cultural achievement are in every sense more highly valued (and hence more effective forms of power) than in Britain, nobody can beat the British in the art of class distinction, and his treatment of the way indices of superiority can be established and maintained independently of mere vulgar money is particularly illuminating. For the most painful thing about class as a social valuation of people is that it is hard to shake off: you can't easily buy your way out of it, and the signs of class membership are often either embodied characteristics (e.g.

regional accent) or early-established patterns of conduct (e.g. the manners and vocabulary of mealtimes) which it requires a prodigious effort to change in later life. Furthermore, the ideological option of taking pride in lower-class membership, even though based on undeniably positive values (e.g. courage and solidarity), cannot disguise the equally undeniable and all too material disadvantages of working-class status.

However, class membership pure and simple is probably no longer the vicious obstacle to social achievement that it was only a few decades ago, and while middle-class status can, for all the obvious reasons, certainly be counted as a valuable resource, being born into a working-class family does not on its own absolutely preclude people, as it once did, from entry to and acceptance in a wide range of social and professional circles. It just makes it much harder.

Home and family life

I hope that by now the crucial importance of parent–child and sibling relations in early life to the formation of character will be abundantly apparent. Those personal attributes that give us the courage to tackle the inevitable obstacles and setbacks of life (in particular the all-important factor of 'confidence'), however much they may seem to be congenital aspects of our personality, are acquired from our experience of the success or otherwise of our first tentative engagements with the social world outside ourselves.

The resources of character are thus the embodied constituents of early experience. Given the current structure of our society, there can be no doubt at all, I think, that the degree to which children are able to acquire skill and confidence in their dealings with the world and with others as they grow up plays a vital part in later vulnerability to emotional distress. And whether or not they are able to acquire such skill and confidence will depend on the readiness of the significant adults around them to afford them power and encourage their early efforts.

There are, of course, other important resources connected with family life. Solidarity with other members of the family – the more extended, the better – provides an important source of proximal power. Parents, children, sisters and brothers, aunts, uncles and cousins may provide comfort, collaboration and support at times of distress or difficulty. Membership of such families (an important feature contributing to the solidarity of the traditional working class) is becoming increasingly rare, and there is no guarantee that being one of a large family will automatically bring such benefits – indeed, family disunity can be as big an emotional liability as family solidarity an asset.

The colossal weight placed in modern society on 'relationships' – by which is usually meant love relationships with spouse or partner – means that more and more frequently they break under the strain. But where long-term relationships are established in which sex and companionship strike a successful balance, there is no doubt that they do provide an enormously positive resource in people's lives. The difficulty is not in understanding why such relationships are so valuable, but in being able to make or maintain them. The greater the desperation with which we seek love, the harder it seems to get to find. A little more will be said about this in the following chapter.

Social life

Friends in whom we can confide (and whose confidences we are ready to receive in return), on whom we can call at times of crisis or acute distress, with whom we can eat and drink, play games and so on, are at least as valuable a resource as good love relationships, and probably quite a bit easier to find.

Belonging to societies, joining political groups, signing up with evening classes for interest or further education are often helpful both in acquiring or extending personal powers and in establishing a degree of communality and solidarity with others, making friends, etc.

The power of association is probably the principal way in which 'ordinary people' in the modern world can hope to extend their influence beyond the immediately proximal. Reduced to the absolute singularity of the private individual, we have little hope of influencing the world beyond appeals to the charity of others on the one hand or brute force on the other. It is by being *part* of something (usually at work) that people acquire status, respect and influence. The potency of association is well recognised by those political influences that seek to 'individualise' and 'privatise' the life of the ordinary citizen (hence, for example, the enormous ideological effort put into discrediting the trade unions). The lone couch potato browsing through electronic shopping malls or lost in virtual reality is scarcely likely to threaten the political status quo.

The social context

Our lives are dominated by a social environment over which we have very little if any control but which may accord us or deprive us of crucially important resources.

The general economic situation may determine whether or not you have a job, and hence not only your financial power and security, but also, in all probability, the degree to which you can regard yourself as having a worthwhile part to play in society. What kind of job you have, where you figure in the hierarchy of power, how creatively you are able to work or how repressed and restricted you are, will all contribute to your level of confidence and sense of freedom.

The quality of the physical environment in which domestic life is lived can be as important as the emotional relations between those in the home. Overcrowding, poor housing, bleak, dangerous neighbourhoods can quickly crush the spirits and extinguish the optimism of those who have to suffer them. Indeed, the emotional, 'psychological' or 'spiritual' qualities that are supposed to sustain us in times of trouble are often fatally weakened by the very material conditions that they are supposed to buttress us against.

We do not, of course, ordinarily think of ourselves as split up into powers and resources of the kinds I have sketched above. If we think about it at all, we are likely to see ourselves as *agents* who consider what we want to do, survey the alternatives and decide on the most appropriate course. In the process of so doing, it seems that we are constantly drawing on resources inside us and enacting our will to achieve our aims.

What we can do, however, is limited to what can be achieved by use of the powers life has afforded us, and when we find ourselves unable to do things we want to do or feel we should so, there is little to be gained from self-reproach. We need to look not at what ails us, but at what we lack, and nothing is likely to make that clearer than when we come to try to change ourselves.

CHAPTER SEVEN

What Could We Do? Learning and Change

The twentieth century, on many counts the bleakest on record (certainly the most violent and destructive), could also be called the most optimistic. For, as the century of psychology, the last hundred years have established in the Western mind expectations of the banishment of distress through therapy far greater than is justified by the actual lessons of experience. Not only do we expect to be able to overcome, with the help of psychotherapy, 'symptoms' of emotional distress seen essentially as forms of illness, but we hope also that psychology may instruct us in possibilities for 'personal growth' which could lead to our becoming unusually adequate or even excellent specimens of our kind.

There is of course nothing unusual about such hopes and aims. As I pointed out in Chapter One, psychology is in many ways continuous with practices of magic which go back as long as recorded time, and it is perhaps only to be expected that our aspirations and longings should, through psychology, seek a suitably 'scientific' garb for themselves in the technological age. And yet there *is* something incongruous about the existence side by side of the kind of uncompromisingly realistic intelligence that can send space probes to Jupiter and the wildly unrealistic fantasy that human beings can be changed from the inside out in accordance with their wishes. Our wishfulness, it seems, is detached from our intelligence so that each in its own way threatens to run out of control.

Something of the flavour of this split was already apparent early in the century as Freud and Jung juggled their esoteric psychological mysteries while barely casting a glance at the wars and revolutions which erupted around them – as if Psyche, contriving an ostrich survival, dared not contemplate the terrifying realities of human society.

Not that striving for moral purity, mental balance or personal development are unworthy aims, nor that staring straight into the mouth of hell is somehow a bracing form of intellectual discipline to be recommended for its own sake. My point is rather that our hopes of what we can do to better our psychological lot need to be tempered by a sober assessment of the restrictions placed on our room for manoeuvre by the world in which we live. The lesson of history is that, with the best will in the world, we inevitably fall well short of perfection,[1] and perhaps it is time we realised that, rather than each of us being the centre of a psychological universe which somehow we can find the secret to manipulate, we are atoms in a social world which we must learn to control *collectively* if we are to make a noticeable impact on our own suffering. Furthermore, if we are to avoid, on the one hand, the fanatical imposition of our views on others and, on the other, unnecessarily crushing disillusion in our personal lives, it is probably important for us to remind ourselves how modest even our collective achievements are likely to be.[2]

By establishing the idea that happiness, emotional balance and mental adjustment are the norm, psychology and psychotherapy serve only to add an edge of despair to the distress most people encounter at least sometimes in their lives. The contrasting view of life as tragic, reflected in particular in the greatest artistic and literary works throughout the ages, is probably not only more accurate than the cosy smugness of so much therapy and counselling,[3] but is actually a solace to those who value the discovery that they are not alone in the boat.

It is almost inconceivable that anyone can live a life without repeated and significant experiences of loss, disappointment, failure and pain; and for millions of people on the globe life is a continuous experience of toil and privation. Death finally punctuates the whole experience with an ironic question mark whose import can be overlooked only by dwindling numbers of resolute optimists and the most steadfastly religious.

If we really knew how to escape the tragic elements of life through the cultivation of therapeutic (or any other) techniques, we would no doubt long since have perfected them, and the endless labours of research workers seeking the demonstrable benefits of psychotherapy would be unnecessary. As it is, we know perfectly well that the best – if far from infallible – insurance against the worst of the world's unkindnesses is the social and economic advantages which give us a measure of ascendancy over others and choice about the conditions of our lives. Global society is structured accordingly.

The whole lesson of life is that change is not easily achieved, and certainly not from the inside out in the manner promised by therapeutic magic. Closing our ears to the woolly rhetoric of psychobabble, we can very quickly see that no one is transformed through psychotherapy, and that making even modest changes to our being-in-the-world is almost always extremely difficult and demanding. Even if we can understand the influence of the past on the formation of character, we cannot step out of the embodied person we have become. Image and make-believe may contribute to a collective delusion that anyone can do and become anything, but the impress of power is in fact not so lightly to be escaped, and Norma Jean inhabits Marilyn to the end.

Above all, the stability of character is what defeats the more sanguine hopes of psychotherapy, but it also makes the world an interesting – not to say bearable – place in which to live. Just imagine how terrible life would be if we really could be therapeutically engineered into clones of some kind of norm of 'adjustment', and how inevitably therapeutic technique would become an instrument of tyrannical repression. As it is, nothing convinces us more of our indelible individuality than watching people struggling to change aspects of themselves that cause them distress.

For better or for worse, the impress of power stamps upon us strategies and projects which we pursue lifelong, as if fated like characters in Greek tragedy. And indeed it is the case that we struggle to appease the powers we first encounter as if they were the gods of Olympus. It may on every rational count be crazy for, say, this harassed and lonely middle-aged woman to strive unremittingly to please the implacable mother who neglected and abused her from infancy, and yet it seems that no argument and no exhortation can divert her from that aim. It seems that we are indeed born as sunflowers, programmed to turn our faces to the most potent force in our environment, dependent for our very sense of existence on the endorsement of power.

We are social creatures and cannot exist independently of the influences that structure our world, and if the most powerful of those influences, when we encounter them as defenceless infants, should turn out to be the overwhelming proximal relation with an adult who hates us, we will nevertheless seek endorsement through it, not out of masochism but because, quite literally, we could not exist without it. For all too many people there *is* no power beyond the cruel or indifferent parent, or later perhaps the abusive spouse, from whom they may seek the affirmation of their being. It is this kind of circumstance which 'therapy' needs to address in order to understand the limits of its enterprise.

Seeing how we need to be different, wanting, no matter how passionately, to change in accordance with obvious goals, may or may not be necessary precursors to tackling our predicament, but they are certainly not of themselves sufficient for overcoming it. Psychotherapy trades on the excitement experienced by people on seeing for the first time that there are comprehensible reasons for the way they feel and the conviction following from this that the solution is at hand. But if they are not in possession of the powers they need to change, therapeutic insight of this kind may lead only to even greater pain and frustration. As we have seen, 'cure' comes about neither as the automatic consequence of insight nor through the most determined efforts of 'will power'.

Many people recognise this, at least implicitly, by seeking salvation not through any inside-out attempts at self-transformation but rather through intimate relationships with others. To young adults in particular it may seem that many of their most painful difficulties would be alleviated by finding someone with whom they can share their lives. Change will come about not through self-transforming efforts of will but through the redeeming power of love. People search for, form and maintain such relationships as their own personal barriers against adversity. 'Relationship' becomes a kind of commodity to be acquired, exchanged or hoarded as the minimal solidarity needed to survive in a harsh world.[4]

The difficulty with this is that the relationship ceases to be about anything but itself. Friendships as well as love relationships (and of course, more basically, sex) become things to have rather than relations through which something is made or achieved. We thus become possessions of each other, with the burden, if we are not to be summarily discarded and replaced, of providing a whole range of satisfactions: sexual, companionable, even 'therapeutic' levels of comfort and understanding. No such burden can be borne for any length of time by one individual, even if 'in a relationship' with another individual bearing a reciprocal burden.

The impossibility of the demand placed upon relationship is what often makes its attainment ultimately disappointing. The commodified nature of 'relationship' as an end in itself – epitomised in the existence of dating agencies and singles clubs – could not distract us more effectively from an understanding of what does make relations built on love the source of strength that they sometimes are. For example, love is often more about forbearance, the tolerance of difference and acceptance of inevitable aloneness than it is about the constant supply of warmth, understanding and satisfaction. It is certainly true that loving relations with another person, friendships in which appreciation and sacrifice are freely given and received, can constitute an enormously important 'resource' to those both fortunate and strong enough to take part in them. The sobering fact is that they are really quite rare.

There are those, I am sure, who will see my dwelling on the difficulties of personal change as an almost destructive erosion of hope. But it is only false hopes that I wish to destroy. To discover that your best efforts to escape from distress or despair are vain not because of your own inadequacies but because it simply isn't possible to do it all on your own may indeed be disillusioning, but in a way which is, I believe, reassuring rather than disheartening. To bring about change you need access to power. You cannot change your 'self', but you may *be* changed by shifts in the powers and influences which structure the social world around you.

Changing the world and not the 'self'

It would be impossible for a normally cheerful person to make a New Year resolution to be unremittingly miserable for the coming twelve months. On the other hand, if our normally cheerful person loses his job in January, suffers a major bereavement in February and is severely injured in a road accident in March, one would have no difficulty understanding or explaining his misery. Your mood depends on what is happening to you, not on what you decide to feel. The obviousness of this observation may seem to make it hardly worth making, and yet it is surprising how difficult people in distress often find it to grasp.

If you want to know why you are unhappy, look into the world around you, and if you want to change how you feel, look to see if the world can be changed. As an individual, this is just about all you *can* do. And yet many people don't even get this far: instead of looking into the world, they look into their 'selves'. 'It's *me*,' they say (encouraged by a century of half-baked 'psychology'). 'I know it's my fault really.' 'I know there are thousands worse off than me.' 'I feel so stupid.' Shame and self-blame are the commonest reactions to feeling distressed, but, as we have seen in earlier chapters, are singularly inappropriate as strategies for identifying the causes of distress and seeing whether anything can be done about them.

It is about as sensible to seek the reasons for distress inside the 'self' as it would be to see feeling cold as a matter of personal responsibility. It should be no mystery to you why, standing lightly dressed in a field in midwinter, you suffer from the cold. You are unlikely to say to yourself: 'I wonder why my body is shaking and my teeth chattering – there must be something very strange the matter with me.' And in order to cure your problem you are likely to institute an environmental change – put a coat on, or go indoors and light a fire.

It is exactly the same with depression, anxiety and so on. Although the causes of such feelings as these may not be so obvious as in the case of feeling cold, part of this lack of obviousness is because we have become so mystified by the popular culture, by 'psychology' and by powerful ideological (political and commercial) interests which are eager for us to construe our miseries as of our own making. Things are made more difficult by the fact that the causes of our problems are often out of sight, in distal regions of the social environment we might not even know about, and possibly also distant from us in time – perhaps having occurred in the past beyond the reach of our memory. But to start with the idea that it is not you but the world that is 'at fault' is the first essential step in tackling those aspects of your difficulties that *can* be tackled.

Changing position

Psychological distress is unlikely to be just a matter of the influence of the past. We may be shaped as characters in many ways, some of which no doubt render us particularly vulnerable to certain forms of noxious influence, but unhappiness is highly likely to be to a significant degree a consequence of things that are happening in the present. Some of these things may be avoidable by changing our position in the world.

Escaping the causes of distress is, however, in all probability not going to be as easy as walking in out of the cold. It is likely that sufferers will already have tried just about everything they can to improve their lot, and indeed it is often the very irresolvability of the conflict they find themselves in that gives rise to the distress in the first place. Difficult marriages are a good case in point: it may be obvious to one of the partners that s/he is profoundly unhappy, but what to do about it is precisely the problem. Wives may be financially dependent and have nowhere else to go; emotional damage to children may seem to either partner too high a price to pay for separation, and so on.

Again, a change in the physical environment – moving out of bleak, noisy, overcrowded or otherwise distressing domestic accommodation – can often bring about a huge reduction in the degree of psychological distress suffered, but anyone with the means to do so would probably have taken the necessary steps before their living circumstances became a significant problem.

Similarly with changing jobs, improving our opportunities through further education, finding someone to love or developing a social life: if these were easy, it would be simple enough to avoid distress in the first place.

People whose distress would be greatly alleviated by a change in their position in the world could do two things. The first is to consider carefully what their powers and resources are; the second is to grasp the nettle of change.

By 'grasping the nettle' I mean recognising that, if they are to *feel* differently, something will have to be *done*. They must abandon trust in the magical blandishments of the various kinds of marketed make-believe which promise painless transformation. There are some situations in which change, though perhaps extremely difficult, is at least possible. This applies particularly in the area of relationships. For women in particular, it is all too possible to get caught up in relationships that do take a terribly destructive toll on their personal development and happiness (Gina is a case in point). Children may certainly be affected by the break-up of a marriage, and finding somewhere else to go may be very problematic. All the same, it is often possible for a woman in this position to be much stronger and more resourceful than she thinks (especially after years of having been undermined by her partner) and to discover that there is in fact more support available to her in the social environment than she had thought possible.

Similarly, challenging parental power, once the victim of it has grown up, is a possibility, even if putting it into practice can seem shatteringly risky. In every case where I have known a grown-up child challenge a tyrannical parent, the tyrant has backed down surprisingly meekly. I have never yet known an aged parent die of apoplexy if his or her daughter has at last refused after thirty years to mow his or her lawn, prepare his or her meals or do his or her shopping at some precisely ordained (and extremely inconvenient) time, but I suppose it's always possible that one might. But that would be the price of tyranny, not of filial rebellion.

However, as I have already argued, determination on its own is not enough to change your position in relation to the rest of the world: to be successful, you need more material powers or resources on your side.

Assessing available powers and resources

In thinking about the forces we may be able to muster in our struggle with life's difficulties, it may help to develop a rather more systematic view of the kinds of power and resources that were considered in the previous chapter and to present them in the form of a diagram.[5]

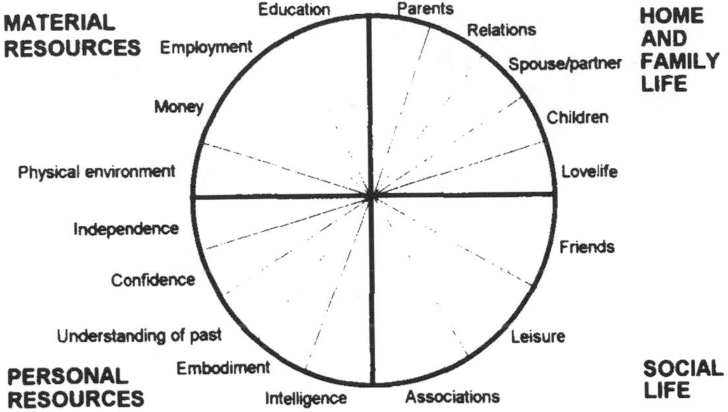

Figure 2: possible availability of powers and resources

The segments that go to make up each of the four main quadrants of Figure 2 are not to be regarded as constituting a definitive or exhaustive, 'scientific' analysis of available resources, but rather an indication of the areas it may be worthwhile surveying when trying to identify what you may have going both for and against you. The more a given segment could be regarded as 'filled', the more possible it becomes for that particular area to be used as a positive resource; the relative 'emptiness' of a segment would indicate not only the lesser availability of the resource in question, but the possibility also of greater pressures and demands in that area.

For anyone suffering significant distress, ***home and family life***, for example, is likely to be as much a source of difficulty as it is of strength. Almost all the examples in Chapter Two indicate how problems in relations with others – parents, spouses or partners, children and stepchildren – have a part to play, if not in directly causing distress, then certainly in stirring up vulnerabilities acquired earlier in life. For obvious reasons problems are more likely to be caused by the absence than by the presence of a lover in the individual's life, but there is no shortage of difficult and destructive relationships which are probably better ended than persevered with.

Consideration of this quadrant is probably as useful for understanding the nature of our difficulties as for indicating what might be changed. Individuals can expect to be able to do very little single-handedly to alter the quality of the family relationships in which they are embedded. Even 'family therapy' or 'marital therapy', which do provide a form of intervention backed by a degree (albeit limited) of power not available to the individual, cannot escape the fact that the families and their members are held in place by environmental and historical powers not amenable to the influence of therapists. Therapies of this kind may provide a useful forum in which family members (particularly parents and children) can reflect on unhelpful 'habits of relating' which may have established themselves, and therapists may play a more or less educational role in clarifying problems and suggesting alternative strategies. As with individual therapy, however, the benefits of 'insight' should not be overemphasised, and difficulties in families are often the consequence of more than just misperceptions or faulty habits.

Married couples or partners may well find marital counselling or therapy helpful in clarifying what they feel about the relationship and each other, and where there is a strong bond of affection between them, having a neutral 'referee' with whom to air difficulties, grievances and sources of pain may quite possibly result in their finding it easier to live together. But there is no way in which counselling of this kind can guarantee to repair difficult relationships, and, depending on what they were hoping for from it, partners are as likely to find the outcome negative as positive. The world has a way of reasserting its influence once the couple are away from the consulting room, and understanding the nature of the problem does not necessarily point the way to a 'cure'.

As indicated in the last chapter, *social life* is a resource of the first importance. Solidarity with others is both one of the most significant and, all things considered, the most available forms of power for 'ordinary' people.

Once again, it is of course extremely difficult for people who find themselves socially isolated to whip up out of nowhere friendships or other forms of association with congenial or influential individuals or groups. But it is often the case that the very people who *feel* most unlikeable, and are therefore particularly vulnerable to emotional distress, are those whom others would take to most readily. The kind of social diffidence that early brushes with power so easily instils tends also to make its victims adaptable and attentive to others, and free of objectionable bombast, so that they are potentially very good (and, if they're not careful, exploitable) friends. It may therefore be possible, at least in principle, for such people to discover that they can make friends much more easily than they had thought.

In times of trouble, when people most need the friends they do have, just such diffidence may make them reluctant to burden people with their problems. Many people *will* burden anyone who cares to listen to the point of ultimate desperation, but these are *not* the people who feel diffident about it. In other words, if you do feel you would like to talk to your friends about urgent or pressing difficulties but really feel reluctant to trouble them – and if, especially, you usually find yourself listening to *other* people's problems – you should almost certainly take the plunge. It would be very surprising if you don't get a sympathetic and helpful response.

As suggested in Chapter Five, it is sometimes helpful for the shy person, who would like but is terrified to approach people who seem congenial, to remember that s/he is 'other for others', and that they are likely to respond to him or her in exactly the way that s/he does to them. In other words, their likely reaction to being approached would be pleased and sympathetic. In order to discover this, of course, there is no alternative to taking the necessary action.

Most forms of broadly cognitive therapy depend very heavily on challenging the assumptions seeming to underlie difficulties that, from every practical aspect, look quite easy to overcome, and it may well be the case that encouragement from a therapist could be a useful source of solidarity in propelling people to take apparent risks it would be very difficult for them to take on their own. As will no doubt be apparent by now, my own view is that while such approaches can be helpful, they do tend to overlook the problem of embodiment – of how deeply 'wired in' are apparently quite superficial ways of conducting oneself – and people should not feel too despondent if they find therapeutic instructions very difficult to follow.

Again, in considerations such as these it is as important as ever to beware of the tyranny of the norm. It is simply not the case that, if we were to expose ourselves to the requisite therapeutic regimen, we would all become averagely sociable human beings, nor is there any particular reason why anyone who wants to shouldn't become a recluse. One aspect of character frequently to be encountered in socially diffident people is that no amount of demonstration of friendship or affection is sufficient to convince them that they are in the least lovable, and while this may in many ways be a painful characteristic, it is certainly not one that makes those who embody it less than human.

It is, however, often the case that making the effort to engage in social activities of some kind leads to great improvement in people's lives and, consequently, considerable mitigation of their distress. Mobilising interests in order to do things with others (hobbies, sports, evening classes, religious or political convictions – pretty well any form of association providing a focus in activity for doing things with people) is probably the best way of developing friendships or deeper relationships. To this end, it may be a good idea, if you wish to widen your social life, to consider what resources you have (of interest, ability or previous knowledge) that could be drawn on or in some way initiated to reposition yourself alongside others.

When it comes to considering ***personal resources*** it may once again be more a question of taking stock than of immediately identifying ways of increasing the amount available. For most people suffering from emotional distress it is highly likely that their stock of confidence will be very low, and, as we have seen, there is no way it could be increased directly by a determined act of will. It is, however, helpful sometimes for people to recognise how much lack of confidence is contributing to their predicament, rather than, say, 'neurotic illness' or moral cowardice. It may also be helpful to note how confidence may sometimes be increased precisely by *not* focusing on it directly, but through the acquisition of powers and resources in other areas.

Both embodiment and intelligence are, again, not aspects of the person that can easily be altered. Quite often, however, these resources are overlooked, especially by people who are feeling depressed or unhappy about themselves. Particularly in the case of intellectual ability, it may be possible to make use of untapped resources to acquire skills or qualifications that can make a very significant contribution to a material increase in power. There are also many people whose education was impaired or interrupted for one reason or another, and who have wrongly concluded that they are 'thick' because, perhaps, they have difficulties with literacy. Although it can be very difficult to walk into adult literacy classes all on your own, without the backing and encouragement of family or friends, it can, for those who somehow manage it, open up worlds almost undreamed of. I have met many highly intelligent and perceptive, but educationally deprived, people who had no idea of their exceptional talents.

Acting on the recognition that they have unrealised potential – maybe by 'going back to school', doing an Open University course, taking evening classes or entering further education by any other available route – may introduce people to a *social* world whose existence they hadn't previously been able to envisage. There are many people who have an unrequited love of truth which they feel as a purely personal pain, and are astonished and overjoyed to find that not only are there others who share their passions and their interests, but that a whole world exists in which such interests are regarded as perfectly normal and in which friends are quite easily to be made.

Much more difficult to swallow (and, happily, in my experience very much less frequent) is the situation in which people need to recognise that their intellectual ability is being stretched beyond its capacity. There are obvious costs to status and self-esteem in acknowledging that, for instance, they are not up to their job, and there may be circumstances in which these costs are not worth paying. On the other hand, there may be times when people find it an enormous relief to retrench to a position in which less is demanded of them intellectually.

Understanding of the past is, on the other hand, something that can be increased relatively easily, and is certainly, through the process of 'clarification' discussed in the opening chapter, one of the main things psychotherapy can help with. Confusion and bewilderment over why we are in the grip of distressing 'symptoms' can often be assuaged quite quickly through a process of relating how we feel to the influences that are affecting and have affected us in a real world over which we have and have had virtually no control. But, as I have emphasised throughout this book, 'insight' of this kind is of limited usefulness, since in and of itself it changes nothing of real significance. It may be, however, that for some people 'knowing the reasons' for things provides a necessary degree of incentive to do something about them. The therapeutic process of clarification, in this way, works best with people who are already in possession of the necessary powers to make changes to their lives: seeing that something needs to be done is fine if you have the wherewithal to do it but may be cruelly frustrating if you haven't.

Independence – most often from some kind of oppressive authority or personal relationship – is again something that may, at least theoretically, be within our power to increase. Those adults I have encountered in life able to be most honest with themselves often say that they still feel like four-year-old children, and for many of us it can easily seem that, like children, we are surrounded by 'grown-ups' who seem to have a handle on the world (i.e. access to powers) well out of our reach. For people (often, of course, those who are most socially oppressed, like working-class women) who find themselves overshadowed or undermined by others in their proximal world, it may be important to recognise that the 'power horizon' of their oppressor is in all essential respects the same as their own, and that, if challenged, he (usually) will back down.

The principle of challenging power in personal relationships should, however, not be turned into some kind of fatuous therapeutic nostrum. While it is very often the case that people who *feel* powerless have, through their normal rights as adults and citizens, much more power than they think they have (or know about) and may, if they can discover it, use it to great effect, it is also true that those whose power relative to those around them *is* restricted (children, women, ethnic minorities etc.) may if they step out of line find themselves at the receiving end of some shattering punishment.

The possibility of exercising our rights as citizens to use the social institutions that offer advice and support in battles with adverse powers is not evenly or fairly distributed among the population. Not only, for example, do we need money to pay for legal advice (except in increasingly rare circumstances), but the knowledge (and hence confidence) to approach authorities, tackle bureaucracies, and so on, is acquired principally as part of a middle-class upbringing. Professional people in official buildings are often bearded with great trepidation, if at all, by people who have been brought up to fear and respect power. It can, for example, be very difficult to persuade those who would most profit from their services even to step inside the excellent Citizens' Advice Bureaux.

Increasing independence need not only be a question of relations with others: there are also relations with the world. It is, for example, surprising how often an extension of mobility, perhaps by acquiring a car and/or learning to drive, can result in a very significant increase in someone's freedom and, consequently, feeling of confidence. Quite literally, someone may be able to change his or her position in the world and open up new horizons of power simply by establishing the means to move around it. Here again, it is quite obvious how increasing independence in this way is not simply a 'psychological' procedure, but depends on very real material resources.

It is precisely the acquisition of ***material resources*** that makes possible the ability to influence our world in practically every other respect. Apart from the fairly routine assessment in research work of people's 'socio-economic status' and the observation that the middle class (in particular those of its members who are 'young, attractive, verbal, intelligent and successful'[6]) tend to profit most from 'treatment', psychotherapy has almost totally disregarded the significance for psychological wellbeing of material advantage.

Money can't buy happiness, but then neither can happiness be assured through psychotherapy. It is easy to highlight the vulgarity of money and to scoff as the crude materialism of the *nouveau riche*, but far more difficult, it seems, to acknowledge that many if not all of what we regard as our most refined virtues and spiritual accomplishments are also acquired through the judicious use of, in the end, financial advantage. When it comes to trying to understand the origins of emotional distress, it helps to realise that what cushions us against the cruelties of the world, what enables us to relax in each other's company, to avoid spiteful competition and invidious comparison (and hence many of the forms of relationship that result in psychological damage), is a degree of material comfort.

This insight, though, as already pointed out, far more the subject of repression than sex and hence rarely openly discussed, lies nevertheless at the very heart of our social structure. At the very moment we adjure each other to 'count our blessings', 'accept responsibility', 'tighten our belts' etc., we scrabble as hard as hell for the most materially advantageous perch we can find.

In view of this, there are not likely to be very many people who have not already, very sensibly, done what they can to maximise their material resources. Nevertheless I want to underline what an important factor the material situation is. So much emphasis has been placed in the general literature in psychotherapy on the idea that 'it's all in the mind' that people often actually overlook the most appalling deprivation in their living circumstances when trying to account for their distress. For anyone who can, it often really does help to move house, change job, invest in further education, have a holiday or even get away for the weekend (all things that affluent people may do as a matter of course – and without reflecting that their ability to do so is what keeps them sane).

Learning to be different

In order to change our position in the world under our own steam (as opposed to being put by powerful forces in a different position, which is a more frequent occurrence), it is often necessary to learn to do things differently. To 'be' different, we may have to alter our characteristic ways of acting in some important spheres.

Challenging unreasonable power in our proximal relationships, or taking the risks involved in making social overtures to others, is often extremely difficult, not least because it is likely to involve going against the grain of deeply embodied habits of personal conduct. Even therapeutic approaches that stress the importance of changing the way we *do* things – like those derived from behaviourism – usually overlook how difficult this is actually to achieve. There tends to be – as usual – a tacit assumption that once the need to change has been established, actually doing things differently is merely a matter of performing the necessary acts of will.

Because we acquire our characteristic ways of conducting ourselves effortlessly (or so it seems), we assume that all that we need to be able to do things differently is a 'good reason'. This overlooks the fact that we can only do things we know how to do. I do not do what I do just because I have good reasons to, but also because I know how to. It may certainly be true that I seem to have acquired that knowledge without even trying, but that doesn't mean that I also know how to do things *differently*.

Speaking a language is a good case in point. I know how to speak English without being conscious of ever having learned to: it seems that I 'just can'. But I do understand clearly why it is that I can't speak Chinese, and I can of course grasp conceptually the fact that I must have *learned* to speak English as an infant just as, if I wanted to speak Chinese now, I would have to *learn* to do so.

The case is not greatly different, in my view, with other aspects of conduct that people appear to perform effortlessly, including activities that enhance or detract from confidence or cause emotional distress. 'Being confident' is, at least in part, a matter of knowing how to act in particular ways in particular circumstances, and for many people the only way to acquire that knowledge may be through a relatively long and arduous process of learning.

Unfortunately, the view of change implicit in the 'learning model' – already considerably more difficult and demanding than the promise of magical transformation implicit in so many nonbehavioural approaches to therapy – is still far too simplistic as a basis for the 'treatment' of psychological and emotional difficulties. For what people can learn is not simply a matter of what they can see as a good reason for learning: they need also an environment that will support their learning.

The learning environment

Learning something new is not simply a matter of deciding to. For example, in order to 'decide' to learn Chinese, you would probably need to have a fairly pressing interest in doing so: an economic, educational or social motivation exerting pressure on you. In addition to this you would need access to books, libraries and teachers, which would cost money. You would also probably need the support and understanding of people close to you: your family would have to be prepared to give you the time to learn and not hinder or ridicule your attempts. In order to keep going, you would almost certainly need a lot of encouragement from people who mattered. You would require the time and space for regular work and revision. For most people, the idea of learning Chinese just for the sake of it would be more than extremely daunting, it would be impossible, and this because they are not inhabiting an environment that makes the learning of Chinese a sensible undertaking.

When you think about it, a great deal of effort is put into our official procedures for teaching people things they are not otherwise highly motivated to learn. Ask any conscientious schoolteacher on a Friday evening how s/he is feeling and you will get some idea of the expenditure of energy necessary to teach even the rudimentary skills of our culture. In order to learn, children need years of intensive effort on the part of others.

Consider also that we make it as easy as we can for children to learn (or as difficult as we can for them not to!). We set up special institutions for them in which to do so, and, while they are learning, we tolerate their making mistakes – we expect them to be ignorant and inexperienced in many respects. As far as we can, we organise the lives and the social environments of children to take account of the fact that they are supposed to be learning.

With adults, things are on the whole very different. The world is not set up for them to learn, especially aspects of conduct and relationships that 'normal' people are supposed to have acquired by their early twenties, and there is unlikely to be anything like the intensity of instruction and tolerance of mistakes that official learners like children are afforded. It is true, of course, that adults may be expected to be more self-motivated than children and that therefore they should not need a similar input of resources, and this is indeed the case with mature students who are, as teachers will often affirm, 'such a pleasure to teach'. But even with willing learners, there is still a need for the material media of their instruction and a lengthy commitment to study and practice, not to mention the social support and encouragement of others.

In comparison, the kind of learning necessary for people to alter their position in the world so that it will become for them a less distressing place receives practically no such support from the social environment. In diagnosing people, in segregating them no matter how subtly as 'abnormal', there is virtually no sign of the provision of the kind of context in which learning to 'be different' could be practised and encouraged. Even in offering 'therapy', the emphasis tends to be more on moral regeneration than on analysis – let alone provision – of a context that would make change possible. And even in those approaches to 'treatment' which do stress learning, it is of course far beyond a therapist's powers to affect any but the most proximal aspects of the person's social environment in ways that would *facilitate* learning.

It is necessary to stress these constraints on 'learning to be different' in order to avoid falling into a kind of narrow 'therapism' which once again suggests that if sufferers don't improve, this time through their own strenuous efforts of learning, it is all their own fault. Having made this point, which cannot be emphasised too strongly, it is possible to make one or two suggestions that might make the process of change, if not easier, then perhaps a little more comprehensible to anyone who has been disappointed by the promises of 'therapy' or who is dismayed by the prospective difficulties of having to learn to behave uncharacteristically.

Doing precedes feeling

For someone to feel differently, something has to happen. Things may of course happen *to* people, in which case they may not have very much control over what they are: uncontrollable events usually lie at the root of emotional distress in the first place. If, on the other hand, you want to feel differently as the result of your own efforts, it is important to recognise that you will have at first to take action (probably to change your position in the world in the way already discussed) while still feeling distressed. Many people expect somehow to 'feel better' *before* undertaking the task of reorganising their lives, whereas in fact 'feeling better' is only likely to come about once the process of 'learning to be different' is well under way.

Most of us recognise that, as in speaking a language, we enact our characteristics effortlessly, and this gives us a sense of who we are. In other words, we are what we know how to do best and most skilfully, even if we would rather be doing something else. Peacemakers who do anything for a quiet life (and hence get unmercifully exploited by others) are likely to say that 'it's not like me to lose my temper'. In order to learn to become more assertive, it is therefore necessary for such people to go through an uncomfortable period of behaving uncharacteristically, during which they may feel horribly false. If they persevere, however, the requisite conduct becomes part of them in a way that feels, and is, perfectly genuine.

You could not 'feel like' a footballer or a concert violinist if you'd never played the game or touched the instrument. It is the same with many psychological characteristics: we do not come ready-made, so to speak, and we only feel like what we are after a long process of learning. The difference between the usual course of character formation and a programme of self-change is that in the first case the learning process is informal and in the second formal. What happens naturally in the case of character formation has to be set about artificially in the case of learning to be different.

It would be dishonest to pretend that there are no important differences between these two processes. For example, therapeutic learning does not simply produce a 'new' character; newly learned characteristics (say, of being 'assertive') do not *replace* old ones, but are superimposed on top of them. This is rather like the difference between naturally speaking with a particular accent and having learned (as an actor, perhaps, or through elocution lessons) to speak with it deliberately. Therapeutic approaches to learning often seem to make a tacit assumption that the client to be changed is a tabula rasa, the therapist a Pygmalion sculpting character from virgin materials. This, of course, is far from the case. The client is already a character with a range of embodied dispositions which are not simply wiped out by new experience.

Someone trying to learn to behave differently in some key situations may have a tacit awareness that the old ways of responding are indeed not far away, and this may contribute to a sense of ungenuineness. It would be a shame, however, if this put them off the process of learning, for learning to be assertive (say) is no more 'ungenuine' than learning Chinese. It may not be, so to speak, your first language, but becoming expert in it is none the less useful for that.

'Walking the plank'

In order to get launched on the process of learning to be different (and thereby to give ourselves the possibility of discovering that acting differently will lead to feeling differently), there is no mediating procedure that will make it easier. By this I mean that there is no procedure the individual can interpose between seeing that action is necessary and carrying it out. There are no 'decisions' to be waited for, no 'courage' to be scraped up out of some illusory internal reserve. Certainly, we may receive encouragement from outside, but in the end the only motto is: Just *do* it.

Going against the grain of embodied experience entails a frightening unfamiliarity which no one should make light of. Behaving in radically new ways challenges deeply embedded certainties, contradicts everything we have learned to expect and undermines an 'expertise' which we have built up perfectly validly over the years. That this expertise no longer serves us as it used to can be discovered only through an act of faith, for otherwise we have no evidence at all that doing things differently will result in anything but the catastrophe which seems most likely.

There is very little in our culture to support the idea that it is sensible or even possible to take the plunge in this way, and most people consult a counsellor or therapist precisely in the expectation (fuelled most enthusiastically by the profession itself) that making changes will somehow be rendered relatively painless. It is true that the solidarity offered by a therapist may provide useful support in walking the plank of change (i.e. in 'just doing' things differently), but reliance on therapeutic tricks and gimmicks is likely to be disappointing.

For the shy person who wishes to become more sociable, for example, there is simply no alternative (other than the passage of time and the inevitable lessons of life) to making an approach to others. It would, of course, be sensible to think about the easiest and least threatening circumstances in which to do so, and there is absolutely no virtue in making the initiation of change any more difficult than it has to be – one of the merits of behaviour therapy has been to emphasise the value of taking it gently. But in the end the first step has to be taken in fear and trembling, with no guarantee that there will be a positive outcome. It is only after the event, and most likely after a considerable period of practice, that things will start to feel different.

Asking people to challenge through their conduct the very thing they are most afraid of – suggesting to someone who suffers from agoraphobia that she should go out for a walk, for example – may seem impossibly demanding, and the active support (the solidarity) of sympathetic others is probably the most helpful way of bringing about the desired result. Otherwise, we can only attempt to strengthen the person's faith that nothing terrible will happen and indeed that in the long run they may 'feel better'. Faith, again, is not an *internal* resource, but the *assurance of power* that something is so.

The need for practice

Learning through our own efforts to be different requires a huge amount of effort. This is again in stark contrast to the magic-infused promises of so many approaches to therapy, and almost no one is prepared for the amount of hard work and practice that has to be put into doing things differently.

To understand this, I think it is helpful to reflect on the processes of learning necessary to acquire forms of skill or knowledge that are more obvious and concrete than those underpinning habits of feeling and relationship. Nobody expects to be able to learn a language or to play a musical instrument, for example, without a great deal – sometimes years – of arduous practice. All the difficulties encountered by people trying to learn to 'be' different, which may often seem to them insuperably disheartening, are familiar enough – and frequently much more easily tolerated – in the acquisition of more clearly defined skills.

For example, the pain of shaping our body to unfamiliar movements in learning musical or sporting aptitudes, the despair of the novice at 'not being able to do it', the embarrassment at our halting attempts to speak another language, the initial clumsiness and inevitability of stupid mistakes – all these are equally to be expected by someone trying to act in new and unfamiliar ways.

Similarly, there is a need to establish a discipline of practice. Many people embarking on some kind of behavioural programme to challenge anxieties or establish uncharacteristic ways of responding to others fail to appreciate the necessity for practising regularly, whether or not they 'feel like it' (and however 'weak' their 'will'), and the temptations to take a line of lesser resistance are exactly as strong – indeed probably much stronger – than they are for the child desperate to evade homework or piano practice.

Keeping change in perspective

In trying in this chapter to give an indication of some of the factors that need to be kept in mind by people struggling to get to grips with their own predicament, there is a danger once again of making personal action the core of 'cure', 'taking responsibility' the road to salvation. The possibility that *perhaps*, if s/he has the necessary resources, the individual can do something to modify the forces that cause distress, does not mean that this is all there is to do, nor that personal action is likely to be the most effective approach to psychological suffering.

All the possible measures I have considered in this chapter are necessarily only applicable in the individual's proximal world. The trouble is that, as we have seen, the powers at work in this world, even though they loom largest in individual experience, are nearly always only mediating much more potent influences which operate at a much greater distance. In relation to these distal powers the individual's possibilities for influencing even those people and events closest to him or her are puny indeed.

The whole point of this book has been to emphasise the fact that we are all in boats not of our own making, and hence that there are other ways of understanding personal distress than merely seeing it as the kind of failure to cope with, or 'manage', our personal life and relationships which is best addressed by some variety of therapy or counselling. It is not only far truer, but also, I think, more productive, to see psychological distress as an indication that there is something wrong with the world than it is to interpret it as a sign of some inadequacy or deficiency of the self. This is not a cop-out, and in no way absolves us from struggle. It just indicates that our struggle should be directed at other targets than our 'selves'.

The proximal world which absorbs so much of our effort and attention is held in place by powers that there is no possibility of our influencing as individuals, and we will make no significant impact on personal distress until we find ways of modifying distal power. The bitterness, fear and exploitation so often poisoning our relations with each other, the defensive blunting of sensitivities which characterises our everyday social intercourse, certainly do give rise to individual distress, but they are not the ultimate cause of it.

The civilised values, freedom and unselfish love which provide the context for truly benign 'personal growth' and psychological stability are built on a foundation of material comfort and freedom from threat which is almost completely absent from our society. For even the most affluent and privileged minority cannot be free of anxiety that its advantages may all be taken away. Indeed, probably the single most destructive factor in our social relations is the fear of loss of power and advantage. From the brutal racism of the least privileged, through the proverbial mean resentment of the petit bourgeois to the paranoid secrecy of the very powerful, we are all haunted by the possibility of slipping from our perch.

I have made a lot in this book of the abuse of parental power within families. Such an emphasis is unavoidable if we are as individuals to make sense of our experience of a proximal world. But it is even more important to see that the shape given to our relations with each other is not simply a matter of personal likes and dislikes, random loves and hates, but is given principally by our need to survive in a difficult and often cruel world and our perception (frequently, of course, imposed upon us by greater power) of the advantages we need to cling on to and the threats we must, if we can, arm ourselves against.

We will not significantly reduce the prevalence of emotional pain in the world through psychotherapy, which sees it essentially as a personal matter, but rather by coming to accept that it is a function of social organisation, which is a political matter. It is distal, not proximal, powers we will have to modify before we 'feel better' to any noticeable extent. As things are, the hugely unequal distribution of power works against the vast majority of people being able to live a life in which insecurity, anxiety, confusion, ignorance and pain are kept to an unavoidable minimum. For things to improve for this majority, power would have to be redistributed.

We have not reached 'the end of history'. Indeed, we must hope that, from a longer perspective, we are still feeling our way in a dark age, gradual emergence from which may yet take inestimable time. Psychotherapy is an irrelevance to the political task of making a more equal society in which 'all the social hierarchies will have to be overthrown, not merely those of money or state power, not only social privilege but the uneven weight of the past and of culture' (see note 2). Perhaps it will never happen. But given intelligence, knowledge, solidarity, unending perseverance and the kind of moral strength and commitment to others seen most clearly in those who suffer most, you never know.

Notes

Chapter One

1. A frequently quoted distinction of Freud's, which he made very early in his career (1895) before he substantially revised his ideas in such a way as to place far more emphasis on 'hysteria' than on unhappiness. (Pelican Freud Library, Vol. 3, *Studies on Hysteria*, 1974, 393.)
2. I considered this issue in a little more detail in my book *The Origins of Unhappiness*, HarperCollins, 1993.
3. See, for example, his *Power/Knowledge*, Harvester, 1980. This is a selection of interviews with and writings by Foucault over the period 1972–77. Some are more accessible than others.
4. To give but two examples: the ideas of the psychiatrist H. S. Sullivan, though influential in American psychiatry around the mid-twentieth century, are virtually unknown today, and yet his view of the development of psychiatric disturbance within the social context was highly sophisticated and brilliantly expounded (see his *The Interpersonal Theory of Psychiatry*, New York: Norton, 1953). Similarly, the psychoanalyst Karen Horney's analysis of the 'neurotic personality' in the context of 1930s American society was not only extraordinarily penetrating, but remains as fresh and relevant today as it was then (her *The Neurotic Personality of Our Time*, New York: Norton, 1937, gives as good an account as one will find of the nature and origins of the kind of basic anxiety underlying a range of 'neurotic' problems).
5. Two who spring to mind are Lucy Johnstone, whose book *Users and Abusers of Psychiatry* (Routledge, 1989) provides a cogent view of the psychiatric scene in Britain, and Peter Breggin, whose *Toxic*

Psychiatry (Fontana, 1993) contains telling, indeed at times courageous, criticism of psychiatry's heavy and unjustifiable reliance on drug treatments.

6. See, for example, Mary Boyle's *Schizophrenia. A Scientific Delusion?*, Routledge, 1990.
7. A good, accessible starting point would be Joel Kovel's *Complete Guide to Therapy: From Psychoanalysis to Behavior Modification*, Penguin, 1978.
8. It is hard to overestimate the complexity, variety and sheer abundance of psychoanalytic ideas, not to mention the stupendous confidence and authority with which they tend to be stated in the vast literature they have generated. I know of no better critical account of psychoanalytic thought and practice than Ernest Gellner's *The Psychoanalytic Movement*, Paladin, 1985.
9. A famous study by the psychologist H. J. Eysenck, published in 1952, indicated that people treated by broadly psychoanalytic methods seemed to recover no more quickly than people not treated at all. Although Eysenck's work was flawed in its methodology, the findings have been modified only slightly by subsequent research. Therapies of a variety of descriptions can be shown to improve on controls where no treatment was given, but differences are not great, and the various forms of therapy cannot be reliably differentiated from each other. An extremely good source of insight into the controversies surrounding psychotherapy and its efficacy is W. Dryden and C. Feltham, *Psychotherapy and its Discontents*, Buckingham and Philadelphia: Open University Press, 1992. Coming to my notice (with thanks to David Munck) only just in time to include in this note before going to press, a swingeing critique of the adequacy of research into psychotherapy, and the claims which rest upon it, has been made by William M. Epstein, *The Illusion of Psychotherapy*, New Brunswick and London: Transaction Publishers, 1995.
10. Not all psychoanalysts adopt the orthodox approach to the 'therapeutic relationship'; indeed, there is plentiful evidence from Freud's writings that he himself often departed very far from the kind of neutrality so strictly observed by some of his less imaginative followers.
11. See Keith Thomas's *Religion and the Decline of Magic*, Penguin, 1973, for an extremely instructive account of this process; some of the parallels between practices in former centuries and those current in recent years are astonishingly close.
12. An excellent overview and critique of the counselling scene is to be

found in Alex Howard's *Challenges to Counselling and Psychotherapy*, Macmillan, 1996.

13. The 'brand name' of Albert Ellis's contribution to the therapy industry.
14. Some psychotherapies have, of course, extended their sphere of operations to groups or even 'systems', but that does not alter the fact that virtually all the most influential theoretical notions of therapy were born in the context of private individual treatment.
15. I think, for example, of Peter Lomas's books *The Case for a Personal Psychotherapy*, Oxford University Press, 1981, and, more recently, *Cultivating Intuition*, Penguin, 1994. R. F. Hobson's *Forms of Feeling. The Heart of Psychotherapy*, Tavistock, 1985, is another rewarding source of insights into the process of psychotherapy. Miller Mair's *Between Psychology and Psychotherapy*, Routledge, 1989, is one of the most honest accounts available of what is involved in the practice of therapy from a clinical psychologist's point of view. My own *Psychotherapy. A Personal Approach*, Dent, 1978, was an attempt to address the implications of therapy as a personal undertaking.
16. I. Suttie, *The Origins of Love and Hate*, Penguin, 1988.
17. P. Halmos, *The Faith of the Counsellors*, Constable, 1965.
18. I prefer the term 'comfort' to 'love' because it seems to me that, with the exception of a tiny minority of exceptionally dedicated therapists, to talk of 'love' overstates the case. Though the therapist's attention to and concern for patients may be concentrated, intense, and genuine enough, it does not in most cases stretch far beyond the fifty minutes or so that they are in the consulting room together, and does not really match the commitment we might expect of one who can truly be said to love another.
19. There is, of course, also the issue that the professional provision of comfort is a poor substitute for the social solidarity in public life and loving generosity in private life that one would hope to see in the kind of 'sane society' which, for example, Erich Fromm writes about in his book of that title (*The Sane Society*, Routledge & Kegan Paul, 1963). Not the least difficulty about the 'professionalisation of love' is that it gives those who dispense it, i.e. therapists, a financial stake in maintaining society's sickness. These are questions which I consider at some length in my book *Taking Care*, Dent, 1987.
20. Criticisms of this kind form the subject matter of Jeffrey Masson's important book *Against Therapy*, Collins, 1989.

Chapter Two

1. Thomas Szasz's *The Myth of Mental Illness* (New York: Harper & Row, 1974) remains the classic text in this respect, and is still well worth reading.
2. Dorothy Rowe has been a relentless critic of the medicalised view of depression, as her several books on the subject will testify. See, for a concise discussion, the chapter on depression in her *Beyond Fear*, Fontana, 1987.
3. The idea of schizophrenics as having a 'split mind', which is sometimes reflected in popular usage, bears no relation to the way in which the psychiatric label is used. 'Clinical schizophrenia' is much more about being confused than it is about being in two minds about something or torn between two incompatible states of feeling.
4. In *The Interpersonal Theory of Psychiatry* (see previous chapter, note 4), H. S. Sullivan provides a masterly account of the ways in which a variety of clinical phenomena, including those associated with schizophrenia, can be traced back to the social ('interpersonal') context in which the individual acquired them. For example, lack of 'consensual validation' (i.e. the failure of crucial figures in the child's early environment to provide a consistent interpretation of reality) may result in a situation in later life in which the absence of such internalised consistency makes it impossible for the individual to grasp the 'reality' which seems so obvious to others.
5. It is a commonplace to observe that the nature of so-called neurotic symptoms has changed quite markedly in many respects from the time when, say, Freud was writing. Our culture sets limits on how we experience and what we are able to say about ourselves. The iconic language of 'hysteria' is, for example, no longer viable as one in which we can attempt to give form to our distress – one does not these days encounter people who are rendered deaf or blind by their troubles.
6. It is common in the language of the 'illness model' to talk of 'precipitating factors' in the present which somehow trigger a slumbering 'predisposition' to breakdown. Although it is easy to see how this manner of thinking can arise, it is, I think, nevertheless misleading as it once again diverts our attention from damaging *worlds* to supposedly *constitutional* weaknesses within individuals.
7. The writings of R. D. Laing are often cited as an example of the unacceptable blaming of parents for the subsequent schizophrenia of their offspring. In fact, I do not believe that a careful reading of

Laing's work substantiates this criticism, but it does seem that a whole range of (extremely interesting) research work implicating family relations in the causation of 'psychosis' in the 1960s and 1970s ran into difficulty because of the slur that seemed to be cast on, in particular, parents, and much of present-day research carries a kind of pious disclaimer of any intention to implicate family relations. It is interesting in this context also to note Jeffrey Masson's argument, in *The Assault on Truth* (Penguin, 1985), that Freud abandoned the idea that, for example, his female patients' neuroses were based on the sexual misdemeanours of their fathers, largely because of a failure of moral courage in the face of the outrage he stirred up.

8. The phenomenon of 'resistance' – another psychoanalytic creation – is commonly invoked to explain patients' unwillingness to accept their therapists' interpretation of their free associations. This is a good example of the moralism that runs deep in so much psychoanalytic and therapeutic thinking: as if the patient is a naughty or recalcitrant child bent on rejecting the sweet reason of adult supervision. Much more often, however, it is a case of patients' being entirely reasonably reluctant to accept without evidence (solely on therapeutic authority) the often highly charged sexual allegations with which the analyst seeks to establish their motivation. In contrast to this supposed battle of wills, patients have in fact a particularly strong and obvious interest in uncovering the reasons for their difficulties and more often than not will readily accept *accurate* explanations.
9. The kind of procedures beloved of behaviour therapy are particularly suitable for the 'treatment' of 'mono-symptomatic phobias' such as specific fear of spiders, winged insects etc. Gradual introduction of the feared stimulus in doses the person feels comfortable with – perhaps first as a photograph, or even as a word, then as graduated specimens in glass jars, and finally as living examples wandering around the room – usually does the trick. It is important that the person is allowed to go at his or her own pace. Many entirely well-meaning amateur 'therapists' have turned an otherwise perfectly helpful approach into trauma by deciding that it's time for their charges to 'go for it' head on.
10. Cognitive-behavioural psychology has, certainly, tried to invent techniques of 'thought-stopping' and other diversionary tactics, but, though they may work up to a point, their plausibility depends on the notion that our attention is indeed ultimately under our own

control, that we have a kind of mental director sitting in our heads deciding the direction of our awareness. How far this may be so is debatable. Is there, for example, another director sitting in *that* director's head?

11. Because of the special difficulties they pose in terms of both physiological involvement and medico-social management – sometimes necessitating hospital treatment – I shall not consider drug and alcohol addiction here. However, the problems of control and the exercise of 'will power' which such addictions present are, I believe, not different in kind from – indeed are virtually prototypical of – the phenomena I shall consider in this section.
12. This is not to say that there is no value in documenting the manner in which social evils such as unemployment cause damage. An excellent article by David Fryer, for example, shows how unemployment and job insecurity have a whole range of adverse effects on victims and their families (D. Fryer, 'Benefit agency?', *The Psychologist*, 8, 1995, 265–72).
13. An extended analysis of this is to be found in Chapter Four of my *The Origins of Unhappiness*, HarperCollins, 1993.
14. According to official government figures published in 1991, the suicide rate in England among men aged 20–24 increased by 71 per cent during the 1980s.
15. See Chapter One, note 4.
16. H. S. Sullivan's work is again of central relevance in this regard (see Chapter One, note 4). The work of Theodore Lidz and others in the USA and of R. D. Laing and others in Britain during the 1960s, together with the writings of Gregory Bateson (on the 'double bind'), Jay Haley and Paul Watzlawick, all focused in one way or another on the way communication may distort experience.

Chapter Three

1. This fundamental point was articulated most fully by Jürgen Habermas in his highly erudite (if for most readers difficult and often obscure) *Knowledge and Human Interests*, Heinemann, 1972.
2. H. J. Eysenck, 'The technology of consent', *New Scientist*, 42, 1969, 688–90. My attention was originally drawn to this quotation by Professor John Shotter.
3. Any credible psychology must be *reflexive*, i.e. must include the psychologist in the scientific equation. Don Bannister ('Psychology

as an exercise in paradox', *Bulletin of the British Psychological Society*, 19, 1966, 21) offered the following neat little parable to illustrate the point:

> The master chemist has finally produced a bubbling green slime in his test-tube, the potential of which is great but the properties of which are mysterious. He sits alone in his laboratory, test-tube in hand, brooding about what to do with the bubbling green slime. Then it slowly dawns on him that the bubbling green slime is sitting alone in the test-tube wondering what to do about him. This special nightmare of the chemist is the permanent work-a-day world of the psychologist – the bubbling green slime is always wondering what to do about you.

4. See in particular his *Discipline and Punish*, Penguin, 1979, for a brilliant and persuasive account of how psychiatric and psychological approaches which could naively be supposed to be 'for the good of humankind' can only be coherently understood once we take into account the purposes of *social control* which underlie them.
5. Foucault was of course not the only person to concern himself with this issue; there is a reasonably large constituency of social critics and historians who have documented and analysed the ways in which psychiatry, psychology, education, social work etc. are intimately associated with the exercise of powers of social control. Andrew Scull and David Ingleby in Britain and Christopher Lasch in the USA are prominent examples of those whose writings are illuminating in this respect.
6. Writing in an unguarded moment to his friend Wilhelm Fliess, Freud even self-consciously described himself as a 'conquistador', and 'actually not at all a man of science, not an observer, not an experimenter, not a thinker' (J. M. Masson, ed., *The Complete Letters of Sigmund Freud to Wilhelm Fliess 1887–1904*, Cambridge, Mass., and London: Harvard University Press, 1985). No doubt Freud meant by this to represent himself as a bold explorer and conqueror of unknown territory, and yet – as he himself could be the last to deny! – our words can reveal more than we realise or intend; the ruthless subjection by the conquistadores of the hapless populations they encountered was surely not an irrelevant aspect of their purpose.
7. Psychology's claim to be a science rests principally on its insistence on the objective measurement of the phenomena it addresses, and for this it is heavily reliant on procedures of statistical analysis.

Population sampling, frequency distributions, measurements of central tendency (means, modes, medians), significance testing etc. lie at the methodological heart of academic, experimental psychology, and many of the most influential figures in the development of, in particular, Anglo-American psychology were first and foremost statisticians. It tends to be forgotten these days that the preoccupations of these gentlemen often had very centrally to do with social engineering and control, particularly where it was felt that significant departures from the norm threatened social stability. My late colleague and friend Richard Marshall was fond of pointing out that, for example, Karl Pearson, one of the revered founders of British academic psychology, enthusiastic eugenicist and inventor of statistical approaches still bearing his name, expressed his admiration in an after-dinner speech at University College London in 1934 for '*Reichskanzler* Hitler and his proposals to regenerate the German people'.

8. See for example John Rowan's *Ordinary Ecstasy. Humanistic Psychology in Action*, Routledge & Kegan Paul, 1976, for a classic example of an account which is stuffed from end to end with aesthetic judgements about human nature and being. The title is itself revealing enough.
9. Probably the most terrifying situation of all is the psychiatric 'case conference', where a roomful of doctors, psychologists, social workers etc. will gather to scrutinise and ultimately pronounce upon the hapless patient – a procedure which R. D. Laing once aptly characterised as a 'ritual degradation ceremony'.
10. H. S. Sullivan, *The Interpersonal Theory of Psychiatry*, New York: Norton, 1953.
11. This kind of observation renders at least dubious a great deal of research in psychiatry which has sought to establish a genetic component to 'mental illness'. Such research has relied on the argument that different degrees of genetic endowment (as between identical and nonidentical twins) can be assessed in relation to constancy of environment (as in the same family) and diagnosis of 'illness' be shown to vary significantly between the two groups.
12. Better than any psychological, or indeed sociological, text that I have come across is Eric Hobsbaum's historical account of the 'cultural revolution' we have endured over recent times. See his *Age of Extremes. The Short Twentieth Century 1914–1991*, Michael Joseph, 1994, especially Chapter Eleven.
13. Sigmund Freud was probably as guilty as anyone of trying to submit

the imagination to moral judgement. His *The Interpretation of Dreams*, full of insight and creativity though it is, is also a *tour de force* of disciplinary moralism. In the course of this work Freud takes the appreciative enthusiasm of his precursor K. A. Scherner for the workings of the imagination and develops in its place a disapproving analysis of the 'irrational' sexual and aggressive impulses he takes to lie at the centre of what he calls 'primary processes' such as imagination and dreaming.

14. Translated by Rosemary Edmonds, Penguin Classics, 1964.
15. This is also, of course, the basis of our *im*morality. Knowing that others hurt as we do is what gives torturers their power.
16. The 'personal construct' psychology of George Kelly is the most carefully and illuminatingly elaborated theoretical approach to take seriously the ways in which people structure and organise their *anticipation* of life in accordance with their *experience* of it. Kelly's *The Psychology of Personal Constructs*, Vols I & II, New York: Norton, 1955, is his major work. His influence on British clinical psychology has been considerable, mediated particularly by Don Bannister (see, for example, D. Bannister and F. Fransella, *Inquiring Man*, Penguin, 1971) and most prominently represented now by Miller Mair (see his *Between Psychology and Psychotherapy*, London and New York: Routledge, 1989) and David Winter (whose *Personal Construct Psychology in Clinical Practice: Theory, Research and Applications*, Routledge, 1992, is a specialist volume, but indispensable for the serious student of the subject). In the field of education, Phillida Salmon is an influential Kellyan – see for example her *Psychology in the Classroom*, London and New York: Cassell, 1995.
17. I have discussed the similarities in this respect between psychotherapy and prostitution at greater length in my *Illusion and Reality. The Meaning of Anxiety*, Dent, 1984.

Chapter Four

1. Anyone wishing to study this evidence in detail can do no better than consult the compendious *Handbook of Psychotherapy and Behavior Change* edited by A. E. Bergin and S. L. Garfield, Wiley, 1994.
2. If this seems unduly cynical, consider a recent account of the significance of conducting research within the British counselling organisation Relate. 'Client (consumer)-dependent evaluation', it is suggested,

'has both facilitated development and suggested clients think well of the organisation for considering their views important. Ultimately this can only increase confidence for all stakeholders associated with counselling practice.' Again, through 'research and development activity', the authors enthuse, a 'counselling agency can harness the skills and methods of psychotherapy research to maintain its place in the market and improve the quality and effectiveness of its services'. (J. Mellor-Clark and D. A. Shapiro, 'It's not what you do . . . it's the way that you do it: the inception of an evaluative research culture in Relate Marriage Guidance', *Changes*, 13, 1995, 201–07). Research is thus conducted in pursuit of market advantage for 'stakeholders' and not of truth; whether or not psychotherapy *works* has become an irrelevance.

3. It is fascinating to see how, throughout the correspondence with Wilhelm Fliess which chronicles the development of his theories about the unconscious sexual origins of neurosis, Freud naively reveals (and utterly fails to notice) how his own preoccupations and worries, not to say motivation, are shaped by more mundane matters. Like the rest of us, he is most concerned by the ability to make a living. On 21.9.1899, for example, Freud writes:

   My mood also depends very strongly on my earnings. Money is laughing gas for me. I know from my youth that once the wild horses of the pampas have been lassoed, they retain a certain anxiousness for life. Thus I have come to know the helplessness of poverty and continually fear it. You will see that my style will improve and my ideas will be more correct if this city provides me with an ample livelihood.

   (J. M. Masson, ed), see Chapter Three, note 6.
4. D. Smail, 'Psychotherapeutic theory and wishful thinking', *Changes*, 10, 1992, 274–81.
5. It is of course to this kind of process Freud meant to refer in his concept of 'repression'. It is unfortunate that, in Freud's writing as in the subsequent development of psychoanalysis, repression came to acquire a *purposive* aspect, as though the individual deliberately strips experience of words so that s/he may not be held morally accountable for it. Repression, in my view, is much better understood as what is done to people than as what is done by them.
6. I have borrowed this term from H. S. Sullivan. His account of the development of the child's conceptual and social understanding is

highly relevant to this discussion. For example, his outlining in *The Interpersonal Theory of Psychiatry* (see Chapter One, note 4) of the development of 'prototaxic', 'parataxic' and 'syntaxic' experience constitutes one of the best accounts I know of the phenomena we are considering. His framework has not, however, been widely taken up in psychology and psychotherapy.

7. For anyone trying to understand the causes of, and possible cures for, much of our distress in the past decade or two, Will Hutton's *The State We're In*, Jonathan Cape, 1995, is worth libraries full of therapeutic literature.

Chapter Five

1. That we are all psychologists is a particularly unpalatable fact for a discipline that attempts to monopolise and, as it were, 'patent' psychology as a professional pursuit. In the end, that attempt must result in obvious absurdity. Psychology, to survive as an intellectual or practical undertaking, needs in my view to cultivate a very strong sense of professional modesty and to strive continually to make clear what the limits of its possibilities are.
2. At times, as for example with the work of O. H. Mowrer (*The Crisis in Psychiatry and Religion*, Van Nostrand, 1961), psychological distress has become linked directly to religious concepts of sin. Ever since C. G. Jung there have been those who see strong connections between religion on the one hand and psychopathology and psychotherapy on the other, and there are several 'pastoral' approaches to psychiatry and psychotherapy which again equate 'cure' with redemption.
3. In fact, Alice Miller achieves precisely this in her illuminating study of Hitler's childhood in her *For Your Own Good. The Roots of Violence in Child-rearing*, Virago, 1987. In this book, as in her *The Drama of Being a Child* (also published by Virago in 1987), there is much to be learned from Alice Miller about the adult abuse of power over children.
4. See note 3 above.
5. Kierkegaard's meditation on this theme in *Fear and Trembling* makes the point powerfully.
6. The most penetrating statement I know on the complexity of 'motivation' comes from the political scientist and philosopher Hannah Arendt (*On Revolution*, Penguin, 1973, 96):

> ... not only is the human heart a place of darkness which, with certainty, no human eye can penetrate; the qualities of the heart need darkness and protection against the light of the public to grow and to remain what they are meant to be, innermost motives which are not for public display.

She goes on to point out that the insistence on dragging motives out into the light of day leads inevitably to profound and widespread mistrust which sees 'intrigue and calumny, treachery and hypocrisy everywhere'. We develop procedures of 'motivational research' which become 'an eerie sort of filing cabinet for human vices, ... a veritable science of misanthropy'.

7. 'Political correctness' can easily become an additional factor making it hard for people to be honest with themselves about what they think and feel. There is a fine line between stipulating what people should be able to say and trying to prescribe what they should think. Regulating conduct offensive to others is one thing, trying to police the contents of our heads, quite another.
8. In this way, for the superconscientious person, Kant's 'categorical imperative': 'So act that the maxim of your will could always hold at the same time as a principle establishing universal law' (*Critique of Practical Reason*) becomes applied to the self with no universality at all. 'Act always for the good of others without expecting, requiring or even wishing that they should do the same for you' is more the superconscientious code.
9. This is poignantly exemplified at the time of writing by the court testimony of the stepdaughter of Rosemary West. West is accused of murdering ten girls and young women, one of them her own daughter and another the witness's sister. Violently sexually assaulted by her stepmother and raped by her father at the age of eight, the witness 'recounted years of abuse and degradation at [their] hands. [She] said she was told that "all loving parents" subjected their children to such treatment as she had experienced in the cellar. At fifteen she had run away from home, but *she had always remembered to send a Mother's Day card to Mrs West*.' (*Guardian*, 19.10.95 – my emphasis.)
10. A preoccupation with 'authenticity' probably came into mid-twentieth-century philosophy ('existentialism') at least in part as a counter to a kind of institutionalised hypocrisy which *pretended* a harmony between outer act and inner motive. But *insisting* that they be harmonious is in the long run no more satisfactory than pre-

tending that they are, mainly because it is only relatively rarely the case that they *can* be.

Chapter Six

1. At first sight it looks as though the Freudian notion of 'psychological determinism' does indeed constitute a challenge to the received view of will, but closer examination reveals a surprisingly confused account of what could be meant by this. For example, modestly claiming 'a triumph for the interpretative art of psychoanalysis' in revealing the origin of 'parapraxes' such as slips of the tongue, Freud wrote that such events were 'strictly determined' and 'revealed as an expression of the subject's suppressed intentions' or 'a clash between two intentions, one of which was permanently or temporarily unconscious' (from the first of Freud's 'Two Encyclopaedia Articles' in Vol. 15 of the Pelican Freud Library, *Historical and Expository Works on Psychoanalysis*, 136–37). All that seems to have happened here, however, is that Freud has transferred the processes of will from the conscious to the unconscious mind; 'unconscious mental acts' come about in exactly the same way as conscious ones, apart, of course, from the individual's not knowing about them.
2. The best account I know of the process I am trying to describe here is in Jean-Paul Sartre's *Being and Nothingness*, even if not always expressed in the most accessible terms. Gilbert Ryle's classic *The Concept of Mind* (Hutchinson, 1949) is another work which, in an altogether drier and more Anglo-Saxon mode, still constitutes an illuminating critique of our usual ways of representing the causes of action to ourselves.
3. Although one might credit the considerable perspicacity of both behaviourism and psychodynamic therapy in recognising the limits to be placed on the person's own account of his or her motivation, both also abused this insight by claiming that only the trained expert was in a position to offer an accurate account – the behaviourist, or the psychoanalyst, 'knew better' than the subject what lay behind the subject's actions. In this way, professional psychologists placed themselves in a position of intransitive power in relation to the subject or patient. Intransitive psychologies of this kind fail to recognise that psychologist and subject are in the *same* position when trying to understand motivation, with neither being especially privileged.

4. The work of the Russian psychologist Lev Vygotsky has been seminally important in demonstrating that the child's 'inner world' is actually a projection from external experience. See for example his *Thought and Language*, Massachusetts Institute of Technology, 1962.
5. An extremely funny article pointing out the dangers to psychotherapy in, among other things, not considering the potential inaccuracy of self-report has been written by Simon King-Spooner: 'Psychotherapy and the white dodo', *Changes*, 13, 1995, 45–51.
6. This view is argued at much greater length, and with matchless subtlety and profundity, by Jean-Paul Sartre in *Being and Nothingness*.
7. The eugenics movement between the wars provides a cautionary lesson concerning the way 'scientific' measurement can be used to attempt legitimation for profoundly dubious sociopolitical programmes (see Chapter Three, note 7).
8. The question of how far 'intelligence' is genetic is of course far from settled in psychology. Much of the controversy which has raged in this area centres on the means that have been used to 'measure' intelligence – tests of so-called IQ. It seems to me to stretch credulity to suppose that genetically inherited physical structures are irrelevant to many of the intellectual gifts and abilities that are necessary for some kinds of human achievement. This does not mean that we know what these structures are. It has been amply demonstrated that their 'measurement' is fraught with difficulty to the extent that, for example, educational discrimination between children on the basis of 'tests' is not rationally justifiable.
9. See his *Distinction*, Routledge & Kegan Paul, 1984.

Chapter Seven

1. In his wonderfully instructive but now unfashionably titled *The Perfectibility of Man* (Duckworth, 1970), John Passmore surveys the principal ways in which, since Greek times, we have sought to achieve the kinds of solutions to our predicament for which we look now so hopefully to psychotherapy and counselling. This work is still extremely well worth reading for the insights it gives into the forerunners of contemporary thought, showing once again that there is nothing new about either our preoccupations or the proffered answers to them.

2. The most healthily sobering observation I know in this respect comes from Fernand Braudel at the end of his magnificent survey of the socio-economic history of modern times (*Civilisation and Capitalism 15th–18th Century*, 3 vols, Fontana, 1985). Quoted at greater length in my *Taking Care*, some of what he says is worth repeating here:

   Jean-Paul Sartre may have dreamed of a society from which inequality would have disappeared, where one man would not exploit another. But no society in the world has yet given up tradition and the use of privilege. If this is ever to be achieved, all the social hierarchies will have to be overthrown, not merely those of money or state power, not only social privilege but the uneven weight of the past and of culture.

3. There are, of course, exceptions to this. One notable one is Roy Schafer, whose book *A New Language for Psychoanalysis* (New Haven and London: Yale University Press, 1976) elaborates a 'tragic view' of psychoanalysis.
4. I discuss the business of 'relationship' at much greater length in *Taking Care*, Dent, 1987.
5. I am very grateful to Dr Teresa Hagan for permitting me to borrow her notion of 'power mapping' in order to construct Figure 2, which is based essentially on her work with people whose distress is the direct upshot of powerlessness. From work currently in progress, Dr Hagan and I hope to develop a more formal mapping structure in which to consider the extent of available powers and resources and relate it to various forms of psychological distress.
6. These qualities, forming the acronym YAVIS, were first identified in 1964 as characterising the kind of patients psychotherapists preferred to deal with (W. Schofield, *Psychotherapy: The Purchase of Friendship*, Prentice-Hall). Very little has changed since.

Index

Printed in the United States
by Baker & Taylor Publisher Services